The Food of ITALY

CLAUDIA RODEN, widely admired as both a great cook and a fine writer, became familiar to a very large audience through her BBC TV series 'Mediterranean Cookery', and her books on Middle Eastern food and Mediterranean cookery have become classics.

Born in Egypt, she was educated in Paris and London, where she now lives.

The Food of
ITALY

CLAUDIA RODEN

ARROW BOOKS

For Simon, Nadia and Anna
and the Italian *appassionati di cucina*
who helped me with this book.

Arrow Books Ltd
20 Vauxhall Bridge Road, London SW1V 2SA

An imprint of Random Century Group

London Melbourne Sydney Auckland
Johannesburg and agencies throughout
the world

First published by Chatto & Windus Ltd 1989
Arrow edition 1990

Text copyright © Claudia Roden 1989
Maps by Anthony Sidwell
Food photography by Graham Kirk

Printed and bound in Great Britain by
Butler and Tanner Ltd, Frome, Somerset

ISBN 0 09 976220 X

ERRATA

Please note that the caption to plate 28 should read:

Piedmontese cooking, once ignored, is now acclaimed as one of the great cuisines – pheasant in red wine (p22) and quails on grilled polenta (p23) are shown here with a mixture of wild mushrooms. Funghi trifolati – fried with garlic (p127) – are popular all over Italy.

The note to plate 41 should read:

Sicilian sweets: cassata Palermo style (p191), coffee granita with whipped cream (p190), and 'almond blossom' – an almond pastry (190)

Contents

Introduction

Travelling up and down the country through every corner of Italy, throughout a year, to research 'The Taste of Italy' series for the *Sunday Times Magazine* was an undreamt of opportunity to get to know the food and the country in an intimate kind of way. This book is based on the series and on further material collected during the many trips.

Every recipe brings a rush of memories – a dinner in a piazza in the warm night air; a discussion about a dish on a train with the whole carriage joining in; the back streets of Naples full of bustle and drama glittering with carnival lights, and shrines to the Virgin Mary; a wedding party in Sicily; fishing boats bringing their catch into a tiny Ligurian port; nuns making almond pastries in a monastery. The taste of basil, parmesan and olive oil, the smell of garlic frying with sage and rosemary, bring back the brilliant light and pure primary colours, with images of Italy and feelings of joy and enchantment.

It is easy to fall under the spell of Italy. The French writer Stendhal wrote in the early part of the last century that in the art and the joy of living Milan was 200 years in advance of Paris. This can hardly be said of Milan today, but everyone can still be irresistibly charmed by a country so full of natural beauty, art, music and tradition; by a quality of life that warms the heart and by food that is simple and unaffected but full of rich flavours and delightful touches.

Part of the fascination of Italy is the incredible diversity. The landscape, the vegetation and the climate constantly change. There are hills, mountains, plains and coastline, and every town and village is quite different from the next. The architecture, the ambience, the way people behave is different and you can hear different dialects and even different languages. The cooking too is different. There is no such thing as Italian cooking, only Sicilian, Piedmontese, Neapolitan, Venetian, Florentine, Genoese and so on. That is what makes a culinary tour of the regions such an enormous pleasure. The extraordinary diversity is a legacy of Italy's fragmented past and its division, until the unification of the country only just over a hundred years ago, into many independent sovereign states. There were kingdoms, duchies, lordships and republics, papal and city states, and each had its own history, culture and traditions.

After the decline of the Roman Empire Italy became a many-centred universe. In the Middle Ages each big town, in central and northern Italy especially, conquered and managed the surrounding land, and the great sea towns had their own colonies around the Mediterranean. These towns and communes were ruled by different laws and institutions and they were constantly divided by economic and political rivalries, bitter conflicts and wars. A kaleidoscope of foreign influences – the French in Piedmont, Austrians in Lombardy, Trentino-Alto Adige and Veneto, Yugoslavs in Venezia Giulia, Spaniards in the south, Arabs in Sicily – reinforced the differences. The south has a tradition of unity in diversity because the regions shared the same rulers and destinies, but in the north and central Italy there are hardly two cities that shared the same succession of rulers or had the same cultural heritage. When King Victor Emmanuel of Piedmont was proclaimed king of a united Italy in 1861 the component parts of the new nation were disconnected and extremely diverse. The great cleavage, partly historical, partly climatic and economical, was that which divided the north from the south, the former Kingdom of Naples whose inhabitants belonged to another civilization.

The twenty administrative regions which were formed after the war correspond more or less to the states that existed before unification and their particularism has not been cancelled out. Each region is a world in itself with its own identity. Local patriotism – *campanilismo* – is such that each feels strongly about its food and lays claim to having the best cooking in Italy.

Italy has changed dramatically since the Second World War and it is still changing. The political writer Giorgio Bocca writes in *Italia che Cambia* (Changing Italy) that it has changed more in these last few years than in the 3000 preceding ones. Although there were some industries in the north at the end of the nineteenth century, until the 'economic miracle' after the war Italy was still an agricultural country, where a system of share-cropping – *mezzadria*, by which peasant farmers lived on estates as tenants and cultivated the land, giving half the produce to the landlord as rent, prevailed. Estates were large and divided into fields or *poderi*, each housing a family community headed by a *mezzadro* or *capoccia*. Farming methods were archaic. Peasants were busy all the year round growing wheat, maize or rice, vegetables and fruit. Wine was made on each estate and in many also olive oil. Every farm kept pigs, rabbits and poultry. In the north and centre they also bred a few calves for the market. They made cheese and cured pork. But the harvest often failed and life was hard. Until then the cooking had remained little changed for hundreds of years.

When Italy was rapidly transformed in the fifties and sixties into a highly industrialized modern consumer society where women went out to work, the old life was swept away. The *mezzadria* system was abolished. The government gave credit to tenants to buy their land at an interest of only three per cent, but peasants still abandoned the land for the cities and factories. People from the poorer south invaded the richer north in search of work and a better life or went abroad. With this industrial, economic and social revolution came a change of eating and cooking habits and a homogenizing of cultures.

Now the culinary borders have been confused and there is no longer a precise geography of food. The great differences were between north and south. Before the war you could divide Italy according to cooking fats. There was butter in the north, pork fat in the centre and olive oil in the south. The Italy of polenta and rice and of boiled meats was in the north, and the Italy of pizza and dry pasta was in the south. Black pepper was used in the north, hot red pepper in the south. In the north they cooked with wine, in the south with tomatoes.

The past twenty-five years have seen the '*invasione pizzaiola*' and the adoption of pasta, both hardly ever eaten in the north before, in every corner of Italy. Mass-production of foods has brought standardization. The same factories make all the different regional salamis and cheeses. The use of olive oil has become widespread (in the past a bottle might have lasted a whole year in a family in the north) and few people now will eat pork fat. Cooks in all the main cities are mostly from the south – from the Abruzzi, Apulia and Sicily – and this has had a major influence on national tastes.

Italy has succumbed to fast foods and has gone through many fashions in eating, from steak and salad after the war (a reaction against meat only once a week which had been the case for most country people) and French cuisine in restaurants, to a proliferation of hamburger, sandwich and salad bars and *nouvelle cuisine*, going through the 'threes and fours' when everything – spaghetti, omelettes, pizza – had three or four cheeses and three or four herbs. Now there is concern with health and dieting and the cult of the new (they call it '*cucina creativa*'). I was offered a *risotto tricolore* in the national colours with chopped tomatoes and kiwi and another with wild strawberries and found menus full of things like prawns with whisky, and ravioli filled with crab and vodka or with smoked salmon. Almost every restaurant offers smoked salmon in various forms – chopped into tagliatelle, sliced with mushrooms or mixed with salad. One could say that smoked salmon from Scotland and Canada is the most important unifying factor in restaurants throughout the country.

But despite all this, regional cooking has survived, and perhaps because of this, it is reflowering. Nostalgia and fascination with the past and the quest for identity have brought a revival of interest in traditional cooking and a respect for genuine produce. As their world changed and the old traditions seemed to be vanishing, and when they seemed to lose touch with their roots, people began to hanker for the good things of the past. Afraid to lose forever their culture and their link with the land, Italians have started to 'rediscover' their individual heritage in the old everyday foods of the countryside. They call it *il ricupero* and *la riscoperta*. The dishes which evoke the 'happy days' when peasant farmers had ten children, and families were close and patriarchal, when the kitchen was the living room and meals were convivial, are very much in fashion. Poor peasant dishes like polenta and bean soup and those based on bread or dried chestnuts or made with offal or wild plants are particularly popular.

In Italy the past is not far away. The generation that cooks in the old way, the *nonnine* (little grandmothers), is still there, and inspired chefs go to them for recipes. Many showed me handwritten recipe books as well as old cookery books, including facsimiles of books written during the Renaissance, which they used. These chefs follow the seasons, use local ingredients, track down home-made produce and band together to get farmers to raise quail, ducks, geese and game (which had almost disappeared). They explained that they wanted to update and revitalize tradition, not embalm it.

There is a certain mystification going on and what someone called 'nostalgic kitsch'. Some of the dishes which are revived never really existed, like tortelloni filled with nettles. At a restaurant in Parma the chef-owner offered me tortelli stuffed with apple, saying it was an old local dish. When Massimo Alberini, the culinary historian, told him not to make up stories, he said that the recipe might not have been codified but that his grandmother made them.

Authentic local food is not easy to find in restaurants because Italians do not want to spend very much to eat what their grandmothers make, and want to try something new. For years French food guides only commended restaurants with 'creative' cooking so there was no incentive to stick to tradition, while state catering schools teach classic French and international cooking with the more well-known Italian dishes, so that students are able to find work anywhere. It is in the trattorias and family-run restaurants that you get the real thing. Since tourists have become more adventurous and started to ask for local specialities, more and more '*piatti tipici*' have begun to appear on menus during the tourist season.

Because the cooking of Italy is so varied and diverse and because it was never formalized as it was in France, there is no 'haute cuisine' or 'cuisine bourgeoise' or classic national cuisine. It is basically country cooking for large families, a combination of peasant food and the grand dishes that belonged to the nobility which were eaten by the peasantry on special occasions – some only once a year at carnival time. The different styles may have a city stamp but they have their roots in the land. Town and country in Italy have always been closely bound. Since the Middle Ages big towns in north and central Italy owned the land around them and the rich and noble spent a good part of the year in their country houses. In the south, feudal landlords had castles in the country while the agricultural population lived in walled hilltop towns for protection and worked in faraway fields every day.

The aim of this book is to feature real traditional recipes from all the regions of Italy. The selection reflects what is popular in Italy today, what I liked best and what I feel you will most enjoy cooking and eating. I did not try to be comprehensive. Many things are missing. I adore snails and frogs, newborn (jelly-like) fish and cardoons, but have found it impossible to buy fresh ones here, and I expect you to be squeamish about frogs, sheep's heads and certain offal. I like the salt cod and stockfish but I hate cooking them, I loved a *pasticcio di tortellini* – a pie filled with a sweet bechamel and tiny pasta stuffed with meat, but it is too fattening and takes too long to make, and although I tried the famous trifle, *zuppa inglese*, in different versions in many places, I never thought much of it. Because many dishes have several regional versions I tried as many as I could and chose the best one.

I have not included many of the old traditional pastries, all part of ancient rituals to celebrate religious festivals. Every town and village has its own version of almond petits fours, of sweet bread rings, fritters in the shape of ribbons and hard dry biscuits to dunk in wine, and they all have pastries filled with ricotta, nuts or candied fruit and pastries made with chestnut flour or soaked in honey or wine must. They are delightful and fascinating but I preferred to include more of the luscious modern sweets which you find in Italy.

Every generation pulls from tradition what suits them best. We are keener now on fish and vegetables and prefer quick and easy, fresh, light foods with rich flavours, less fat and less stodge. The intention was to keep to the original authentic way of preparing the dishes and to make the kind of improvements which young Italian chefs are making, in a way that both respects tradition and takes into account modern tastes. Generally, it has been a matter of reducing the amount of fat and using oil in preference to butter and pork fat – if you wish, you can use exclusively olive oil, and sunflower oil which is also used in Italy – and of cooking vegetables and fish for less time. This, and the importance of presentation are what the Italians have learnt from *nouvelle cuisine*. They make their food look exquisite in a natural, simple kind of way and that is what you should do too.

The owner of a restaurant in Umbria was angry that I wanted only traditional local foods. 'Why must we remain stuck in the past?' he complained. Food is always changing and that is natural, but now that changes come through the media and that all the world is getting to be the same, what appeals and fascinates and touches the heart is that which distinguishes Italy, which recalls her past and which is part of her precious heritage and traditions.

Piedmont and Valle d'Aosta

The region of Italy which played the most important part in Italy's struggle for unification during the last century, whose King Victor Emmanuel II became the first king of Italy, has recently gained a reputation as the great gastronomic region with centres like Alba and Asti and Monferrato. A region whose cooking is based on the most perfumed truffles and the best wine in Italy, and on wild mushrooms and game, is bound to be gastronomic, yet, until not very long ago, the cooking of Piedmont was generally thought to be only a derivation of the French because the dialect is French and cooking terms are French. One of the first cookery books published in Turin in 1767 was _Il Cuoco Piemontese – Perfezionato a Parigi_ (The Piedmontese cook – Perfected in Paris).

In those days the cooking from across the mountains (the border with France runs north as far as Mont Blanc) was followed in all the well-to-do families, not only in Piedmont but in the whole of Italy and Europe. But Piedmont was part of the once French province of Savoy that became the Kingdom of Savoy (of which Turin was the capital from 1559) and French was the language of the court until the middle of the nineteenth century while the French influence continued to dominate in the kitchens of the court into the twentieth.

But there was also a rich tradition of country cooking, and today the cooking, especially of the gastronomic enclave of the wine country in the area of the Langhe, attracts thousands of people from all over the world. They come mainly in the truffle season when the famous white truffles are hunted in the hills around Alba, Asti and Monferrato.

White truffles are a rarity (the only other place you find them is Morocco where they are quite different) and, although less prized abroad than the black ones of France, are highly scented. In their season, in the autumn, they appear in all the restaurants in almost every dish, shaved on at the last minute with a special slicer, and you can smell them from one part of the restaurant to the other. The medieval city of Alba, capital of the Langhe, is the most

6

important market and its October truffle fair is a great attraction for gourmets.

The people of Piedmont – of Asti and Alba especially – are great ones for festivals and pageantry. They have them all the time and everyone has a medieval costume and a flag ready to bring out. The most important are the wine and gastronomic festivals. For the festival *delle sagre* (festival of festivals) people come from all around the countryside, in ox carts, dressed in pre-war clothes, bringing mountains of their own local specialities for the great feast in the main square.

The truffle season, which comes at the same time as the grape harvest, at the end of October, is also the wild mushroom season, the game season and the season for frogs and snails. So autumn is the time when Piedmontese cooking blossoms and comes into its own. Truffles have become so expensive that few can afford to buy them and the alternative perfume which you can detect everywhere is that of garlic, married often with anchovies.

When Piedmontese cooking was thought to be derivative, it was the middle class cooking of Turin alone that people were thinking of. The extraordinarily rich variety of country dishes was ignored until they arrived at the capital with the influx of peasants who were to form the new working class (it is now massive, with immigrants from the south), and restaurants opened offering the dishes of the hinterland.

The great industrial and business city; the most hard-working city in Italy; the elegant baroque city of gracious squares, tree-lined streets and lovely gardens with graceful bridges over the river Po – Turin has no cooking of her own and few things which can be called entirely hers. The most representative is *giandujotti* – hazelnut chocolates, which take their name from the carnival mask *gianduja*. Turin is said to be the place where chocolate was first introduced in Europe. At the end of the sixteenth century the Duke Emanuele Filiberto brought cocoa back from Spain and, at the end of the eighteenth, Turin became the centre of a great chocolate industry (Suchard, the founder of the Swiss chocolate firm, went there as a young man to learn chocolate-making).

Another product of Turin known all over the world is grissini, the little hard sticks made with bread dough. In Turin people only want the hand-pulled, uneven, long, thin and crisp ones, sometimes with a dusting of flour clinging to them. There are two varieties: *stira* is thin, one-and-a-half-metres long, and dusted with rice flour; *rubata* is fatter and less even, with finger marks as it is made by rolling rather than pulling. Napoleon is said to have sent regularly for supplies of '*les petits bâtons de Turin*' from the city which the French affectionately named 'Grissinopoli' and 'the *commune* of San Grissino'.

The Turinese are famous for their passion for pastries and desserts and pastry-making is more developed here than anywhere else in Italy. Many of the wonderful sweets they serve in the old cafés, where you go to drink coffee and hot chocolate, were developed by cooks at the court of Savoy. These cafés also make their own ice-creams and are among the most enjoyable features of city life. Otherwise Turin has absorbed the culinary traditions of the countryside.

Turin is the only real city in Piedmont. Everything else is the antithesis of the city: entirely rural with small provincial towns filled with the smell of the country, love of the good life and people whose energies are directed towards wine and gastronomic festivals and singing sessions. The contrast is amazing.

Piedmont lies within an arc of high mountains which embraces its northern and western borders and fans into the gentle hills of the Langhe and Monferrato and down into the plain around Vercelli and Novara. The Valle d'Aosta, the smallest region of Italy, to the north-west of Piedmont, has deep river valleys alternating with high mountains which make it one of the loveliest tourist spots in the Alps. Because the geographical variety is so great, this part of Italy has the greatest possible agricultural differences. There are maize, barley and wheat and also rye and oats in the plain. Novara and Vercelli produce 60 per cent of Italy's rice. The celebrated vineyards are in the hills, where vegetables and fruit also grow: apples and pears in the Aosta valley, peaches around Canale, walnuts at Feisuglio, hazelnuts at Alba. Each valley and hillside specializes, and that is also the case with cherries and strawberries. Cattle-rearing in the mountain pastures makes Piedmont the greatest producer of meat in Italy, and one of the most important in butter and cheese. In the old days the cooking fats used were butter, pork fat, hazelnut and walnut oils. Now olive oil (from Liguria) is important.

The numerous alpine valleys produce a vast range of cheeses. Fresh cheeses are served as antipasti, sometimes dressed with olive oil and also herbs; a Piedmontese meal must always finish with sharp, piquant cheeses, served with red wine, followed by fruit and sweets served with Asti Spumante. Bread and cheese is a favourite accompaniment for wine-tasting.

The most famous cheese, fontina, is made in the Valle d'Aosta. Others are paglierino (the name comes from the straw – *paglia* – in which it was originally ripened), and robiola (also called tuma), a sharp, creamy goat's cheese. Piedmont is strong on goat's cheeses. There are dozens of different ones – soft and creamy, hard and semi-hard, sweet and aromatic, piquant, slightly acid and almost bitter – even when they look the same, they taste different in every valley. And there are mixtures: *brus*, from around Cuneo and Asti, is a mixture of different cheeses, mashed together, flavoured, left to ferment then enriched with grappa or other alcohols to make a powerfully piquant cream which can only be savoured in tiny quantities. *Sargnon*, a speciality of Vercelli, is made from remaindered pieces of gorgonzola and other fermented cheeses mixed with alcohol and left for a month to become a rich strongly flavoured cream.

There is quite a large range of home-made pork sausages and salamis. One of the most characteristic is *salamin d'la duja* which is kept in pork fat (the air is too humid for drying out), traditionally in a clay pot called *duja*, hence the name. And the region is also famous for its goose and donkey salamis (tender young donkeys less than one year old are used), its cured goose (*prosciutto d'oca*), smoked goose breasts (*petti stagionati*) and goose liver pâtés, and also *violini*, salted and cured venison.

A Piedmontese meal can be an overwhelming experience with from 5 to 30 antipasti which they call *assaggi* (tastings), followed by several often substantial courses. People have reduced the amount they eat in these diet and health-conscious days, but the habit of the important meal, especially on Sunday, remains an institution.

The countryside, to which all those with roots in the land and memories of parents and grandparents pruning the vine and feeding the chickens are deeply attached, has remained much the same, although everyone has become rich as the wine industry has prospered. The peasants here always put money aside, and when the landlords were forced to sell them their homes cheaply, they bought them and a bit of land. Their children went to work in local factories and the wages helped to invest in machinery. Half the agriculture is still in the hands of the old farmers, and their farmhouses (*cascine*), where once they had a bit of everything including ducks, geese, a few cows in the stable and a pig which made them self-sufficient, are still there next to modern villas in a sea of vines, vegetable gardens and fruit trees.

Giovanni Goria, a lawyer from Asti and the great Piedmontese gastronome who organizes festivals, advises and encourages restaurants and even teaches cooking (all for love), remembers the long list of typical dishes which figured year after year in the ritual cycle of feast days. To celebrate the *svinatura*, when they put the newly-made wine in the barrels, they ate *bagna cauda*, a strongly flavoured sauce kept simmering on a little stove on the table and a plate of raw vegetables for dipping. It was a convivial affair, with everyone dipping into the same bowl, eating masses of bread, drinking rivers of wine and singing. The Piedmontese are not spontaneous and exuberant like the Italians of the south, quite the opposite. They are quiet, reserved, hard-working, a little taciturn and closed in, so these moments of conviviality are extra precious.

For the *Festa dei Santi e dei Morti* (the Feast of the Saints and the Dead) they prepared a huge *minestrone*. On the feast of killing the pig, farmers invited their friends to come and enjoy the perishable parts. The basis of the Piedmontese *fritto misto* is the brains, sweetbreads, liver (all the parts which had to be eaten at once), and *batsoa*, boiled pig's trotters (the word comes from the French '*bas de soie*' – silk stocking), boned, and cut into slices, dipped in egg and bread-crumbs and fried.

Christmas Eve (a day of abstinence from meat) always began with *lasagne della Vigilia*, pasta simply dressed with butter, garlic and Spanish anchovies (since the Middle Ages every farmhouse had a barrel of salted anchovies brought to them from Spain by Provençal 'anchovy men'), great spoonfuls of parmesan and masses of black pepper, and continued with fried tench, stewed eels and salt cod. Christmas lunch started with a variety of pâtés made with liver, pheasant, goose and rabbit, followed by agnolotti, large ravioli stuffed with meats. Then came a very concentrated meat broth with *pasta reale*, omelette cut into little squares, and tiny peas, followed by a great big pike and the festive turkey stuffed with minced veal and parmesan. Dessert was *dolce Monte Bianco* with chestnuts and cream, perfumed with rum – the Piedmontese adore rum.

The great New Year's dish was the *gran bollito misto*, a selection of boiled meats, accompanied by an array of strongly flavoured sauces. The *bollito* was preceded by rice with *fonduta*, and followed by sliced fruit cooked in butter with sugar, then finally, a Milanese *panettone*. The list continues with dishes for the Carnival, Lent, Easter, the Resurrection and Spring.

Recently hundreds of trattorias and restaurants have sprung up where these and other traditional dishes can be found.

Every little part of Piedmont has its specialities and different influences although there has been a symbiosis between them. Until the fifteenth century, the region had been divided between a small aristocracy into numerous little autonomous dukedoms and marquisates, continually fighting one another and continually fighting off French and Austrian invaders. The house of Savoy, which had been mainly in the mountains, gradually affirmed itself, and by the eighteenth century all the domains were united under the Savoy dynasty. Piedmont, which had always been in the margin, went into the heart of Italian history and, during the period of the *Risorgimento* (1849–1861), it became the protagonist of Italian unity, providing the ideology, and the basis for government and driving the Austrians out of Italy. Count Camillo Benso di Cavour, the leading architect of Italian unity and the new nation's first prime minister, and Giuseppe Garibaldi (he was born in Nice which was part of the kingdom of Savoy), who led the bitter wars to unite the reluctant south, are the great heroes of Italian unity, with streets named after them in every city.

Cavour promoted the agricultural and industrial prosperity (mainly silk production) of the region, but while Turin grew into a powerful political and industrial capital, rural Piedmont continued with the old traditions, some of which date back to and reflect the diversity of the time of the old dukedoms and marquisates.

PÂTÉ DI FEGATO

Liver pâté

The recipe for this pâté comes from Danilo, the young owner-chef of La Cròta at Roddi d'Alba. Most of his customers ask for *assaggi* – small tastings of everything, a way of eating which has come into fashion in the last ten years.

250g (½lb) calf's liver
250g (½lb) chicken liver
125g (4oz) butter
Sprig of rosemary
3 tablespoons Marsala
Salt and pepper
3 tablespoons Cognac
1 small truffle diced (optional)

Clean the livers and remove the veining. Cut the calves liver into small pieces.

In a frying pan melt a knob of butter with the rosemary and sauté the chicken livers for moments only till browned but still pink and juicy inside. Remove, and sauté the calves' liver also moments only and on high heat till lightly browned but still pink inside. Pour in the Marsala and let it bubble for a second. Add salt and pepper and put the livers and pan juices through the blender.

Let the paste cool a little, then blend in the butter and the Cognac and finally stir in the truffle if used. Pour into a bowl and let it cool in the refrigerator for a few hours to a firm paste. Serve with toast.

BAGNA CAUDA

Hot garlic and anchovy dip

This hot garlicky sauce with vegetables to dip in is the most representative of Piedmontese foods. It is eaten all the year round but is associated by the Piedmontese with grape picking and pressing; the smell of fermenting grape juice; and the electric atmosphere which accompanies the rituals and celebrations of winemaking.

A drinking party invited me to join their long, thin table. They explained that a group around a *bagna cauda* must be large, uninhibited and jolly. Actually it was euphoric and they sang Piedmontese ballads.

Once upon a time the local hazelnut and walnut oils were used as a base for the sauce, but now a light and delicate olive oil from Liguria is used, and often it is mixed with melted butter.

Serves 4

200ml (7fl oz) olive oil
4–5 cloves of garlic, crushed
12 anchovies, drained and chopped
100g (4oz) butter

Put the oil in a pan, add the garlic and heat until garlic is soft but not brown. Add anchovies and cook, stirring, over a low heat until the anchovies dissolve, being careful not to burn the garlic. Add the butter and as soon as it has melted serve, standing it on a spirit stove on the table so it does not get cold.

TO SERVE Have a variety of raw vegetables cut into pieces – in Piedmont they use peppers, celery, carrots, cauliflower, mushrooms, fennel, artichoke hearts, cardoons, turnips, spring onion, beetroot, boiled potatoes and Jerusalem artichokes. Serve lots of bread to mop up the dip.

FONDUTA

Cheese fondue

Fonduta, a speciality of the Valle d'Aosta, the smallest Italian region, which has a very strong French character, can also be found in Piedmont. Fontina cheese, with which it is made, takes its name from Mount Fontin at Quart in the Valle. It is often served over polenta or rice.

Serves 6

500g fontina cheese, diced
300ml (½ pint) milk
5 egg yolks
50g butter, melted
White pepper
White truffles (optional)

Put the cheese in a bowl, cover with milk and leave for at least an hour to soften. Then heat in a double boiler stirring continuously until the cheese melts and starts to make threads. Add the butter and take off the heat. Beat in the egg yolks, return to the double boiler and stir vigorously until the mixture becomes smooth and creamy and thickens slightly. Do not let the mixture boil or the eggs will curdle (I find this way is quicker and works better than the usual one of starting with egg yolks then adding the cheese and milk). Add pepper, and if you have truffles, sprinkle with the shavings. Serve in soup plates with plenty of bread or toast to dip in.

NOTE Swiss gruyère is a good alternative to fontina.

PEPERONI ALLA PIEMONTESE

Peppers with anchovies and capers

Serves 6

4 fleshy peppers
6–8 anchovy fillets, finely chopped
1–2 cloves garlic, crushed
1 heaped tablespoon capers, finely chopped
A few sprigs of fresh oregano, finely chopped
4–5 tablespoons olive oil

Roast the peppers in a 200°C (400°F, gas mark 6) oven for 20 minutes or until they are soft, then put them straight into a polythene bag, close it tight and leave them for 10 minutes to loosen the skins. Peel the peppers, remove the seeds and cut each into 4 pieces or into ribbons. Dress with the rest of the ingredients, well mixed.

UOVA IN CAMICIA

Poached eggs with tomatoes and basil

Serves 4

1 small onion or ½ medium one, chopped
2 cloves garlic, crushed
2 tablespoons olive oil
400g (14oz) peeled and chopped tomatoes
3 tablespoons basil, chopped
2 tablespoons parsley, chopped
Salt and pepper
2 teaspoons vinegar
4 eggs

To make the sauce, fry the onion and garlic in oil until soft, add the tomatoes and simmer a few minutes until slightly reduced, then add the herbs and seasoning. Put a high-sided frying pan on the heat filled with salted water and the vinegar. When it comes to the boil, break the eggs in one by one and reduce the heat to simmering point. When the white is set, put a spoonful of sauce on to four dishes, remove the eggs with a draining spoon and place on the sauce.

CIPOLLE RIPIENE DI MAGRO

Onions stuffed with pumpkin

6 large (Spanish) onions
500g (1lb) sweet yellow pumpkin
175g (6oz) amaretti, reduced to crumbs
125g (4oz) mostarda (fruit in syrup with mustard essence)
A good pinch of nutmeg
Salt and pepper
1 egg
Butter

Boil the whole peeled onions in salted water for about 30–35 minutes till tender. Peel the pumpkin, remove the seeds and stringy bits and boil till tender (you can put it in with the onion and lift it out when it is done). Drain the onions, let them cool then cut them in half horizontally and remove the centres leaving a shell about 3 layers thick. Patch up any holes left at the bottom with a piece of onion.

For the filling, mash the pumpkin, add the *amaretti*, *mostarda* (you can buy it in jars), finely chopped, with a little of the syrup, season with nutmeg, salt and pepper and add an egg to bind it. You can put it all in the blender.

Fill the onion halves and place in a buttered baking dish. Top with butter shavings and bake in a 200°C (400°F) Mark 6 oven for about 40 minutes till nicely coloured.

NOTE You can do the same with small onions and serve them with an array of mixed little stuffed vegetables.

CIPOLLE RIPIENE

Onions stuffed with meat

4 large (Spanish) onions
250g (8oz) veal, minced
4 tablespoons grated cheese
2 cloves garlic, crushed
A sprig or two of oregano or marjoram, finely chopped
A bunch of parsley, finely chopped
2 tablespoons tomato paste
Salt and pepper
1 egg
Oil

Boil the peeled whole onions for about 35 minutes till tender. When they have cooled a little, cut in half horizontally and remove the centres leaving a shell of about 3 layers and patching any little hole left at the bottom with a piece of onion.

Mix the meat (if it is not already minced you can turn it to a paste in a food processor) with the cheese, garlic, herbs, tomato paste, a little salt and pepper and the egg, and work well to a smooth paste. Fill the onions with this mixture, arrange them in an oiled oven dish, brush the tops with oil and bake at 200°C (400°F, gas mark 6) for 40–50 minutes.

Serve hot.

IL FRITTO MISTO
PIEMONTESE

Mixed fried delicacies

The tradition of deep-frying spreads right across the country. *Figittori* or *frittolini* – some of them street vendors, specialize in frying. But the combination of little delicacies that are put together in a *grande fritto misto* can be something so special that it makes you gasp with surprise and pleasure.

Fritto misto belongs to the great tradition of Italian cooking for grand occasions. It is part of the rituals celebrating births, weddings, saints' days, anniversaries and special events such as a return from abroad. Piedmont, Emilia-Romagna, Lombardy, Rome, Tuscany and Naples are all famous for the variety they offer. The Piedmontese *fritto* is the richest. Until only a few years ago many restaurants there, especially in the region of the Langhe and in Turin, owed their reputation to their sumptuous selection of *fritti*, which could go up to as many as twenty-five. But now, because it is so rich and so finicky to make, a *fritto misto* is never on a menu more than once or twice a week, and usually it has to be ordered and the ingredients discussed in advance.

Traditionally, in Piedmont they fry in a mixture of oil and butter, but now many fry meat in sunflower oil, and that is what I prefer. Most things are first dipped in flour, then in beaten egg and finally in fine dry breadcrumbs, but some vegetables and fruit are dipped in a batter.

Some ingredients need to be cooked beforehand. All have different frying times. When they are a nice golden brown, they must be drained, salted, and brought to the table piping hot. Although it is possible to do all the frying in advance and to heat everything up in the oven when you are ready to serve, the result will not be quite the same as when the dark golden crust is still crisp and light from the hot fat. The components vary according to the season and to individual tastes. There can be chicken cutlets, potato and cheese croquettes, pieces of meat, all kinds of offal, vegetables and fruit. I once got a skewer with alternating pieces of bananas and strawberries. You could also be offered frogs, the cooked and flattened meat of pig's trotters, cockscombs and snails.

METHOD Have ready a bowl of beaten egg, a plate of flour and one of fine breadcrumbs.

For a batter, mix 100g (3½oz) flour with 1 egg and 1 tablespoon of oil and beat in about 120ml (4fl oz) water or milk or enough to make a light creamy batter.

Here are some of the usual meats

Lamb's or calves' kidneys – trimmed, the first cut in half, the second sliced (for preparation see page 21).
Lamb's or calves' brains – remove as much of the thin membrane as you can, blanch in salted water with 1 tablespoon of vinegar for a few minutes until firm, lift out and cool, then cut into large pieces.
Lamb's or calves' sweetbreads – peel off the thin membrane and blanch in salted water with a tablespoon of vinegar for about 10 minutes, then lift out, pull off the remaining membrane and cut into pieces.
Calves' or lamb's liver, cut into small thin slices
Tiny lamb chops
Frying sausages, cut into bite-sized pieces

Vegetables

Porcini mushrooms cut in slices or small mushrooms left whole
Aubergines, cut in slices
Asparagus – use only the tender part, up to 13cm (5in) from the stalk
Courgettes, cut in slices diagonally

14

Pumpkin flowers, the pistil removed and the stem trimmed, washed and dried – dip in batter.

Tomatoes, cut into thick slices and the seeds removed

Peppers

Artichoke hearts, cut in slices

Cauliflower, boiled in salted water till tender, then cut in florets

Fruit, sweet things and other foods

Sweet dessert apples, cut into slices – dip in batter

Amaretti (almond biscuits) slightly moistened in milk

Polenta cut into small 1cm (½in) thick slices

Fried sweet semolina cream is always present and is a must

To make this, bring to the boil in a saucepan 500ml (16fl oz) milk with 2 tablespoons sugar. Add 125g (4oz) semolina all at once and cook for about 15 minutes, stirring occasionally, over very low heat. Remove from the heat and mix in 1 egg yolk. Pour the mixture in a layer about 1cm (⅜in) thick on a wetted tray or dish and, when it has cooled, cut into parallel lines, then diagonally into lozenges. Turn them out and dredge first in flour, then in beaten egg and finally in breadcrumbs and deep-fry till golden.

NOTE In Lombardy they use butter for frying; elsewhere it is oil.

INSALATA DI CARNE CRUDA

Raw meat salad

I had this raw meat salad at the Castello Grinzane Cavour which once belonged to Cavour's family and now belongs to the *commune*. The castle houses a wine museum, an *enoteca* where you can taste local wines, and a trattoria which specializes in the cooking of the Langhe.

Serves 4 or 8

500g (1lb) very tender fillet of beef or veal
3 lemons
6–8 tablespoons olive oil
Salt and plenty of pepper
2–3 cloves garlic, crushed
A good bunch of parsley, finely chopped
4 pickled cucumbers, cut in thin slices
2–3 tablespoons capers

Chop the meat very finely. Beat the juice of 2 lemons with the olive oil, add salt and pepper and garlic, and mix very well with the meat. Let the meat absorb the dressing for 2 hours, covered, in the refrigerator. Serve spread on a flat dish, sprinkled with parsley, and garnished with lemon wedges and slices of pickled cucumber and capers spread around the edges.

VARIATIONS There are those who add 1–2 finely chopped anchovies to the sauce and those who present it with a crown of truffle or parmesan shavings or very thin slices of raw *porcini* mushrooms.

A modern version, the Venetian *carpaccio* invented at the grand hotel Cipriani, is to serve a very thin slice of raw beef dressed with the oil and lemon dressing, sometimes embellished with shavings of truffle or parmesan.

LINGUA IN SALSA ROSSA

Tongue with red sauce

Tongue with red sauce is a speciality of Asti where they serve the dish warm as an antipasto, but elsewhere it often comes as a main dish. Tender tongue and strongly-flavoured and fragrant sauce make a delicious combination.

In this country beef tongues are nearly always sold cured in saltpetre, which preserves their red colour. They will not be too salty if you cook them without soaking, but you may prefer to remove the saltiness (as I do) by soaking overnight in a bowl of cold water.

Serves 10–12

1 beef tongue weighing about 2kg (4lb)
1 onion
5 cloves
1 carrot, cut into large pieces
1 celery stalk, cut into pieces
2 bay leaves

Wash the tongue, put it in a large pan with plenty of water to cover, bring to the boil and remove the scum, then add the onion stuck with cloves and the rest of the ingredients and simmer gently, adding water to keep the meat covered, for about 4 hours, until it feels very tender when you pierce it with a pointed knife.

Take out the tongue, peel the skin off while still hot and return to the broth. Cut into slices just before serving, hot or cold, and accompany with the hot or cold red sauce. An alternative sauce is the herby green sauce – *salsa verde* (see page 19).

SALSA ROSSA

Red sauce

1 onion, chopped
1 celery, diced
1 carrot, diced
2–3 cloves garlic, chopped
1 red pepper, diced
2 tablespoons olive oil
2 anchovy fillets, finely chopped
1kg (2lb) tomatoes, peeled, seeded and cut into pieces
2 sprigs rosemary
Salt
Up to ½ a teaspoon chilli pepper
1–2 tablespoons red wine vinegar
1–2 tablespoons sugar
1 bunch of basil, chopped
A bunch of parsley, chopped

Fry the onion, celery, carrot, garlic and pepper in oil till soft, stirring often. Add the anchovies and let them melt, then add the tomatoes, the rosemary and salt, and simmer for 30–45 minutes until much reduced. Take out the rosemary twigs (they will have lost their leaves), blend the sauce to a cream and return it to the pan. Now add vinegar and sugar and chilli pepper and more salt if necessary, simmer for about 10 minutes, tasting to make sure that the flavouring is rich and strong, and add basil and parsley.

TAGLIATELLE CON TARTUFI

Tagliatelle with white truffles

If you want to try the old-style Piedmontese tagliatelle called *tajarin*, the dough is made with 400g of flour, 2 eggs, 1 tablespoon of grated parmesan and about 5 tablespoons of water, or see the recipe on page 84 and cut the noodles thin.

Serves 4

1 small white truffle
100g (3½oz) butter
40g (1½oz) grated parmesan
Salt and pepper
Pinch of nutmeg
500g (1lb) tagliatelle
or fettuccine

Scrub the truffle with a brush and wash it well. Melt the butter in a pan and add grated parmesan and a little salt, pepper and nutmeg.

Boil the tagliatelle until *al dente*, drain quickly and serve immediately, tossed with the melted butter mixture. Shave a little truffle over each serving.

ANTICO RISOTTO SABAUDO

Risotto with ham and cheese

Serves 4–6

50g (2oz) butter
1 medium onion, finely chopped
50–75g (2–3oz) cooked ham, diced
Sprig rosemary
400g (14oz) Arborio (risotto) rice
150ml (5fl oz) white wine
1.25 litres (2 pints) chicken or veal stock
100g (4oz) fontina or gruyère cheese, cubed
Freshly grated parmesan
Jellied meat juice (optional)
Sliced white truffle (optional)

Melt the butter in a saucepan, add onion and cook for five minutes until soft but not coloured. Add the ham and cook one minute, the rosemary and rice, stirring until the rice is transparent.

Add wine, stir and cook until it is absorbed. Add stock, ladleful by ladleful, stirring until each is absorbed. After about 20 minutes the rice should be creamy but *al dente*. Stir in fontina or gruyère and cook five minutes more. To finish, add three to four tablespoons of parmesan and the meat juice. This is sometimes crowned with a few shavings of white truffle.

RISOTTO AL BAROLO

Risotto with Barolo wine

Wine is one of the most important ingredients in Piedmontese cooking – there are wine soups; game is marinated in wine; stews are simmered in wine; *agnolotti* (meat ravioli) are served with wine poured over them, and fruits are cut up and dropped in wine for dessert.

This risotto from the Langhe has been adopted by restaurants in Turin. In the truffle season they add truffle shavings.

Serves 4

350g (12oz) Italian risotto rice
1 litre (1¾ pints) light chicken stock (you may use 1½ stock cubes)
Salt and pepper
1 onion, chopped
50g (2oz) butter
About 300ml (½ pint) Barolo or a good red wine
Grated parmesan

Bring the stock to the boil, add the rice, season with salt and pepper and simmer gently for 15 minutes, stirring occasionally, then drain. In the meantime, in another large pan, fry the onion in a knob of butter till soft and transparent, add the rice, pour in the wine a little at a time, and cook, stirring often, for 5–10 minutes, until the rice is tender. The risotto should be moist and creamy. Stir in the rest of the butter and let it melt in. I prefer to leave the parmesan for everyone to help themselves at the table.

IL BOLLITO MISTO

Mixed boiled meats

The tradition of boiling meat belongs to the north of Italy, especially to the cattle- and pig-raising valley of the river Po where they have made an art of boiling different types of meat together. Emilia Romagna (and Modena in particular) have a reputation for *bollito misto* and Lombardy once had.

But in Piedmont, where although it is considered more a meal for big eaters than a dish for gourmets and where it is offered on market days in the provinces, the *bollito* is an institution with a place of honour in restaurants – it features on Saturdays and Sundays on provincial menus and arrives in a splendid, silver trolley, *il carrello dei bolliti*, and is always present on great occasions.

Usually it is a matter of only two meats – beef and chicken (they call it *bollito di seconda*) or of three meats – *di terza*, with added tongue; while *di quarta*, with four, is the richest. You only find the dish in full regalia as the *gran bollito misto* with seven (it's the magic figure) traditional components, and at least three sauces in a few grand restaurants and at great family or civic events.

The typical Piedmontese protagonists of a *gran bollito misto* are beef, chicken, tongue, leg of veal, and, less commonly, calf's head, a joint of pork and *cotechino* (a coarse-cut boiling sausage). In Lombardy you may find calf's or pig's feet. In Emilia-Romagna sausages and pork products such as *cappello da prete*, *salame da sugo ferrarese* and the *zampone* (stuffed pig's foot) are prominent while in the Veneto, apart from Verona which is the regional capital of *bollito*, the usual offering is likely to be sausage or chicken – often stuffed with bread and herbs.

In the days before the stock cube, when stock-making for soups and risotti was all-important, the rich and noble Piedmontese families made a habit of regularly boiling meats and chicken for stock. The practice was to put the meats in cold water and then to bring them to the boil which extracted the best from the meat for the broth. The impoverished meat formed the servants' meal.

Now the meats go into boiling water which is supposed to seal in their juices and allow the meats to cook to melting tenderness (you should be able to eat them with only a fork) while preserving their succulence. *Bollito misto* is now more often eaten out than at home because families are no longer large enough for the amount of meat it requires.

There is a little prejudice in this country against boiled meats but everyone who eats them is usually won over, especially when there are wonderful sauces to enliven them.

Make it as simple or as complicated as you like with 2, 3, 4 or more meats – the choice is up to you. There is no merit in making it difficult for yourself. A good selection is chicken, beef or veal and tongue.

Serves 16–20

2 carrots, cut into chunks
2 stalks celery, cut into chunks
2 onions, cut into chunks
1.5kg (3lb) ox tongue (if you use a pickled one, cook it separately (see page 16) or its flavour will dominate the broth)
1 pig's trotter or calf's foot, scrubbed and blanched (optional)
1kg (2¼lb) brisket, topside or silverside of beef
Salt and pepper
1.5kg (3½lb) boiling chicken
900g (2lb) boneless veal (boned rump or rolled shoulder)
1 cotechino sausage, available pre-cooked in Italian shops

Place the vegetables, tongue and pig's trotter or calf's foot if you are using one, in a really large saucepan with enough boiling water to cover them, bring to the boil again and skim the scum from the surface. Then add the beef and season to taste. Reduce the heat and simmer, covered, very gently for an hour. Add the chicken and veal and simmer slowly for two more hours. Add the pre-cooked *cotechino* sausage towards the end of the cooking time and heat through thoroughly.

Leave the meat in the broth while you remove the tongue, skin and trim it and return it to the broth. Bring the meat, still in the broth, to the table and carve in thick slices – or carve in the kitchen, cover the slices in broth and keep hot until you are ready to serve.

TO SERVE Accompany with potatoes, carrots, baby turnips and onions, boiled separately; and serve with a selection of sauces (you must have the green which follows and red sauce (page 16)) and if you like, also pickles, olives, *mostarda di Cremona* (fruit in syrup with mustard essence which is served in Lombardy), *peperonata* (see page 56) and other sauces such as the horseradish *salsa di cren* (see page 51) of Friuli and Alto-Adige and the old-fashioned *saussa d'avie*, which is ground almonds or walnuts, mustard and honey mixed to taste.

VARIATIONS For a Modenese (Emilia-Romagna) version of *bollito misto* add a *zampone* – a pig's trotter stuffed with sausage meat. They are sold here already cooked and vacuum-packed. Follow the packet instructions and drop them in at the end.

BAGNET VERD

Green sauce

This green sauce to be served with boiled meats is far better made with the 'continental' parsley which is now more readily available at small fruiterers and no longer expensive. It is best made an hour before serving.

Serves 8

1 large 175g (6oz) bunch 'continental'
parsley, finely chopped
1 25g (1oz) bunch of mint, finely chopped
3 anchovies, finely chopped
1 tablespoon capers, finely chopped
4 small pickled cucumbers, finely chopped
4 tablespoons fine breadcrumbs (optional)
2 hard-boiled egg yolks, mashed (optional)
2 cloves garlic, crushed
2–3 tablespoons vinegar
1 tablespoon sugar
Salt and pepper
About 150ml (¼ pint) olive oil

Everything can be done in the food processor but not all at once. First chop the parsley and mint and put them in a bowl. Then blend the anchovies, capers, pickled cucumbers, breadcrumbs or hard-boiled egg yolks. Add them to the chopped herbs and mix in the garlic, vinegar, sugar, salt and pepper. Finally beat in the olive oil. The sauce should be slightly fluid.

MOSTARDA D'UVA

Fruit preserve in grape juice

This delicate sweet preserve is made when it is grape-picking time and grapes are pressed. It is kept in jars for serving with boiled meats.

About 600ml (1 pint) red grape juice
2 large hard pears
2 apples
1 teaspoon cinnamon
5 cloves
3 tablespoons walnut pieces or coarsely chopped and toasted hazelnuts or almonds (optional)

Boil the grape juice in a large pan until reduced by about half. Add the pears and apples, peeled and cored, and the cinnamon and cloves, and simmer gently, covered for most of the time, for at least an hour – cutting the fruit into little pieces when it is soft – until the fruit falls apart and the almost disappeared liquid has the consistency of syrup. If you like, add walnuts (but make sure they are not stale as they often are) or other nuts.

VARIATION In Asti they make *mostarda* with pears and quince.

Serves 8

3 tablespoons olive oil
2 stalks celery, finely chopped
3 carrots, peeled and finely chopped
2 cloves garlic, crushed
1 onion, chopped
Sprig rosemary
900g (2lb) beef topside in a piece, or rolled silverside
600ml (1 pint) Barolo wine
Salt and pepper
Freshly ground nutmeg

Heat oil in a pot or casserole, add celery, carrots, garlic and onion and cook for about five minutes until soft. Add rosemary and topside. Brown lightly then pour in wine, cover and simmer for two hours or until tender.

Remove the meat and keep warm. Pour liquid and vegetables into a blender and process until smooth. Season to taste with salt and pepper and nutmeg and reheat. Slice the meat and serve with sauce poured over.

At the restaurant it is usually accompanied by potato purée and carrots.

BRASATO AL BAROLO

Beef braised in Barolo

Every region of Italy makes stews (*stufati*). In the Veneto they call them *pastizzade*, in Venezia Giulia *gulasch*, in Emilia Romagna and Tuscany they are *stracotti* and in the south *ragù*. The *brasati* of Piedmont are different in that the piece of meat stays whole and it is first browned in fat, while the cooking medium is wine.

This recipe is from Signor Rocca of the Giardino da Felicin in Monforte d'Alba.

ROGNONI TRIFOLATI

Sautéed kidneys

Serves 4

4 veal or 12 lambs' kidneys, cleaned
2 tablespoons butter
1 tablespoon sunflower oil
1 onion, chopped
Salt and pepper
4 tablespoons cognac or 3 tablespoons Dry Marsala
Bunch of parsley, finely chopped

Split the kidneys in half, remove the cores and white membrane, then wash and cut into slices (they do not need soaking in water with vinegar to remove strong flavours as large beef kidneys do). Small lambs' kidneys can be left cut in half. Fry the onion in a mixture of oil and butter till soft, add the kidneys, season with salt and pepper and fry very briefly stirring on high heat, until they change colour. Sprinkle with cognac or Marsala and parsley and cook for a moment or two longer. They toughen if they are overcooked. Serve hot.

FEGATINI DI POLLO AL MARSALA

Chicken livers with Marsala

I was first offered this as an hors d'oeuvre but I like to serve it as a main course or as a sauce with noodles.

Serves 2

250g (8oz) chicken livers
1 small onion, chopped
1 tablespoon butter
2 slices pancetta or unsmoked bacon, chopped
Salt and pepper
6 tablespoons dry Marsala

Clean the livers and leave them whole. Fry the onion in butter till soft. Add the bacon and fry two minutes, stirring, then add the chicken livers and sauté quickly, turning over the pieces, till browned all over but still pink inside. Add salt and pepper and Marsala and cook for a minute or two.

ANATRA DI PALMINA

Duck stewed in wine

Serves 4

1 duck, jointed
1 onion, chopped
1 carrot, chopped
1 celery stalk and some leaves, chopped
Salt and pepper
300ml (½ pint) dry white or red wine
4 tablespoons cognac or brandy

It is simpler to buy duckling pieces – 2 legs and 2 breast fillets – for this dish. The best way to get rid of the fat is to remove the skin entirely from the start. Pull it off with the help of a sharp knife.

Heat a piece of skin, fat-side down, in a pan until you have released about 2 tablespoons of melted fat, and throw away the skin.

Fry the chopped onion, carrot and celery in the fat till soft, then put in the duck pieces. Pour in the wine, season with salt and pepper and simmer gently, covered, for an hour or until tender. Add the cognac or brandy, cook a few minutes longer and serve very hot.

NOTE The sauce can be served with pasta as a first course.

FAGIANO IN SALMI

Pheasant in red wine

This is a nineteenth century court dish, made a little differently now from the way it was prepared in the royal kitchens.

Serves 6

3 young tender hen pheasants
50g (2oz) tablespoons butter
2 tablespoons oil
2 unsmoked bacon slices, chopped
1 large onion, chopped
1 large carrot, chopped
2 cloves garlic, finely chopped
2 anchovies, finely chopped
1 stick celery and leaves, chopped
150ml (¼ pint) Marsala
Bottle of red wine
1 sprig of sage
2 sprigs of rosemary
3 bay leaves
5 cloves
1 teaspoon cinnamon
12 juniper berries
Salt and pepper

Sauté the pheasants in a mixture of butter and oil in a large casserole, turning them to brown them all over, then take them out. Drain off a bit of the fat, leaving some to fry the bacon and onion. When the onion is soft, add the carrot and garlic, and when the aroma rises add the anchovies and celery. Pour in the Marsala and the wine and add sage, rosemary, bay leaves, cloves, cinnamon, juniper berries, salt and pepper. Put the pheasants back in the casserole, add a little water and simmer, covered, for 30–45 minutes until tender, turning them over at least once.

Ladle most of the sauce into another pan and boil down to a rich consistency, then pour back over the birds and heat through.

Serve on toast or on grilled polenta (see page 64) with the sauce poured on top.

NOTE You can also bake the pheasants covered, in a 200°C (400°F, gas mark 6) oven for 45 to 60 minutes.

FAGIANO CALDO IN CARPIONE

Soused pheasant

Serves 4

4 hen pheasants
Sprigs of sage, rosemary and thyme
3 tablespoons olive oil
1 stick celery, finely chopped
1 medium carrot, finely chopped
1 onion, finely chopped
1 bottle medium dry white wine
25g (1oz) butter
3 shallots, finely chopped
2 tablespoons vinegar
2 egg yolks
Salt and pepper

Stuff pheasants with herbs and brown in the oil. Add vegetables, pour in wine, add water to cover, and bring to the boil. Season and simmer covered for 30–45 minutes. Remove the birds and keep warm.

Melt the butter in a pan, add shallots, cook until soft and golden.

Strain the liquid into shallots, add vinegar, boil to reduce to 400ml (15fl oz). Stir two tablespoons into egg yolks and return to saucepan. Stir over gentle heat, a moment only to prevent curdling, until slightly thickened. Serve pheasants with the sauce poured over (for a smoother sauce, liquidise it in a blender).

QUAGLIE SU CROSTONE DI POLENTA

Quail on grilled polenta

There is a long tradition of cooking game birds and *polenta e osei* (polenta with birds) is a famous northern dish which arouses romantic nostalgia. Now that there is little to be caught, farmed quail is the usual alternative.

Serves 4

8 quail
300ml (½ pint) white wine
Few sage leaves
2 sprigs of rosemary
Pepper
100g (3½oz) unsmoked bacon slices, cut into small pieces
3 tablespoons vegetable oil
Salt
8 slices of polenta (see page 64)

Marinate the quail overnight in wine with sage, rosemary and pepper.

Fry the bacon in oil for a few minutes, then add the birds, lifted out of the marinade. Turn to brown them all over, then pour in the marinade. Add salt, and simmer for 20–30 minutes until the quails are cooked and the sauce is reduced, adding more wine or a little water if it becomes too dry and turning over the quail.

Toast the slices of polenta under the grill, turning them over once. Serve the birds on top and the sauce poured over.

VARIATION For grilled quail, cut the birds open at the breast, then pull them out and flatten them as much as you can so that they cook more evenly. Marinate as above. Brush with oil and cook over glowing embers or under the grill turning them over once and leaving them longer with the open, bone side towards the fire. Be careful not to overcook.

LEPRE IN SALMI

Hare in wine sauce

Serves 4

½ onion, chopped
½ carrot, chopped
1 small stick celery and leaves, chopped
1 clove of garlic, chopped
2 tablespoons sunflower or other light oil
1 hare, cut into four pieces
420ml (¾ pint) red wine
1 bay leaf
4 cloves
1 teaspoon cinnamon
Salt and pepper
3 tablespoons Marsala

In a large pan fry the onion, carrot, celery and garlic in oil till soft. Add the hare and turn to brown the meat all over then pour in the wine. Add the bay leaf, cloves, cinnamon, salt and pepper and simmer for 30 minutes. If you have the liver, put it into the pot and cook for a minute. Now blend the liquid with the liver (to make a thicker sauce), return to the pan and cook a few minutes longer, until the meat is tender (with the young tender hare available now it takes less than 45 minutes altogether). Add Marsala towards the end.

NOTE It is quite usual to use the sauce to dress pasta, which is served as a first course.

TARTARÀ DOLCE

Almond pudding

Tartarà is one of the old farmhouse foods that have been 'reborn'. A savoury *taratrà* with milk, eggs and cheese is also popular.

Serves 4

4 egg yolks
6 tablespoons sugar
½ litre (18fl oz) milk
The grated peel of 1 lemon
100g (3½oz) almonds, very finely chopped
6 bitter almonds, finely chopped or a few drops of almond essence

Beat the eggs with sugar in a bowl sitting in boiling water till pale and fluffy. Boil the milk with the grated peel, cool slightly and add to the egg mixture and cook, stirring (to avoid lumps forming), till it thickens (it does so only a little). Now add the almonds and essence and continue to cook, stirring occasionally, to a thick cream. Serve hot or cold.

ZABAIONE

Zabaglione

In the countryside, *zabaione* is eaten hot for breakfast.

Serves 6

8 large egg yolks
75–125g (3–4oz) sugar
250ml (8fl oz) dry Marsala or red wine

Beat the egg yolks with the sugar until they are pale, then beat in the Marsala. Pour into a large saucepan and heat gently by standing the pan in a larger pan of barely simmering water. Beat constantly – an electric beater is a help – until the mixture swells to a thick foam. serve in warm glasses with dry biscuits.

BONÈT

Rum and chocolate custard

Serves 4

5 eggs
7 tablespoons sugar
½ litre (18fl oz) warm milk
100g (3½oz) plain amaretti (dry macaroons), finely crushed
2 tablespoons bitter or dark cocoa
200ml (7fl oz) good strong coffee
3 tablespoons rum

Beat the eggs with 4 tablespoons of sugar. Mix in the milk, amaretti, cocoa, coffee and rum. Heat the remaining sugar with 2 tablespoons of water and let it become golden brown. Pour it into a warmed mould and coat the inside. Let it cool, then pour in the milk mixture. Bake at 150°C (300°F, gas mark 2) for an hour or until the cream sets. Chill and turn out.

TORTA DI NOCCIOLE

Hazelnut cake

1 tablespoon baking powder
3 eggs, separated
200g (7oz) sugar
125g (4oz) butter, melted
200g (7oz) flour
200g (7oz) hazelnuts (bought without skins), coarsely chopped and toasted
Grated rind of 1 lemon
4 tablespoons milk

Beat the baking powder with the egg yolks, add the sugar, butter, flour, hazelnuts and milk and mix thoroughly. Beat the egg whites stiff and fold in. Pour into a 20cm (8in) buttered, floured cake tin and bake at 180°C (350°F, gas mark 4) for 35 minutes or until browned and a skewer comes out almost dry.

Liguria

A tiny narrow arc on the sea below Piedmont framing the bay of Genoa, Liguria is all hills rising up spectacularly from the sea into the high mountains of the Alps and the Apennines. The towns are all perched on the coast and almost a quarter of all Italian tourism is there, attracted by the lovely beaches, the sun and the deep blue sea. Every kind of vegetable is squeezed into the thin strip between the sea and the hills which are terraced and planted with olives, vines and fruit trees, particularly peaches, apricots, oranges and lemons. The brilliant sun makes everything grow profusely. Colour bursts out from every corner. Bright flowers grow out of crevices and cascade down the walls which support the banks above roads, and even in the winter mimosas and bougainvillaea bloom. There is an intensive commercial cultivation of carnations and other flowers, and the Ligurian coast is called the *Riviera dei Fiori* (the Riviera of flowers).

The hills are covered with wild herbs entangled in the scrub – thyme, sage, rosemary, oregano, marjoram and basil. They perfume the air and characterize the cooking. While Piedmontese food is winter fare with all its *bolliti*, *fritti misti* and *brasati* (stews), the cooking of Liguria is at its best in the summer months. Both are highly aromatic – the Piedmontese with truffles, wild mushrooms and garlic, the Ligurian with garlic and herbs. Ligurians adore herbs and greenery: they cook everything with their delicate olive oil, one of the best in Italy.

Their cooking is surprising in many ways. It has none of the characteristics which are common to the other northern regions, nor is it a cuisine based on the sea, as you would expect from a region with so much coastline. Instead it makes great use of vegetables and its most striking feature is the abundant use of aromatic herbs. The difference from its northern neighbours can be explained by the natural barrier of high mountains which left it isolated in the days when transport was difficult. All Liguria's traffic and exchanges were made across the sea: it received pine nuts from Pisa, pecorino cheese from Sardinia, and salted

25

anchovies in barrels from Spain. The list of special local dishes is extraordinary for such a small region; the cuisine owes more to the country than the sea because it grew out of the hankerings of her sailors.

For centuries all the men of Liguria were sailors. Christopher Columbus was born in Genoa, which is still Italy's most active port, and La Spezia is one of Italy's two naval bases. In the days of sail when voyages took months, sailors lived on foods which kept for ever, like beans, chickpeas, dry salami and hard biscuits and, of course, they ate fish. They yearned for fresh vegetables and greenery and fragrance, and during their time ashore this is what their women made to please them. The Ligurians adore herbs and make a cult in particular of basil. Everyone grows their own in every available space, in little plots, in window boxes, around the house. Their most famous food – they call it their flag – is the basil sauce *pesto*. Provence in the south of France makes a similar sauce: *pistou*. Liguria became briefly part of the French Empire in 1806 and Nice was Ligurian until 1859. Liguria is the most truly Mediterranean region of Italy and you find here more than in any other part similarities with southern France, Spain, Greece and the Arab world. Square lasagne are *mandilli di sea* (*mandil* is the Arab word for handkerchief and *sea* means silk in dialect). Trenette or linguine are also called by an old Arab name, *tria*. There were Saracen coves on the coast until the tenth century but the culinary legacy may have come from the trading colonies Genoese merchants established on the coast of North Africa. Ligurian cooking is the cooking of Genoa and, like all the great Mediterranean ports, many of the influences come from far away.

Another reason why the cooking of the sea is not greatly developed is that this part of the coast is not rich in fish. There are plenty of shellfish-like a type of clam called *tartufi di mare*, sea dates (*datteri di mare*) and mussels (a hairy type, which the Ligurians call *cozze pelose*). They eat shellfish raw, sprinkled with lemon and pepper or take them out of the shells, dip them in batter and deep fry them.

Until 1815 when it was incorporated in the kingdom of Savoy, Genoa was the capital of the Ligurian republic, which in its heyday had been one of the great financial and commercial powers of the Mediterranean, a rival to Venice and Pisa. But Liguria always suffered from the division of the land into myriads of small, constantly warring estates of the local nobility. Some of the history is visible in the medieval city centre of Genoa where the walls of the tall houses seem to close overhead leaving only a slit of piercing sunlight to illumine the labyrinth of streets. It is visible in the Romanesque, Gothic and Baroque churches and splendid Renaissance villas and palaces and the castles that dot the mountains and it is also present in the dishes.

1. Baked courgette boats (p123), peppers stuffed with rice (p182), tomatoes filled with vermicelli and a mixture of herbs (p174), onions stuffed with pumpkin (p13)

2. *Mushroom market in Treviso*
3. *Palermo market*
4. *Venice: vegetables arrive by boat*
5. *Piazza Campo di Fiori in Rome. A* norcineria *is a butcher's which specialises in sausages
and pork meat.*

*Nowadays markets have most vegetables all the year round. Wild mushrooms and wild salad
leaves are enormously popular.*

6. Brodetto alla Marchigiana – *fish soup with sea bream, red mullet, squid, mussels, clams, langoustines and king prawns (p117)*
7. *Scallops, mussels, oysters and clams are eaten raw, steamed or placed on a grill until they open. Crabs and prawns are boiled, and they are all served with oil, lemon and chopped parsley*

8. *At the fish market in Marsala, Sicily*
9. *The Trieste fish market*
10. *Fish sold out in the street in Naples*

*The cooking of fish and seafood is now very
much the same all around the coast. There is
seafood salad, seafood pasta and seafood
risotto, grilled and fried fish and fish soup, but
every port and every seatown has its own special
selection for the traditional mixed fry and for
fish soup, which may have tomatoes or not,
white wine or vinegar. In Venice they put fish
straight on to the grill, in the south they dip it
first in breadcrumbs.*

11. Popular antipasti *of the south are simple and tasty: garlic bread with tomatoes (p159), roast pepper salad (p169), aubergines country style grilled and marinated with garlic, oregano and mint (p159)*

FOCACCIA

Flat bread

In Tuscany they call this *schiacciata*.

Serves 8 or more

1kg (2lb) flour
Salt
50g (2oz) fresh or 25g (1oz) dried yeast
About 500ml (18fl oz) or more warm water
A pinch of sugar
150ml (¼ pint) olive oil
Coarse salt
2 sprigs of rosemary or sage

Put the flour and a pinch of salt in a bowl and make a well in the centre. Dissolve the fresh yeast in about half a glass of the measured warm water, adding a pinch of sugar to activate it. Leave it to froth then pour into the flour, stirring it in with a wooden spoon. Or follow the packet instructions for dried yeast. Then stir in 4 tablespoons of oil and enough of the remaining warm water, working it in with your hands, to make a soft dough. Knead for 10–15 minutes until soft and elastic, adding a little flour if it is too sticky. Then roll the dough in a tablespoon of oil so that a dry crust does not form, cover it with a damp cloth and leave to rise in a warm place for an hour or until it doubles in bulk. Punch it down and knead it again briefly, then divide it into 2 balls and roll each out onto a lightly floured surface with a lightly floured rolling pin to a thickness of about 1cm (⅜in). Lift each onto an oiled baking sheet, brush the top generously with oil and sprinkle with salt and rosemary or sage leaves. Press your finger in the dough to make indentations all over and let the dough rise again for about half an hour on the sheet. Bake it in the hottest part of your oven at the highest marking for about 20 minutes until golden brown. Brush with olive oil and serve warm.

FOCACCIA CON LE OLIVE

Flat bread with olives

Serves 8

1kg (2lb) flour
Salt
50g (2oz) fresh or 25g (1oz) dried yeast
350ml (12fl oz) warm water
1 pinch of sugar
150ml (¼ pint) olive oil plus 6 tablespoons
to brush on at the end
150ml (¼ pint) dry white wine
400g (14oz) black olives, pitted and coarsely chopped
1 tablespoon thyme
2 tablespoons oregano

Put the flour and a pinch of salt in a bowl and make a well in the centre. Dissolve the fresh yeast in about half a glass of the water, adding a pinch of sugar to activate it. Leave it to froth then stir into the flour. Or follow the packet instructions for dried yeast.

Stir in 150ml (¼ pint) olive oil and the wine, then add the rest of the warm water, working it in with your hands – just enough so that the dough sticks together in a ball. Knead well for 10–15 minutes until soft and elastic, adding a little flour if it is too sticky. Then work in two-thirds of the olives and the thyme. Leave the dough to rise in a bowl covered by a damp cloth for 1–2 hours until doubled in bulk, then punch down and work for a minute or two. Roll out on a floured surface with a floured rolling pin to a thickness of about 1cm (½in) and place on oiled trays, spreading it out with your hands. Sprinkle with salt and oregano and spread the rest of the olives over the top. Make many depressions all over the dough with your finger. Bake at the hottest possible heat for about 25 minutes till lightly brown. Brush with the remaining oil and serve hot.

FUNGHI RIPIENI

Stuffed mushrooms

Liguria, like the French Riviera, is known for its great variety of stuffed vegetables.

Serves 6

500g (1lb) large flat mushrooms
Olive oil
Salt and pepper
Large bunch of parsley
2 slices of dry white bread, crusts removed
Milk
2 or more cloves of garlic, crushed
2–3 tablespoons brandy or rum (optional)

Wash the mushrooms and cut off the stalks, then briefly fry in 2–3 tablespoons of oil for 5 minutes or until just tender, sprinkling with salt and pepper and turning them over once. Arrange them, stem side up, side by side in a heatproof dish.

For the stuffing, chop the mushroom stalks and parsley finely in a food processor. Add the bread, soaked in milk and squeezed dry, and process a little longer. Turn into a bowl and add as much garlic as you like and a little salt and pepper. Moisten with brandy or rum to taste and with 2–3 tablespoons olive oil and mix well. Press a little stuffing into each mushroom cap and put under the grill for about 5 minutes. Serve hot.

VARIATIONS You can also bake the mushrooms. Place the stuffing in the raw caps brushed with oil and bake at 200°C (400°F, gas mark 6) for about 20 minutes.

The more common Ligurian stuffing has 100g (4oz) grated parmesan and 50g (2oz) breadcrumbs moistened with milk mixed with 2 eggs, some chopped oregano and marjoram and salt and pepper. I found restaurants baking huge trays of many different vegetables, all tiny and all with this filling, which makes a charming display but which makes all the vegetables taste the same.

ZUPPA DI LATTUGHE RIPIENE

Stuffed lettuce with a mushroom filling in broth

Serves 4

400g (14oz) shiitake or other mushrooms
2–3 tablespoons olive oil
4 cloves of garlic, crushed
3 tablespoons fresh marjoram, chopped
200g (7oz) ricotta
2 eggs
2–3 tablespoons parmesan
Salt and pepper
1 large iceberg or romaine lettuce
1 litre (1¾ pints) light meat broth
4 slices coarse-textured bread, toasted in the oven and brushed with olive oil

Chop the mushrooms finely in a food processor. Lightly fry in the oil with the garlic and marjoram for about 10 minutes until tender, stirring occasionally. Then mash the ricotta with the eggs, add the mushrooms, parmesan, salt and pepper, and mix well.

Discard the outer leaves of the lettuce and separate the rest. Blanch them in boiling water for a few seconds until they soften, then drain. Open each carefully, put a heaped tablespoon of filling at one end and roll up towards the end where the rib is thickest, tucking in the sides before the roll is finished so that the filling does not fall out.

Pack the rolls into a wide saucepan. Pour on the boiling broth and simmer a few minutes.

Serve the rolls in soup bowls on the toasted bread with a little of the broth poured over.

PESTO

Genoese basil and pine nut sauce

Pesto is the prince of Ligurian dishes. Its making is a joyful ritual and the perfume which fills the air is a powerful appetite whetter. There is no place in the world which makes as much use of basil as Genoa, and no place where the plant has as much perfume. Every town has its own version. This is the way they make it at 'Da 'O Vittorio' in Recco. It is served with trenette, tagliatelle or corzetti (coin-shaped and stamped with a motif) and with gnocchi.

Serves 4

2 or more cloves garlic, crushed
50g (2oz) pine nuts
Salt
4 tablespoons grated pecorino sardo or parmesan
50g (2oz) basil weighed with the stems (or 8 supermarket bunches)
150ml (5fl oz) light olive oil
2–3 tablespoons prescinsoa (a creamy acid ricotta) or fromage frais (optional)

Pound the garlic and pine nuts in a large mortar with a little salt. Add the chopped basil leaves (the amount takes into account that the basil we get here is less perfumed than theirs), a few at a time, pounding and grinding the leaves against the sides of the bowl. You can also put everything in the blender. Now stir in the grated cheese and mix very well, then gradually beat in the olive oil (the olive oil of Liguria is very light, delicate and perfumed) and the prescinsoa or fromage frais.

MINESTRONE CON PESTO

Vegetable soup with pesto sauce

This is the kind of soup which is best made the day before to give the flavours time to mingle.

Serves 6–8

4 medium potatoes, peeled and diced
1 slice (about 250g/9oz) pumpkin diced, or a few sliced courgettes
1 small cauliflower, broken into small florets
75g (3oz) mushrooms, roughly chopped
100g (4oz) fresh or frozen peas
150g (5oz) broad beans, or green beans cut in pieces
1 medium can (400g/14oz) cannellini beans
1 onion, finely chopped
2–3 tablespoons olive oil
6 ripe tomatoes, peeled and chopped (or 1 medium can plum tomatoes)
3 tablespoons parsley, finely chopped
Salt and pepper
100g (4oz) rice or pasta (ribbons or broken tagliatelle)
Pesto
4 tablespoons grated parmesan or pecorino

Fill a pan with plenty of salted water and bring to the boil. Add the potatoes, pumpkin, cauliflower, mushrooms, fresh peas and broad beans and simmer for about 40 minutes or until the vegetables are very tender. Add the cannellini beans and heat through. In the meantime, fry the onion in oil until soft, add the tomatoes and parsley and cook a further five minutes, then pour the mixture into the soup and check the seasoning.

Twenty minutes before serving, bring to the boil and add the rice, or add pasta 10 minutes before serving. When the rice or pasta is cooked, stir in the pesto, or pass it around along with the grated cheese and let everyone help themselves.

TRENETTE AL PESTO ALLA GENOVESE

Noodles with pesto sauce

Serves 4

Pesto sauce (page 29)
2 medium waxy new potatoes, peeled and sliced
4–6 french green beans, strings removed
Salt
400g (14oz) trenette (thin egg noodles) or fettuccine
Grated pecorino or parmesan

Put the potatoes and green beans to boil in a large pan with plenty of salted boiling water and cook until both are nearly done, then throw in the trenette and cook until these are *al dente*. Drain, reserving a ladle of the cooking water. Serve with the pesto sauce, diluted if you like with a little of the cooking water, and with grated cheese.

MANDILLI DI SEA

Pasta squares with pesto

For *mandilli di sea* (which means silk handkerchiefs in dialect) make egg pasta as described on page 84 – there are those who mix a little white wine with the water – roll it out as thin as you can, let it dry for 30 minutes on a cloth, and cut into 15cm (6in) squares. Cook, four at a time, in boiling salted water with a tablespoon of oil to prevent them sticking, until done *al dente*. Serve as they are with plenty of *pesto*. You may also use bought lasagne.

This is not the kind of food you can make for a party because you can only make a few *mandilli* at a time and you must serve them right away. It is the kind of food you eat in the kitchen while the next batch is being cooked.

PANSOTI CON SALSA DI NOCI

Triangular herb ravioli with walnut sauce

Pansoti means 'pot bellied'. Different kinds of wild Ligurian herbs and leaves (*preboggion* is the general term) may go into the filling. I have made *pansoti* with spinach and cress, but you may try adding herbs of your choice.

Serves 10

For the filling

1kg (2lb) mixture of beets, swiss chard or spinach and borage or 500g (1lb) frozen spinach
200g (7oz) cress weighed with stems (2 bunches)
Salt
200g (7oz) ricotta
50g (2oz) grated parmesan
25g (1oz) butter, melted
2 eggs
Pepper
1/4 teaspoon nutmeg

For the dough

400g (14oz) flour
A pinch of salt
1 whole egg
1 egg yolk, plus another to stick the edges
120ml (4fl oz) water

Make the filling: wash all the green leaves, remove the stems and cook in very little salted water, turning them over with a wooden spoon until they crumple to a soft mass. Drain and squeeze every drop of water out, then chop finely – in a food processor if you like, and mix well with the rest of the filling ingredients. Frozen spinach need only be defrosted and squeeze-dried.

Make the dough: mix the flour and salt with the egg and yolk and add only just enough water so that it holds together in a ball, working it in with your hands. Then knead for 10–15 minutes until the dough is smooth and elastic, adding a little more flour if it is too sticky. Wrap in clingfilm and leave to rest for 30 minutes. Then roll out as thinly as you can on a lightly floured surface with a floured rolling pin. Cut the sheet into 10cm (4in) squares and brush the edges with the remaining egg yolk. Put a heaped teaspoon of filling in the centre of each square and fold over the filling into a triangle, pressing the edges firmly to stick them together (you can bring the ends together to make the traditional headscarf shape but it is not worth doing if you risk tearing the dough).

Cook the pansoti in plenty of salted boiling water for 3–5 minutes until *al dente*, then drain and serve covered with the following sauce.

SALSA DI NOCI

Walnut sauce

300g (10oz) shelled walnuts
1 clove garlic, crushed
2 slices of country bread, crusts removed
300ml (½ pint) milk
50g (2oz) grated parmesan
5–6 tablespoons light olive oil
Salt and pepper

Blend the walnuts and garlic, the bread soaked in the milk, the cheese and olive oil (the Ligurian oil is light and delicately flavoured) to a cream, adding salt and pepper.

TORTA DI RISO E SPINACI

Rice and spinach cake

Serves 8

500g (1lb) fresh or 250g (½lb) frozen whole leaf spinach
250g (½lb) Italian short-grain risotto rice
Salt
1 onion, chopped
1 tablespoon of oil
25g (1oz) butter
3 eggs
4 tablespoons parmesan
Pepper
Good pinch of nutmeg

Wash the spinach and remove the stems. Cook until it softens (frozen spinach needs only to be defrosted) then drain and chop fine. Boil the rice in salted water for about 10 minutes until nearly done, throw the spinach in with the rice, stir well and drain at once.

Fry the onion in oil till golden and put it in a bowl with the rice and spinach. Add butter, eggs and cheese, pepper and nutmeg. Mix well and press into a buttered non-stick mould or cake tin. Bake in a 200°C (400°F, gas mark 6) oven for about 25 minutes until golden.

Turn out and serve hot. It is also good cold.

VARIATION For *preboggion con riso*, add a bunch of chopped herbs such as mint, basil, marjoram, oregano, thyme, sage, rosemary, parsley and 1 or 2 crushed cloves of garlic with the spinach.

TRIGLIE ALLA LIGURE

Red mullet with olives

This is how Gianni Bisso cooks red mullet at Da 'O Vittorio in Recco.

Serves 2

*2 × 225g (8oz) red mullet, cleaned and
scaled
4 tablespoons olive oil
150ml (5fl oz) white wine
Pinch salt
50g (2oz) black olives, stoned
1 lemon, halved
2 tablespoons fresh parsley, chopped
2 cloves garlic, chopped*

Put the mullet in an oven dish with the oil, wine, salt, olives, garlic and lemon halves. Cover with foil and bake at 180°C (350°F, gas mark 4) for 20 minutes, or until the fish flakes easily when tested with the point of a knife. Serve sprinkled with parsley.

SPINACI ALL'UVETTA PASSOLINA E AI PINOLI

Spinach with raisins and pine nuts

The more common way of doing this Genoese dish is with olive oil and anchovies and without tomatoes. I prefer this recipe, and I like using butter which softens the taste of spinach.

Serves 4

*1kg (2lb) spinach
4 ripe tomatoes, peeled and chopped
3 tablespoons light olive oil or a mixture
with butter
2 tablespoons raisins, soaked in water
Salt and pepper
Pinch of nutmeg
2 tablespoons pine nuts*

Wash the spinach well and remove the stems. Drain and squeeze the water out. In a large pan heat the tomatoes in butter and oil till soft. Put in the spinach and the drained raisins and cook, stirring, and turning the leaves over until they crumple. Season with salt, pepper and nutmeg, stir in the toasted pine nuts and serve hot.

COTOGNE IN COMPOSTA

Quinces in syrup

This old-fashioned preserve makes a ready dessert which keeps well in a jar.

Serves 6

*1kg (2lb) quinces
250g (½lb) sugar
Thinly pared peel of ½ lemon
Juice of ½ lemon
1½ teaspoons cinnamon
6 cloves
150ml (¼ pint dry white wine)*

Wash, peel and core the quinces and cut them into thick slices. Put them with the peels and cores (these lend a jellied quality) in a pan with the rest of the ingredients and about 300ml (½ pint) of water to cover.

Simmer for about an hour until the fruit is tender, then lift out the quince slices and arrange in a serving bowl. Reduce the syrup a little and strain it over them. Serve cold.

Lombardy

Lombardy is the richest of all the regions. It accounts for a third of all Italian exports but it is not a smoky industrial monster. Industries are studded around the most luxuriant and fertile of countrysides. The basin of the River Po is an immense flat plain with pale green fields alternating with wheat, maize and rice fields, cut by rivers and canals; fringed to the north by a succession of the most beautiful lakes in Italy (Maggiore, Lugano, Como and Garda) and by pre-alps which rise to high snowy-crested peaks. Woods scramble over hills, bell towers spring out from behind trees, a hazy mist gives an air of nostalgic melancholy. Towns with historic names and palaces, castles and medieval streets carry you into the heart of the Renaissance.

Lombardy was already well advanced in agriculture by the fifteenth century. It was ruled by noble families who owned the land; first by the Viscontis and later the Sforzas who were the richest and most powerful *signorie* in the peninsula (there were also the Gonzagas in Mantua and the Estes). By draining the marshes and irrigating the fields they made Lombardy the most productive region in the world at the time. They grew wheat and maize and introduced the cultivation of rice, bred and stabled cattle and made cheese. At that time Italy was the centre of Europe. Italian could be heard in the kitchens of the European courts and the banquets of noble families were complex spectacles of gastronomic architecture and choreography.

The eighteenth century saw a growing movement of capital towards the countryside. Merchants and the nobility built villas and gardens and began to invest in large-scale agriculture. Large farm settlements and capitalist methods of production appeared, and the old feudal order fused into semi-feudal systems such as the *mezzadria* in which tenant agricultural families gave half their produce to landowners.

This was when the cuisine of Lombardy took its shape, combining the rustic cooking of the hungry *mezzadro*, who remained personally and economically dependent, locked in a cycle of subsistence, with a kind of cosmopolitan *haute cuisine* which retained elements of the old tradition of the court and was practised by a middle class passionate about the pleasures of the table.

The court cuisine had been in the great Italian Renaissance tradition which was codified by Bartolomeo Sacchi of Piadena (known as Platina), in his *De honesta voluptate* (1457), the first cookery book to be published in Italy, in which most of the recipes came from Mastro Martino, a cook from Como who worked for the Patriarch of Aquileia. In almost every restaurant I went to where they served regional dishes, chefs brought out facsimiles of books written by men who cooked at the courts, from which they picked ideas for their menus. The most commonly used is one published in 1662 by Bartolomeo Stefani, a Bolognese who was a steward at the Gonzaga court in Mantua. But the chefs also gave me lyrical accounts of the 'poor food' of the old peasantry; of the offal (tripe, heads, tails, feet, lungs) and cured meats and sausages they ate only a few times a year; of the one-pot *piatto unico* in which the poor combined meat and vegetables; of the pheasants and partridges and birds they caught (illegally, as they belonged to the landlords); of the eel and trout of the lakes, the chestnuts gathered in the mountains, the wild strawberries with their extraordinary perfume; and the mushrooms and truffles they found in the woodland.

It is impossible to speak in general of the cooking of Lombardy because, apart from these rich and poor traditions, and differences in the cooking of the plain, lakes, hills and mountains, every town is different and does not know the dishes of the next. It is, more than in any other region of Italy, a real mosaic. Bergamo, once part of the Serenissima, is more Venetian; Mantua, which was the seat of the Gonzagas and has refined aristocratic cooking traditions, is more like Emilia to the south; the Valtellina has the resources of the mountains, including game. But they do have things in common: they use enormous quantities of butter, lard and cream and all the cuisines are based on risotto, polenta and *minestre*.

Lombardy is the region which grows and consumes the most rice. The culture of the grain expanded throughout the plain in the sixteenth century, but not without difficulties; it was blamed for the malaria which prevails in the watery areas, and fields were constantly destroyed by edict. Before it was mechanized rice picking was the work of women – the *mondine*, who spent their days wading in the marshy waters, their dresses stuffed into their drawers. The rice is short-grain and there are many varieties: the round originario and padano which fall apart and stick together quickly are preferred for soups and for stuffing vegetables. Of the rice used for risotto the most prized are carnaroli, vialone nano, razza 77 and the famous arborio, which retain a certain firmness and bite. In the past, rice was the food of the urban rich and even now, in some parts, risotto is a wedding dish, and Sunday is not Sunday without it. As in the

Veneto, almost every ingredient you can think of – vegetable, fish and meat – is made into a risotto. But here the risotto is dry (*asciutto*), not almost liquid as in Venice.

Polenta, the porridge made with maize flour and water, was the food of the rural poor. Before maize arrived, peasants made porridge with wheat, barley, oats, millet and buckwheat. Maize flour polenta was introduced relatively late, spreading inland from Venice. But by the beginning of the eighteenth century, maize cultivation was widespread in Lombardy and polenta was the staple food – and until the Thirties, with many rural workers in the area eating little else.

In Lombardy polenta is made in many ways: with water, with milk, and mixed with other grains including buckwheat and black flour – *fraina*. Bergamo is said to make the best: its speciality is *polenta e osei* for which a mound of polenta is topped with small roasted birds threaded on skewers. Pasta has largely taken the place of both rice and polenta because the latter take so long to make, and must be stirred constantly. But polenta – once called *'stramaledetta'* (the cursed) and *'il cibo della miseria'* (the food of poverty), is still an important part of mountain cooking and it has now become fashionable, presented in elegant portions and crisp little grilled rectangles.

The third staple food to be found throughout Lombardy are the *minestre*, rich soups of peasant origin made with dried beans, rice or pasta (sometimes all three) and vegetables, and sometimes including bacon or sliced sausage.

Lombardy is the most important livestock and milk-producing region in Italy, though you never see the cows because they never leave the cow sheds. Their milk is used to make every kind of cheese, including those traditional to the south, but the region has its own cheese repertoire: bitto, bransi, bagoss which has a powerful flavour, furmai maioch, formagella and scimud. Other cottage-industry cheeses are certosa, straness and quartirolo, crescenza, uso monte, zincherlino, fiorett and cupeta. Four great cheeses, stracchino, robiola, runny taleggio and tartufelle are matured in caves in the Valsassina. Rich creamy mascarpone is eaten as a sweet. Of the factory cheeses which can be found in British supermarkets there is the famous green-flecked gorgonzola, made in the province of Novara around Mortara, and bel paese. The hard and sharp grana padano, made into huge wheels and aged between ten months and two years is used like parmesan for grating.

There is plenty of meat throughout Lombardy. Veal, pigs, chicken, rabbit, even lamb and their offal go into making the boiled meats (*bolliti misti*), roasts (*arrosti*), stews (*stracotti*) and breaded and fried morsels (*fritti misti*), which are characteristic of the 'belt' that runs along the valley of the river Po.

Lombardy is also pig country and the areas of Brianza and Cremona are famous for their sausages. They manufacture specialities from other regions, but their own are the fine cut pork and beef *salame di Milano*; bastardei, also with pork and beef; coarse cut pure pork *salamella di Cremona*; and varzi which is pork flavoured with salt, pepper, garlic and wine. Luganega needs to be fried or grilled; *mortadella di fegato* made with liver and *sanguinaccio*, black pudding, are cooked and eaten hot. Bresaola is air-dried spiced beef. Red culatello and fiocchetto are salted and spiced lean hams in sausage casings which are matured for up to a year. Other meats are used: in the Lomellina, where geese are reared, there is goose salami and goose liver pâté, while violin is cured goat's meat. It is no wonder that the favourite antipasto of the region is a selection of cured meats and salami – served with pickles.

Two centuries of Spanish rule, which began in 1535 when Charles V made his son, Philip, Duke of Milan, brought saffron and rice growing to the Po valley and dishes like risotto and *cassoeula* – a stew made with sausages and pigs trotters, ears and ribs that derives its name from the Spanish clay pot in which it is made. The other main foreign influence is Germanic, and it is evident in the heavy dishes of meat and cabbage, the schnitzel-like *costoletta milanese* and the range of panettone and other brioche-type cakes. It comes not from the Teutonic Longobards who ruled Lombardy for 200 years and gave the region its name, but from the Austrians when Lombardy passed from Spanish to Austrian rule in 1713 at the end of the war of the Spanish Succession. It was Austria who introduced a land tax in 1760 which encouraged small landowners and led to a fairer division of wealth and agriculture. There is also a French connection which came mainly through Turin and the House of Savoy.

Lombardy's chief city, Milan, which has led the country into industrialization and modernization, is a European city in the centre of Europe and it has lost its culinary traditions entirely. No one in Milan wants to cook Milanese dishes (which survive in the *Bassa*, south of Milan). They say they have no time for lengthy cooking and prefer the healthier Mediterranean diet of southern Italy. After the war they ate steak and salad. Now many have become hardened eaters of bread rolls and pizzas – *paninari* and *pizzetari*. Milan is a world of fast foods, of sandwich bars, hamburgers and pizzerias (in 1956 there were 6, now there are 500) but it is also the city where you can eat the best food – at Tuscan, Apulian and other regional trattorias as well as at restaurants which serve international cuisine and '*cucina creativa*'. And Peck, perhaps the greatest food shop in Europe, is here.

The mountains and lakes of Lombardy are now resorts for city people. The harsh life of villagers has gone and, with the sub-alpine civilization practically dead, traditional variety is hard to find. But around Cremona and Mantua and in other centres of the more leisurely life lost long ago in Milan, people are still attached to the good things of the past.

INSALATA DI CAPPONE

Chicken salad

This salad is from a book published in 1662 by Bartolomeo Stefani, chief cook at the court of the Gonzagas in Mantua. It is one of the ancient recipes which Franco and Silvana Colombani have on their menu at the Albergo del Sole at Maleo which has been in the family for 100 years. Franco has a rare collection of antique Italian cookery books and manuscripts, and also collects cooking utensils which are in a gigantic tangle in the attic (when Mussolini asked the Italians to give their pots and pans for the manufacture of bombs, many hid them in their attics and forgot all about them).

Serves 4

450g (1lb) cooked chicken (or turkey)
2 tablespoons sultanas, softened in water
20g (1oz) candied lemon peel, finely chopped
Salt and pepper
6 tablespoons fruity olive oil
1 tablespoon wine vinegar
1 teaspoon balsamic vinegar or 1 tablespoon red wine vinegar with a pinch of sugar

Remove the bones and cut the meat into very thin strips. Put in a bowl, add the sultanas, candied peel, salt and pepper to taste. Stir in the oil, vinegar and balsamic vinegar. (The balsamic vinegar we buy here is not very strong, so you may want to use more.) Arrange on individual plates on a bed of salad leaves dressed with oil and vinegar. Franco suggests serving the chicken salad with crisply cooked green vegetables, such as French beans.

MINESTRONE ALLA MILANESE

Vegetable soup with beans and rice

There are many versions of this heartwarming winter soup which becomes a cold soup (served at room temperature) in the summer.

Serves 10

250g (½lb) pancetta or unsmoked bacon, cut into small pieces
1 large onion, finely chopped
1 clove of garlic, finely chopped
Small bunch of parsley, finely chopped
4 carrots, diced
4 celery sticks, sliced thin
4 floury potatoes, diced
500g (1lb) tomatoes, peeled and chopped
250g (½lb) borlotti or dried white beans, soaked overnight or tinned ones weighing about 500g (½lb) drained
Salt
1 small white cabbage, shredded
250g (½lb) peas
4 courgettes, diced
200g (7oz) Italian rice
Good bunch of basil, cut into strips
Grated grana or parmesan cheese

In a very large pan, heat the bacon until some of the fat melts, then fry with the onion until the onion is pale gold. Add garlic and parsley and stir until the aroma rises. Then add the carrots, celery, potatoes, tomatoes and dried beans (drained). If you are using tinned beans these must be added at the end. Cover with plenty of water; bring to the boil and simmer with the lid on for about 2½ hours, adding salt when the beans have begun to soften and water if necessary (the soup should be thick, but not too thick). Add the cabbage, peas and courgettes and simmer 15 minutes more, then about 20 minutes before serving, add the rice. At the end of the cooking, stir in the basil.

ZUPPA DI ZUCCA CON LE MANDORLE

Pumpkin soup with almonds

This is a recipe from Jolanda Migliorini who cooks at her husband Valentino's restaurant at Caorso, south-west of Cremona in the Piacentino.

Serves 4

450g (1lb) pumpkin, peeled and diced
900ml (1½ pints) milk
Salt and pepper
Freshly ground nutmeg
300ml (½ pint) single cream
4 tablespoons chopped almonds, toasted

Put the diced pumpkin into a saucepan, add milk, salt and nutmeg to taste. Bring to the boil and simmer for about 30 minutes. When it is tender, pour into a blender and process until smooth. Pour back into the saucepan, stir in the cream, taste and adjust seasoning. Reheat and serve, sprinkled with the toasted almonds.

NOTE The success of this soup depends on the flavour of the pumpkin. With so many varieties available, it is worth experimenting.

TORTELLI DI ZUCCA

Pasta stuffed with pumpkin purée

On the road between Mantua and Cremona there is a huge stall selling pumpkins of every size, shape and colour. Pumpkins have always prospered in the plain around those two cities and they have always been exceptionally sweet and yellow.

These large pumpkin tortelli are a speciality of Mantua and well represent the aristocratic cooking traditions which go back to the court of the Gonzagas. They are tradi-

tionally made for Christmas Eve but they are eaten all the year round.

Although this is a fashionable dish, not everybody likes it in Italy. In Parma, Mantua and Cremona, where I found it, there were always great discussions about whether crumbled *amaretti*, (almond macaroons), and *mostarda* (fruit in syrup with mustard essence) should be used. Also controversial is whether the pumpkin should be boiled, baked or fried in butter. I liked all the versions I tried. The important thing in this country is to find a pumpkin with a really good sweet taste.

Serves 6

For the filling

1.5kg (3lb) piece of pumpkin
100g (4oz) mostarda di Cremona, finely chopped
100g (4oz) macaroons, crushed
100g (4oz) fine breadcrumbs
100g (4oz) amaretti or macaroons, crushed
2 eggs
Freshly grated nutmeg
Salt
Grated peel of half a lemon

For the dough

450g (1lb) plain flour
4 large eggs
Salt
1 egg yolk to stick the dough

For the garnish

80g (3oz) or more butter
80g (3oz) parmesan cheese, grated

Peel the pumpkin and remove the seeds. Wrap in foil and bake at 200°C (400°F, gas mark 6) for 1 hour. Mash to a purée and add the mostarda, amaretti, breadcrumbs, parmesan, eggs, nutmeg, salt and lemon rind. Stir well and leave to rest for a couple of hours at least.

To make the tortelli, work the flour, eggs and a pinch of salt into a soft dough and roll out very thinly into two equal rectangles. Upon one of these place small mounds of filling, the size of a walnut. Brush around them with egg yolk. Cover with the second layer of dough and press the edges down well to make sure they are completely sealed and there are no air pockets. With a pastry cutter, cut the tortelli into squares – and let them rest.

Cook a few at a time in boiling salted water for about 3–4 minutes until *al dente*. Drain and serve with plenty of butter and parmesan.

VARIATION Finely chopped almonds with a few drops of almond essence may be used instead of amaretti.

MALFATTI

Cheese and spinach dumplings

They are called *malfatti* ('badly done') because they are like the filling of ravioli without the dough.

Serves 6

2kg (4lb) spinach
Salt
500g (1lb) ricotta
2 large eggs
125g (4oz) parmesan
Pepper
Pinch of nutmeg
Flour
75g (3oz) melted butter

Wash the spinach and remove the stems. In a large pan with the lid on, steam the leaves with a little salt in the water that clings to them, turning them over, until they crumple. Strain and squeeze every bit of water out with your hands – this is all important and the secret of success (otherwise they would fall apart) – and finely chop the leaves.

Mash the ricotta and stir in the eggs, half the parmesan, salt, pepper, nutmeg and spinach. Work very well, shape into balls the size of a large walnut, and roll in flour.

Half-fill a large pan with water, bring to the boil, and very carefully drop in the dumplings. Keep the water barely simmering until they rise to the surface – they do so very quickly.

Lift them out very carefully with a slotted spoon and serve very hot with melted butter and the remaining parmesan.

RISOTTO CON LA ZUCCA

Pumpkin risotto

Serves 4

Piece of pumpkin weighing about 300g (1lb)
1 onion, chopped
1 tablespoon olive oil
Salt and pepper
¼ litre milk (8fl oz) milk
1 litre (1¾ pints) light chicken stock (you may use 1½ stock cubes)
350g (12oz) risotto rice
50g (2oz) butter
Grated parmesan

Peel the pumpkin, remove seeds and stringy bits and cut into small cubes. Fry the onion in oil till soft, add the pumpkin, season with salt and pepper and cover with milk. Simmer gently till the pumpkin is tender (from 5–15 minutes). Now bring the stock to the boil in a large pan, throw in the rice and let it simmer gently for 18 minutes, stirring occasionally, and adding salt and pepper, and stock or the milk in which the pumpkin cooked, or water, if necessary, until the rice is tender and the liquid absorbed. Now stir in the pumpkin mixture and the butter and heat through. Serve with grated parmesan.

RISOTTO ALLA MILANESE

Saffron risotto

You find this yellow risotto everywhere in Milan but I wonder how often it is made with real saffron pistils (generally powder is used), real stock and bone marrow, but that is how chef Fulvio de Santa makes it at the new restaurant Peck in Milan where they offer two menus – a 'modern' one and the old traditional classics of Milanese home cooking.

This is the traditional partner to *osso buco*.

Serves 4

1 small onion, chopped
Small piece of marrow from a beef bone
(optional)
50g (2oz) butter
1 litre (1¾ pints) meat or chicken stock
125ml (4fl oz) dry white or red wine
275g (10oz) arborio or risotto rice
Salt
1 envelope saffron powder or ½ teaspoon chopped stamens
50g (2oz) grated parmesan

In a large pan, fry the onion and marrow in half the butter until the onion is soft. In a separate pan, heat the stock. Add the wine to the fried onion and boil until much reduced. Add the rice and stir to coat the grains well. Add salt, and the boiling stock, by the ladleful, stirring all the time as it becomes absorbed. Add the saffron towards the end. When the rice is done – there should be enough liquid to make it creamy, but the grains must still be firm – add the rest of the butter and the parmesan.

RISOTTO CON GLI ASPARAGI

Asparagus risotto

Serves 6

1kg (2lb) asparagus
1.25 litres (2¼ pints) chicken stock made with 1 stock cube
Salt
1 onion, chopped
50g (2oz) butter
350g (12oz) risotto rice
1 bottle dry white wine
Pepper
3–4 tablespoons grated parmesan (optional)

Wash and peel the asparagus. Cut off about 7cm (3in) of tips and keep them aside. Boil the stalks in the stock till very tender. Lift them out and put them through a food processor with a little stock, strain off the hard stringy bits and return the cream to the pan with the stock. In another pan cook the asparagus tips in salted water for a few minutes until only just tender.

In a third large frying or shallow pan, fry the onion in half the butter till soft. Add the rice and stir to coat the grains well. Pour in the wine, bring to the boil, add salt and pepper, and simmer gently, stirring. Then add the stock containing the creamed asparagus gradually as it becomes absorbed, stirring often, and continue adding water as required – you may need about 600ml (1 pint) – until the rice is *al dente* and creamy. Stir in the rest of the butter and the grated parmesan and serve at once, garnished with the heated asparagus tips cut into two or more pieces.

POLENTA E GORGONZOLA

Baked polenta with gorgonzola cheese

Serves 4

300g (10oz) maize flour (meal)
Salt
75g (3oz) butter
Pepper
250g (8oz) gorgonzola cheese

Make polenta as described on page 64 with the maize flour, and 1.5 litres (2½ pints) of salted water. When it is done, stir in the butter and pepper. In a buttered ovenproof dish pour a layer of hot polenta, cover with a layer of cheese pieces, then continue with another layer of polenta and one of cheese, finishing with polenta. Bake in a 220°C (425°F, gas mark 7) oven until browned.

VARIATION Use taleggio instead of gorgonzola (in the Valle d'Aosta they use fontina).

For a *pasticcio di polenta*, add alternating layers of a reduced and thick tomato sauce (see page 150).

ROSTIN NEGÀA

Veal chops in wine

This is a recipe from Sergio Torelli, the head chef at Savini's in Milan.

Serves 4

4 veal chops
1 tablespoon flour
Salt and pepper
15g (½oz) bacon, cut in small cubes
50g (2oz) butter
1 tablespoon rosemary, chopped
Half a glass of dry white wine

Dip the chops in seasoned flour. Fry the bacon in butter with the rosemary and add the chops. Brown on both sides. Add the wine, season, cover and cook slowly for 35 minutes until tender. Uncover and reduce the sauce to a glaze. Serve immediately.

OSSO BUCO ALLA MILANESE

Braised shin of veal

Serves 4

4 thick slices of shin of veal cut with a piece
of marrow bone
Flour
50g (2oz) butter
125ml (4fl oz) dry white wine
225g (8oz) tomatoes, peeled and chopped
Meat stock or water
Salt and pepper

For the gremolata

4 tablespoons finely chopped parsley
1 tablespoon finely grated lemon rind
1 small clove garlic, crushed
1 anchovy, finely chopped (optional)

Coat the meat with flour and brown in butter on both sides. Add the wine and simmer for 10 minutes, then add the tomatoes and stock or water to cover and season. Cook with the lid on for 1½–2 hours, stirring occasionally to make sure it does not stick, until the meat is so tender it comes away from the bone. Add stock or water to keep the meat covered at first. The sauce should be thick at the end.

Make what is called a *gremolata*: a mixture of parsley, grated lemon rind and garlic (and anchovy if you like). Place a little on each piece of meat and cook a few minutes longer. Serve with *risotto alla milanese* (see page 40) or plain white rice.

ANIMELLE IN AGRODOLCE

Sweet and sour sweetbreads

Serves 6

2 tablespoons capers in vinegar
4 tablespoons olive oil
1½ tablespoons sugar, or to taste
4 tablespoons wine vinegar
750g (1lb 11oz) sweetbreads
50g (2oz) butter
50g (2oz) raw ham, diced
1 large onion, peeled and diced
1 large carrot, peeled and diced
Stick celery, diced

First make the sauce: strain and squeeze the capers well and chop them finely. Put them in a small bowl, add the oil and beat well. Heat the sugar in a small saucepan with the vinegar, to dissolve, then add the oil and caper sauce, stirring constantly. Take the sauce off the heat before it boils, pour it into a bowl and leave to cool.

Heat plenty of water in a saucepan and plunge the sweetbreads into it as soon as it comes to the boil. Simmer for 6 minutes, then plunge into cold water and remove the membrane that covers them. Cut into 2cm (1in) chunks.

Melt the butter in a frying pan, add the ham, onion, carrot and celery and cook over a medium heat until they begin to brown and soften. Then add the sweetbreads, stir, season, and cook gently for a further 15 minutes. This dish should be served very hot, with the sweet and sour sauce poured over.

TACCHINO DI NATALE

Christmas turkey

Serves 8

1 turkey weighing about 3½kg (7lb)
Salt and pepper
2 sprigs of sage, chopped
2 sprigs of rosemary, chopped
50g (2oz) butter

For the filling

3 Golden Delicious apples, cut into pieces
125g (4oz) moist pitted prunes, chopped
200g (7oz) chestnuts, roasted and peeled or 150g (5oz) tinned ones
300g (10oz) luganega sausage, skinned and cut into small pieces
Salt and pepper
75g (3oz) butter, cut into pieces

Mix the filling ingredients and stuff the turkey with them – the cavity as well as the skin at the neck. You may add the heart, stomach and liver of the turkey, cut into pieces, but I prefer not to as the liver sometimes tastes bitter and the stomach remains tough. Sew up the openings with thread and sprinkle with salt, pepper, sage and rosemary and with butter shavings. Place the bird, breast side down on a baking dish and bake at 150°C (300°F, gas mark 2) for about 2½ hours or until done to your liking, turning it over for the last ½ hour to let the breast become crisp and brown.

ANATRA ALL'ACETO BALSAMICO

Duck breasts with balsamic vinegar

At the Ristorante del Pescatore at Canneto sull'Oglio, Antonio Santini has introduced some of the grand old dishes of nearby Mantua in addition to the local peasant dishes.

Serves 4

1–2 tablespoons sunflower oil
4 duck breasts
1–2 tablespoons balsamic vinegar (or red
wine vinegar with a pinch of sugar)
Salt and pepper
¼ teaspoon cinnamon
4 tablespoons blueberries or cranberries

Heat the oil in a frying pan. Put the duck breasts in, skin side down, and cook on a low flame. Turn over when the fat under the skin has melted and the skin is golden. Add the vinegar, salt and pepper, cinnamon and berries. Cover and cook for a further 10–15 minutes (the duck breasts should be juicy inside). The berries will have melted to make a delicious sauce. Spoon off any excess fat and serve the breasts with the sauce poured over them.

RISOTTO CON LE QUAGLIE

Rice with quails

Serves 6

---

6 quail
1 onion, chopped
3 tablespoons sunflower oil
100g (3½oz) butter
2 sprigs of sage
Salt and pepper
300ml (10fl oz) dry Marsala
500g (1lb) Italian risotto rice
1½ litres (2¼ pints) light chicken stock
seasoned with salt and pepper (you may use
stock cubes)

Burn off any remaining feathers and rinse the quail. In a large frying pan fry the onion in the oil with 2 tablespoons of butter till soft. Put in the quail and turn to brown them all over. Add salt and pepper and the sage leaves, pour in the Marsala and cook gently for about 20 minutes until the quail are done, turning them over a few times.

In the meantime boil the rice in plenty of stock for about 18 minutes, until cooked *al dente*, then drain quickly. Stir in the remaining butter and serve with the quail on top and the sauce poured over.

RANE IN GUAZZETTO

Frogs cooked in wine

I went with another frog enthusiast, Lucia Alberini, wife of the distinguished culinary historian Massimo Alberini, to try several dishes at Piero Bolfo's elegant Ristorante Canoviano in Milan. We had frog soup, frog stew and frog risotto – all marvellous. It is possible now to buy frogs' legs in Britain: this is a good way to use them.

Serves 4

800g (1¾lb) frogs' legs
80g (3oz) butter
225ml (8fl oz) dry white wine
4 tomatoes, peeled and chopped
Salt and pepper
Handful chopped parsley
Juice of half a lemon

Rinse the frogs legs and fry quickly in half the butter. Add the wine and tomatoes, season with salt and pepper, and simmer vigorously for at least 20 minutes to reduce the wine sauce.

Add the parsley towards the end and, just before serving, stir in the rest of the butter and the lemon juice.

PESCHE AL VINO

Peaches in wine

Serves 6

6 large ripe peaches or nectarines
400ml (14fl oz) red wine
2 tablespoons sugar or to taste (optional)

Pour boiling water over the peaches or nectarines and skin them. Slice them into a bowl or individual wine glasses and pour the wine over them. Add sugar if the peaches are not sweet enough and leave them to macerate for an hour.

PESCHE RIPIENE

Stuffed peaches

There are not many old Italian desserts, but this is one of the classics. It is Sergio Torelli's recipe, the head chef at Savini's, Milan's famous restaurant in the Galleria near the Duomo. It appears in *Le Migliori Ricette della Scuola del Gritti*, edited by Massimo Alberini.

Serves 6

12 yellow peaches
50g (2oz) butter
12 macaroons (amaretti – the small, slightly
bitter ones)
2 egg yolks
2 tablespoons maraschino, Marsala, or
almond liqueur (amaretto)
50g (2oz) finely chopped almonds
100g (4oz) sugar
1 teaspoon cocoa powder
Grated rind of half a lemon
White wine
Caster sugar, to serve
Butter

Cut the peaches in half, stone and hollow out some of the flesh. Lightly grease an ovenproof dish with butter. Place the peach halves in it, cut side up. Chop the peach pulp, crush the macaroons and stir together in a bowl with the yolks, maraschino or liquer, almonds, sugar, cocoa and grated lemon rind. Mix well. Fill the peach halves with this mixture, sprinkle with white wine, dust with sugar and put a shaving of butter on each. Put the dish in a moderate oven, 180°C (350°F, gas mark 4) for 20–30 minutes, until golden. Serve dusted with caster sugar.

ALBICOCCHE RIPIENE

Stuffed apricots

For the filling

4 apricots pitted
1 egg
125g (4oz) ground almonds
125g (4oz) sugar
Few drops of almond essence

800g (1½lb) apricots
25g (1oz) butter
6 tablespoons Marsala

To make the filling, blend the apricots and egg together and mix with the rest of the ingredients into a paste.

Cut the apricots in half and remove the pit. Lay them close to each other, cut side up, in a lightly buttered baking dish. Cover each half with almond filling, sprinkle a few shavings of butter, pour the Marsala into the dish and bake in a 200°C (400°F, gas mark 6) oven for 25 minutes or until lightly browned.

PERE AL FORNO

Baked pears

Serves 6

1kg (2lb) large firm pears
250g (9oz) caster sugar
250ml (9fl oz) dry Marsala or red wine
1 stick cinnamon
1 vanilla pod or a few drops of vanilla essence
150ml (¼ pint) water

Stand the pears, unpeeled, in a large oven-proof dish with the rest of the ingredients. Bake, uncovered, for 1½–2 hours at 150°C (300°F, gas mark 2). Serve hot or cold.

MASCARPONE

This delicious rich creamy cheese made by curdling thick cream with citric acid originates in Lodi, but it has become so popular in Italy that many regions produce it. It is served with the cheese course, spread on a slice of bread or mixed with sugar and cognac, Alchermes or rum, in an emptied wine glass or coffee cup.

Mascarpone is used instead of cream to sauce fruits and pastries. The classic *crema di mascarpone* has 2 egg yolks, 150g (5oz) sugar and 3 tablespoons of rum mixed into 200g (7oz) mascarpone. The stiffly beaten whites are folded in and the fluffy cream is chilled.

A favourite way of serving it is *al caffè*. Stir into 250g (½lb) mascarpone, about 2 table-spoons finely ground or preferably pulverized coffee (a dark roast is good), 3 tablespoons or more caster sugar and 2–4 tablespoons of rum. Let the flavours infuse for a while and serve chilled.

TORTA DI CIOCCOLATO

Chocolate dessert

Turin had a dominating influence on Lombardy in the 19th century and this is a legacy. The recipe comes from Franco and Silvana Colombani's delightful *Cucina d'Amore*.

Serves 8

200g (7oz) fine quality dark chocolate
100g (3½oz) unsalted butter
4 large eggs
200g (7oz) sugar
2 tablespoons flour plus 1 to dust the dish
Icing sugar (optional)

Melt the chocolate and butter in a bowl placed in boiling water. Mix the yolks with the sugar and flour, then mix well with the butter and chocolate, and finally fold in the stiffly beaten egg whites. Butter a round baking dish or mould about 30cm (12in) in diameter and dust with flour. Then pour in the chocolate mixture and bake in a 140°C (275°F, gas mark 1) oven for 45 minutes. Serve cold in the baking dish, dusted if you like with the icing sugar. The sweet is soft and best served with a spoon.

VARIATION A *torta* which is both incredibly easy and incredibly delicious is made by beating 350g (¾ pint) double cream until very stiff, then beating in 250g (½lb) semi-sweet or Menier chocolate which has been melted then cooled a little. Chill it or put it in the freezer. I discovered it at the River Café in Hammersmith and it serves eight.

Trentino–Alto Adige

There are two different worlds in this spectacular region of dark forests, mauve-coloured mountain peaks and valleys, which below Bolzano turns into gentle slopes and terraces: German-speaking Alto Adige in the north and Italian-speaking Trentino in the south. Salorno, a village above Trento, represents the dividing line.

Alto Adige takes its name from the river Adige and is a prosperous tourist region full of old castles, turreted houses and fortified convents which have become hotels and restaurants for people going skiing and taking local health cures. It attracts mainly German and Austrian tourists and produces some of the best white wines in Italy and a great variety of fruit including apples, pears, plums and grapes. Until the First World War it was the Austrian South Tyrol and it has clung fiercely to its traditions.

The cooking is Tyrolean and based on the pig. Its heart and soul is *Speck*, a delicious salted and smoked pork which is eaten for breakfast, as an appetizer and as an afternoon snack and is also used in cooking. Shops in Alto Adige are full of the great blackened chunks. The best *Speck* is made in the old wooden farmhouses which have just the right ventilation and no central heating. Pigs are killed in winter and the legs are boned, opened like a book, covered with a mixture of salt and saltpetre, with pepper, bay leaves and juniper berries and left for three weeks while the liquids run out. After that the meat is hung in the fireplace and smoked with fruit wood and juniper for a few hours a day and allowed to get cold after each smoking. This continues for up to three months; then it is left to mature in well ventilated attics for six months more.

The repertoire of Tyrolean dishes includes bread dumplings, *Knödel*, the size of small oranges which are dropped into soups and stews, or eaten with roasts and boiled meats; *Gulasch*; trout from the lakes and torrents and game cooked in wine and vinegar. The main vegetables are cabbage (especially as sauerkraut) and potatoes. Red cabbage is cooked in red wine with onions and bacon. They use apple sauce, bilberry jam and sour cream and all kinds of sausages and salami.

Bread is all-important. There are many different kinds, some dark, with mixtures of wheat, rye and barley flours and every village has its own.

Sweets are Austrian yet with a difference: *Krapfen* (doughnuts) are filled with jam and poppy seeds or with cream; strudel is filled with apples, raisins and pine nuts; with poppy seeds, honey and cream, or with ricotta and sour cream. There are plum tarts, prune dumplings, chestnut cakes and puddings, stuffed pancakes and pastries filled with nuts and marzipan.

The cooking of Trentino is a mixture, similar to that of the Veneto mountains but with a German and mid-European influence because of neighbouring Alto Adige and because Trentino was once part of the Austro-Hungarian Empire – there are also pockets of ethnic communities whose ancestors came to mine coal in the eleventh century who speak an old German dialect. The cooking is based on polenta which is made differently in every valley, using water, milk or even wine, sometimes combined with mashed potatoes. A dark *polenta nera* is made from a mixture of maize and buckwheat flour. They also have rice and pasta, and they sauce their pastas with veal stew and thick cream, and with mashed sardines.

In Trentino they make all kinds of gnocchi including a German-inspired *gnocchi di prugne*, stuffed with prunes, and their *canederli* are the German bread dumplings. They poach trout and eel in white wine and vinegar, and fry frogs in batter. *Baccalà dei frati* (salt cod cooked in broth and milk with mashed anchovies and tomato paste) is so called because it was made by priests and sold with steaming polenta by convents on Fridays. Salted and smoked herring from the North Atlantic are soaked in milk and cooked with onions in vinegar. Meat is simmered long and slowly with wine, vinegar or milk, rabbit is Hungarian style with white wine, paprika and juniper berries and they also make *Gulasch* and *crauti* (sauerkraut). Potatoes are favourite vegetables – they grate them raw to make tarts, cakes, fritters and omelettes.

During the mushroom season there is a little market in the heart of the old centre of Trento that sells nothing but mushrooms and a few other wild things. Gatherers arrive from the hills and valleys to sell what they have found – porcini, porcinelli, chiodini, finfireli, vesci, russole – as many as 250 different types have been seen. The commune employs experts to vet them. A speciality of the Trentino region is a mushroom stew with wine, *misto di funghi,* which accommodates the unremarkable and is served with polenta, risotto or pasta.

WEINSUPPE

Wine soup

This is one of my favourites from this region. The recipe is from Andreas Hellrig, owner chef of the restaurant Andrea in the mountain resort of Merano. Andreas uses old traditional recipes from local families as well as his own creations.

Serves 4

4 egg yolks
½ litre (18fl oz) meat broth (you may use a beef stock cube)
200ml (7fl oz) or more white wine
120ml (4fl oz) double cream
1 teaspoon powdered cinnamon
Small bunch of chives, finely chopped

Beat the yolks, wine and cream with salt and a pinch of cinnamon in a saucepan and stir vigorously over very low heat until the mixture thickens slightly and becomes creamy. Serve hot with a sprinkling of cinnamon and chives.

CANEDERLI TIROLESI

Tyrolean dumplings

These dumplings are called *Knödel* in German-speaking Alto Adige. They are served with melted butter or grated cheese or in a soup of delicate meat or chicken broth.

They are very large and very filling and one or two are enough per person.

Serves 6

3 eggs
250ml (8fl oz) milk
250g (9oz) stale white bread, crumbled
150g (5oz) speck or smoked raw ham in a piece
1 tablespoon chopped chives
2 tablespoons chopped parsley
Salt and pepper
Pinch nutmeg
200–225g (7–8oz) plain flour
1.5 litre (2¾ pints) approx. stock

Beat the eggs with the milk, add the bread and the *Speck* or ham, both cut into very small cubes, and chives, parsley, salt, pepper and nutmeg. Stirring continually, add enough flour to make a consistency that will hold together. Mix it well then, with wet hands, make balls a little larger than an egg.

When all are ready, flour lightly and simmer in the stock for about 20 minutes.

CANEDERLI AI FUNGHI PORCINI

Bread dumplings with mushrooms

These dumplings are served with melted butter and grated parmesan or in chicken or meat broth and served as soup.

Serves 6

200g (7oz) white bread, sliced and crusts removed
125ml (4fl oz) milk
1 onion, chopped
40g (1½oz) butter
250g (½lb) mushrooms
2 eggs
2 tablespoons flour
Salt and pepper
Large bunch of parsley, finely chopped

Break up the bread, sprinkle with milk and mix it well with your hands.

Fry the onion in butter till soft, then add the mushrooms, cut into pieces, and cook till they are done and the moisture is absorbed. Put through a food processor and mix with the crumbled bread squeezed dry and the rest of the ingredients. Work into a paste and let it rest for a few minutes.

Then with wetted hands roll into little balls the size of a walnut (they sometimes make balls as big as tangerines but smaller ones are best). Drop a few at a time into boiling salted water and simmer for about 2 minutes until they rise. It is good to test one for consistency at the beginning so that if it falls apart you can add a little more flour to the rest. Lift out with a slotted spoon.

SCHLUTZKRAPFEN OR RAVIOLI DELLA PUSTERIA

Ravioli with spinach and ricotta

A version of ravioli with spinach and ricotta – a speciality of northern Italy, can be found in almost every corner of the country. In this region they make pasta dough with eggs and milk. But you can also make it with the usual flour and egg mixture on page 84.

Serves 4–6

½kg (1lb 2oz) plain flour
2 eggs
Pinch of salt
150ml (¼ pint) milk, warmed

For the filling

750g (1½lb) spinach (weighed without stems) or half this amount frozen
300g (10oz) ricotta
1 tablespoon butter
½ onion, chopped
2 tablespoons grated grana or parmesan cheese
Salt and pepper
½ teaspoon nutmeg

1 egg yolk to seal the dough
Salt
75g (3oz) butter, melted
Grated grana or parmesan cheese

Prepare the filling: Wash the spinach and remove the stems. Boil the leaves till they crumple, in very little water. Drain, squeeze out all the water that you possibly can and finely chop. Fry the onion in butter till soft. Add the spinach and stir well. Then add the cheese, salt if necessary and nutmeg. Take off the heat and mix with ricotta in a bowl.

Make the dough: Mix the eggs into the flour, add the milk gradually – just enough for a firm dough, and knead well for about 10 minutes until the dough is smooth and elastic. Leave it for quarter of an hour wrapped in clingfilm. Then roll it out as thin as you can (it is easier to divide the dough in 2 and roll out smaller amounts).

Cut into rounds about 7.5cm (3in) in diameter with a pastry cutter. Brush round the edges with egg yolk mixed with a teaspoon of water so that they stick more easily. Place a tablespoon of filling in the centre of the dough, fold over to form a half moon and press the edges firmly together. Or use the methods given for ravioli on page 86.

Throw into plenty of boiling water and cook for 3–4 minutes until tender. Drain well and serve with melted butter accompanied by grated cheese.

SCHLUTZKRAPFEN CON FUNGHI

Mushroom filling for ravioli

This is an alternative and most delicious filling for the previous recipe.

1kg (2lb) shiitake or other mushrooms
3 tablespoons butter
1 tablespoon oil
3–4 cloves garlic, crushed
Salt and pepper
Large bunch of parsley, finely chopped
150ml (¼ pint) double cream (optional)

Fry the mushrooms in a mixture of butter and oil with the garlic till they are tender and the liquid has disappeared. Finely chop, then add parsley and cream.

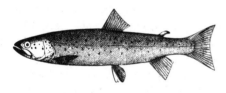

TROTE ALLA PANNA ACIDA

Trout with sour cream

Trout is the favourite freshwater fish all over Italy. In many parts they now used farmed trout, but here the fish comes from mountain streams and torrents. Fresh cream is sometimes used instead of sour cream.

Serves 2

2 trout, cleaned and the heads left on
Juice of ½ a lemon
120ml (4fl oz) wine vinegar
Salt
25g (1oz) butter
150ml (¼ pint) sour cream
Few sprigs of parsley, chopped

Into a pan put just enough water to cover the fish. Add lemon juice, vinegar and salt and bring to the boil. Put in the trout and poach, covered, the heat turned down as low as possible so that the water barely trembles, for about 6–8 minutes.

Melt the butter in a small pan, add the sour cream and heat through, stirring.

Lift the trout out of the pan and serve with the sauce poured over, sprinkled with parsley.

GRIGLIATA DI CERVO

Grilled venison

The venison we get in our supermarkets now is young tender meat, which you can grill as you would beef.

Serves 6

6 venison chops or steaks
½ bottle red wine
3 tablespoons olive oil
1 onion, chopped
2 cloves garlic, finely chopped
5 cloves
1–2 teaspoons cinnamon
Grated peel of 1 lemon
Salt and pepper
1 bay leaf
10 juniper berries, crushed

Put the venison chops in a bowl with the rest of the ingredients, well mixed, and leave, covered, for a day in the refrigerator, turning the meat over once or twice.

Cook the meat under the grill for about 10 minutes until done, turning it over once.

Pour the marinade into a saucepan and boil to reduce it to a rich sauce. Serve the meat, with the strained sauce, accompanied by polenta if you like and *salsa di cren*, the horseradish sauce in the following recipe.

SALSA DI CREN

Horseradish sauce

This strongly flavoured sauce of Alto Adige (it also belongs to Friuli) is served with all kinds of boiled and roast meats. It varies greatly and is of the kind you make up to taste.

You can start with 250ml (8fl oz) whipped double cream, then add a pinch of salt and 1–2 teaspoons of sugar, and grate in (on a cheese grater) as much as you like of a (peeled and washed) piece of horseradish root.

Or grate about 125g (4oz) of horseradish and add 3 tablespoons fresh breadcrumbs soaked in about 5 tablespoons of milk, a pinch of salt and 1 teaspoon of sugar.

Serve it as it is or add 4 tablespoons white wine vinegar or the juice of ½–1 lemon or a little mustard or a pinch of cayenne. There are those who simply mix the horseradish with boiled mashed apple.

FRÜCHTEPUDDING

Fruit pudding

Serves 8

175g (6oz) white bread, crusts removed
600ml (1 pint) milk
65g (2½oz) butter, softened
3 large eggs
65g (2½oz) almonds, finely chopped
100g sugar
1 teaspoon cinnamon
Zest of 2 lemons
2lb (1kg) fruit such as apple, pear, seedless grapes and plums, cubed

Break up the bread in a bowl and pour in the milk, working it in with your hands and crumbling the bread.

Beat the butter with the egg yolk then add the sugar, cinnamon and lemon zest and beat into the soaked bread. Beat the egg whites stiff and fold them into the mixture. Then fold in the fruit (apples and pears should be peeled).

Pour into a wide oven dish and bake at 180°C (350°F, gas mark 4) for over an hour, until firm and golden on top.

Serve hot or cold. The plums give a beautiful red colour where they touch the surface.

APFELNUSSTORTE or TORTA DI MELE

Apple and nut cake

100g (3½oz) blanched hazelnuts or almonds
(or a mixture of both)
6 apples (such as Golden Delicious)
4 eggs
140g (4½oz) sugar
Juice of 1 lemon
140g (4½oz) flour
2 tablespoons butter

Chop the hazelnuts or almonds (or both) and toast them in a dry frying pan, shaking the pan so that they brown all over. Peel, core and slice the apples. Beat the egg yolks with the sugar. Add the lemon juice, then the flour gradually, beating well. Beat the egg whites stiff and fold them in, then fold in the nuts.

Grease a 23–25cm (9–10in) spring form tin with butter and dust with flour. Pour in half the cake mixture, then arrange a layer of apples on top and pour the remaining cake mixture over them. Arrange the rest of the apple slices in circles on top, brush with melted butter and sprinkle with 1 tablespoon sugar.

Bake in a 180°C (350°F, gas mark 4) oven for 1 hour and 25 minutes or until a skewer pushed into the cake comes out clean. You can put the cake under the grill for a minute at the end to give the top a caramelized look.

Veneto

Italians describe the cooking of the Veneto as delicate and colourful. They compare it to Venetian mosaics and tinted marbles, use words like 'poetic' and 'spiritual' and explain that Venetians have Venice and the paintings of Bellini and Titian to inspire them. They talk of the Middle Ages and Venice's central role in the spice trade, of the dried fruit and nuts that came from the East, of the Saracens and Byzantium and the feasts of the Doges.

But the people I met in the Veneto, in Verona and Vicenza, Padua and Treviso, and in Venice too, said their cooking was 'poor food', *la fantasia dei poveri*, and stemmed from the days when the region lived (meagrely) off the land. There is no trace, they claim, of the grand dishes of the old noble families, *i signori*, such as the Della Scalas of Verona.

The Veneto consists of the plain between the rivers Po and Tagliamento, bounded in the north by the spectacular Dolomite mountains. The plain is a region of small industries: factories are dotted amid fields and woodlands, and busy modern agglomerations contrast with ancient villas and *palazzi*, noble cities and serene villages. Most people have either moved to the nearest town or remained in the village and gone to work in the nearby factory, so there has not been a complete break with the countryside.

The main feature of the cooking in town and country is the all-important influence of Venice, the lagoon city, which developed as a refuge for main-landers running away from northern invaders and became the ruling economic and political power of the Venetian republic which remained independent for 1,000 years. Venice was once the richest, most powerful city in the world, mistress of the Mediterranean, an international market and a great maritime power, with her own fleet and her own trading posts in the Levant. She was like a bazaar city, with foreign communities – there were Germans, Turks, Greeks, Arabs, Jews and Armenians, each with their own quarters – traders from everywhere at her quayside and her own merchants and seamen in the four corners of the world. Marco Polo was Venetian.

Venice was Europe's point of contact with the East and Venetians absorbed culinary ideas from the Arabs and Byzantium (Arab-style sweet and sour fish, *pesce in saor*, with raisins and pine nuts is typical of the region). But they translated everything into their own, very simple, style. When I asked the owner of the popular Madonna restaurant in the Rialto why, despite the sumptuous past and the spice trade, the cooking of Venice was so uncomplicated, he explained that their cooking was simple because it was based on fish.

If you could see the fish come in live at dawn in barges on the Grand Canal straight on to the market stalls round the corner from the Madonna you would understand why all they want to do is lightly fry, poach or grill it.

The entire Veneto is a region of water with rivers and torrents, lakes, canals and lagoons, so much of the cooking revolves around fish. The best antipasti are seafood. Prawns, scampi, crab, squid, cuttlefish, baby octopus, and all kinds of shellfish are served simply dressed with olive oil, chopped parsley and lemon, but the lemon seems superfluous. My own favourites are the tiny soft-shelled crabs, *le moleche*, of Murano, netted when they change their shells in the spring and autumn, dipped live in egg batter with garlic and parsley and fried.

Although most dishes in the Veneto are variations of Venetian ones, each city also has specialities of its own. Horsemeat stew is a speciality of Verona, an old garrison town where once upon a time, when they were surrounded, they ate their horses. Also from there is *peara*, a peppery sauce made with bone marrow and breadcrumbs, the secret of which Veronese girls are supposed to receive when they marry. Verona is also the city of potato gnocchi (dumplings). Every year on Good Friday they celebrate a *Baccanale del gnocco* with a procession in fourteenth century clothes, and they elect a *papà del gnocco* who rides on a donkey holding a *gnocco* at the end of a fork. Padua is known for mutton with a wine sauce called *piperata*, Treviso for a pigeon stew, Vicenza for stockfish, Belluno for bean soups and its ice cream. Every city is famous for something.

What is special about the cooking of the Veneto is the cosmopolitan and exotic touch. Meat is marinated in wine then simmered in milk; turkey is bathed in pomegranate juice; fish is garnished with pine nuts and raisins. It is the result of Venice's old connections with both Germany and the Orient.

Spices were much used in the Middle Ages: the old cookery books are full of ginger, saffron, cumin, cloves, cinnamon and nutmeg. By the end of the eighteenth century, under the influence of the French after Napoleon had conquered Venice, they went out of fashion in favour of herbs. But Venetians never forget that pepper was once worth its weight in gold. They also have great respect for the salt which comes from their marshes and has a special flavour.

The Veneto is in the polenta, bean soup and risotto belts that run right across the north of Italy. Polenta was once eaten for breakfast, lunch and supper, and is an accompaniment to most foods. (It was blamed for the old skin disease pellagra because many of those who suffered ate hardly anything else.) Maize was brought from America to Venice in the sixteenth century but called *granoturco* because it was believed to come from Turkey. In Venice they like *polenta* soft and creamy and use a coarser grind of maize flour which is supposed to keep better by the sea. In other parts of the Veneto they make it firm, turn it out on a board, cut it into slices then grill or fry it. Some cooks mix milk with the water, and there are various refinements.

Minestre (soups), are a strong point of the cooking of the Veneto and *pasta e fagioli* (pasta and beans) is the queen of soups. The chocolate-coloured soup is made with the borlotti beans which came from Mexico, also via America, straight to the village of Belluno in the region of Lamon where they still grow.

The rice dishes of the Veneto are one of its glories. Rice was introduced by the Arabs and many short-grained types grow in the marshlands around the river Po. Italians have their way of cooking risotto with stock and also sometimes with wine, adding more liquid and stirring as it becomes absorbed, so that it attains an almost creamy consistency while the grain remains firm, but in Venice they make their *risotti* almost liquid, *allonda*, with a velvety consistency, and eat them cold as soups, *minestre di riso*. The merit of the Veneto *risotti* lies in their delicacy of flavour, their jewel-encrusted look and most of all in their versatility, for every possible ingredient is used depending on the season. Peas, green beans, artichoke hearts, asparagus tips, mushrooms, spinach, fennel, celery, carrots, potatoes, cabbage, cauliflower, leeks, courgettes, pumpkin and courgette flowers, all these go in. There are *risotti* with herbs, with chicken livers, cubed chicken or mutton, quails, sausage, tripe, snails and frogs. A risotto with raisins and pine nuts is a legacy of the Arabs.

The Veneto is richer in vegetables than any other region. That is what makes Venetian food so colourful. The Venetians do not eat much meat, but they like offal, and liver is their favourite. They cook chicken and the myriads of wild migrating birds trapped when they alight on the beaches and marshes. Inland there is plenty of game, and farmyard animals like rabbits, hare, geese, ducks, guinea hen and turkey.

In the hills and mountains in the north they raise cows and pigs and make cheeses, hams and sausages. Their most famous cheeses are the hard, strongly flavoured asiago and vezzena which are aged from six to eighteen months. They also make smoked ricotta. Their hams are lean and savoury and each mountain province has its own special recipes for making salami and sausages (you can still occasionally find them hanging in cellars in country homes). There is a Venetian saying, '*chi no ga' orto ne' porco, porta el muso storto*', 'the one who has no vegetable patch and no pig has a sad twisted face'. It was said that the pig was the king of the peasant table and that the queen was polenta. One accompanied the other. Their special sausages are the soft soppressa, fatty ossocolo, musetto made from head meat, fat boiling cotechino and luganega which is grilled, fried or stewed in broth. Bondola is coarsely minced pork with red wine and plenty of pepper stuffed in a turkey bladder. The making of salami, sausages and ham was governed by the Venetian Statutes since the Middle Ages and today it is guaranteed by an association with a roaring St Mark's lion as trademark.

Sweets and pastries here have always been for special occasions such as weddings, baptisms and anniversaries and many are attached to religious holidays. Every town has its own specialities which are made by bakers. Venice has an Easter *focaccia* – a yeast cake in the shape of a dove. The town of Este has one too that is highly esteemed in all of Italy because of its delicate flavour, a secret of the family which has been making it for generations. Vicenza has the Marsala-flavoured sponge called *bussolano* and Padua has *pinza* which is packed with dried and candied fruit. Verona became a capital of industrial pastry-making before the Second World War with yeast cakes in the Viennese tradition which were introduced when Napoleon handed Venice over to Austria. *Pandoro* and *nadalin* are its Christmas specialities, rivals of the Milanese *panettone*. Verona also have the *brassadela* flavoured with grappa and the famous *mandorlato*, also called *il miracolo del miele*, made with almonds and honey and produced by the same family for 150 years. There is a *Festa del Mandorlato* with flags, tastings and banquets in Verona. The *torta sabiosa*, a light sponge made with potato flour and perfumed with vanilla and anis-flavoured alcohol, is one of the most popular cakes.

There are many old traditional sweets like fried cream (*crema fritta*), rice fritters (*fagottini di riso*) and carnival fritters (*frittelle*) with pine nuts, raisins and candied peel or with apples and wine, as well as creamed rice (*crema di riso*) and other milk puddings. Sweet lasagne with nuts and poppy seeds, a bread pudding called *torta Nicolotta* and a tagliatelle cake are other old specialities, but it is their new ones which are the stars in Veneto today. Treviso claims to have invented *tiramisu*, the most popular dessert in all of Italy (it means 'pick-me-up'), made with mascarpone (a Lombard cream cheese) and sponge fingers, and the men of the Valle del Zoldo near Belluno, who are professional ice-cream makers, have developed some of the best ice-creams I have eaten.

After dinner, in the Veneto, they bring out a bottle of home-made grappa, a powerful spirit made from grapes, plums or juniper berries, sweet wines and hot chocolate or coffee, and biscuits to dunk in, from the famous yellow maize flour *zaleti* to the *bigaroni* of Bassano del Grappa and the Venetian *baicoli* – the hard ship's biscuits perfumed with cinnamon, nutmeg and orange zest which, long ago, were taken on long sea voyages because they kept so well.

ASPARAGI CON SALSA ZABAIONE

Asparagus with egg and wine sauce

Bassano del Grappa in the Venetian Alps is famous for the fat, white wonderfully flavoured asparagus which grow on the banks of the tumultuous river Brenta. A green sauce (page 19) and this very delicate one are the best accompaniment I have found.

Serves 4

750g (1½lb) asparagus
Salt
4 egg yolks
150ml (¼ pint) dry white wine

Rinse the asparagus, peel away any hard skin and cut off the tough ends. Tie them up in bundles and simmer in salted water for 10–12 minutes or until you can pierce the stalks with a pointed knife, being careful not to over-cook. Then lift out carefully, drain well and keep warm.

To make the sauce, beat the egg yolks with the wine and a little salt in a heatproof bowl over a pan of boiling water and continue beating until the sauce is thick and smooth. Serve at once with the asparagus.

PEPERONATA ALLA VENETA

Peppers, Venetian style

Peperonata is originally Neapolitan, but the Veneto has its own version, from Treviso, where peppers are so good they hold a festival for them each year.

Serves 4

2 small aubergines cubed
Salt
4 tablespoons oil
1 clove garlic, peeled and crushed
300g (10oz) small onions, peeled
3 large sweet yellow or green peppers, seeded and sliced
150ml (¼ pint) white wine
5 tomatoes, peeled and chopped

Sprinkle the aubergines with salt and leave for an hour to degorge the juices. Wash and drain them.

Heat the oil in a frying pan with the garlic (remove this as soon as it browns). Add the onions, and cook over a low heat until soft and golden, shaking the pan every so often. Then add the aubergines and the peppers.

Pour in the wine, cover and cook gently for 20 minutes or until tender. Uncover, add tomatoes, turn up heat and boil rapidly for 10 minutes, or until most of the liquid has evaporated. Season to taste. Serve cold or warm.

CALAMARETTI E GAMBERONI FRITTI

Deep-fried squid and prawns

The Adriatic has the tiniest squid and the largest prawns. The most popular way of doing them is deep-fried in oil. One or the other can be served alone but often they come together as a little appetizer.

Serves 4

250g (½lb) small or medium squid
250g (½lb) large prawns
Salt
Flour
Olive oil
1 lemon cut in wedges

Clean and rinse the squid (see page 207). If they are tiny leave them whole, if they are medium cut the bodies into rings. Shell the prawns and rinse well.

Roll both in salted flour. Deep-fry briefly in not too hot oil and, with a slotted spoon, lift them out quickly when golden. (Squid become hard if over-cooked.) Drain on absorbent paper, and serve at once accompanied by lemon wedges.

GRANSEOLA ALLA VENEZIANA

Dressed crab in the shell

They have many types of crabs in Venice. Only one, the *granseola*, is large enough (like our own) to cook in this way.

Serves 4

4 medium crabs
Olive oil
Pepper
Bunch of parsley, finely chopped
1 lemon, quartered

Here crabs are mostly sold already boiled and the fishmonger will usually open them for you and remove the inedible parts. Plunge live ones into boiling salted water and boil hard for 3 minutes with the lid on, then simmer for 10–15 minutes until the shell turns red. Drain and let them cool.

Twist off the claws and legs, crack them with a nutcracker or hammer and remove the meat. Holding the crab upside down, pull the shell away from the body with the help of a rounded knife. Pick out the brown and white meat from the body with the knife. Throw away the mouth and the grey stomach sack along with the intestine that is attached to the top of the shell and the long pointed white gills that are attached to the bony body. The soft tomalley is a delicacy, as is the coral found in the female crab. Break away the inner rim marked with a line and scrub and rinse the shell. Chop the meat, including the flesh from the claws, and dress with olive oil, pepper and a sprinkling of parsley, then return it to the empty shell.

Serve the shell on crushed ice accompanied by lemon wedges.

SOPA DI CAPE SANTE

Scallops in white wine

Serves 4

400ml (14fl oz) dry white wine
12 scallops
25g (1oz) butter
2 tablespoons olive oil
½ clove garlic, crushed (optional)
Salt and pepper
Bunch of parsley, finely chopped

Simmer the wine in a pan for 10 minutes to reduce it (it acquires a mellow flavour).

Take the scallops out of their shells and remove the intestinal thread.

Cook the scallops for a moment only in a mixture of butter and oil with a little garlic in a large frying pan, turning them over carefully. Add salt and pepper and pour in the reduced wine then simmer for 1–2 minutes only until the scallops become translucent. Be very careful not to overcook them as they quickly become tough.

Add the parsley and serve in soup plates.

PESCE IN SAOR

Baby soles marinated in a sweet and sour sauce

Saor is dialect for *sapore* which means 'flavour'. Marinating in vinegar was an old Italian way of making fish last in the days before refrigeration but this recipe has a particular Arab flavour.

Around the end of the twelfth century in Venice, an Arab treatise on dietetics, including 83 recipes, written by a Baghdad doctor, Gege son of Algazael, was translated from the Arabic into Latin by a certain Jambobinus of Cremona who called it *Liber de coquina* (cookery book). Much later, in the sixteenth century, a scholar from Belluno, Andrea Alpago, who spent 30 years in Damascus and later became professor of medicine in Padua, published, in Venice, a translation of the works of the famous Arab physician and philosopher Avicenna (Ibn Sina), a great part of which was devoted to dietetics and cooking. Quite a few of the dishes described were embellished with raisins and pine nuts.

According to an old Venetian saying, social class was once characterized by what fish was used for *pesce in saor*: the poor used the popular sardines, the middle classes used *passarini* and the rich used soles.

Serves 6

500g (1lb) onions, finely chopped
2 tablespoons olive oil
120ml (4fl oz) white wine vinegar
250ml (8fl oz) dry white wine
2 tablespoons raisins
2 tablespoons pine nuts, toasted
2 bay leaves
Salt and white pepper
6 little soles (you may use lemon soles, dabs or other fish)
Flour
Oil for frying

Fry the onions in oil till lightly browned and very soft. Then add the vinegar and wine, raisins and pine nuts and bay leaves, season with salt and pepper, and let the sauce simmer for about 15 minutes.

Now lightly salt and flour the fish and fry quickly in hot oil, turning them over once. Drain well and place in layers on a serving dish, pouring some of the sauce over each fish. Allow to rest and absorb the marinade for several hours before serving cold.

PASTA E FAGIOLI

Pasta and bean soup

Pasta e fasioi (dialect for beans) is an old peasant dish that is now so popular it is served at elegant parties and appears on every restaurant menu in the Veneto. The soup varies from one city to another. There are small differences – wide tagliatelle are used in Vicenza, wholewheat bigoli in Verona, lasagne in Este and Padua, and thin fettuccine in other parts.

This recipe comes from the family of a Verona lawyer and famous *buongustaio* (food lover), Vito Quaranta.

Serves 4

200g (7oz) dried borlotti or haricot beans, soaked overnight
100g (4oz) rindless bacon, chopped
1 stick celery, finely chopped
1 onion, finely chopped
1 carrot, peeled and finely chopped
1 medium potato, peeled and chopped
2 tomatoes, skinned and chopped
Salt and freshly ground pepper
150g (5oz) bigoli, small, tubular macaroni or tagliatelle
Very pure olive oil
Grated parmesan or grana padana

Put the drained beans, bacon and vegetables into a saucepan. Cover with water and simmer for about two hours until the beans are tender. Take out a few tablespoons of beans and put them through a blender before returning them to the soup. Add salt and pepper and the pasta and cook for 10 minutes until it is tender.

Serve the soup warm, with a little freshly ground pepper and a dribble of olive oil on each serving, and pass the cheese.

PAPARELE E FIGADINI

Tagliatelle with chicken livers

The Veneto is not a region of pasta yet, like every part of Italy, they like to claim that pasta originated there. The basis of their claim is that Marco Polo brought noodles back from his voyages to the East. The typical pasta of the Veneto are bigoli (wholewheat noodles), pappardelle (wide tagliatelle) and *maltaja'* or *maltagliatti* which are cut into uneven triangles. In this lovely speciality of Verona there should be some liquid but not so much that it becomes a soup.

Serves 4

250g (8oz) tagliatelle or maltagliatti
250g (8oz) chicken livers
1½ tablespoons butter
Salt and pepper
1 litre (1¾ pints) light beef or chicken stock
(you may use 2 good stock cubes)
Plenty of grated parmesan or grana

Clean the chicken livers and cut a few up into pieces, leaving the rest whole. Fry them quickly in the butter for less than a minute, stirring, so that they are brown outside but still pink inside. Season with salt and pepper and take off the heat.

Throw the pasta into the boiling stock, stir well and after 2 minutes throw in the livers. When the tagliatelle are cooked *al dente* serve hot with the stock in which they have cooked and plenty of grated cheese.

GNOCCHETTI DI RICOTTA AL GORGONZOLA

Gorgonzola cheese dumplings

This recipe from *Le Migliori Ricette della Scuola del Gritti* was contributed by the brothers Celeste and Giuliano Tonon, owners of Da Celeste at Venegazzù, in Volpago del Montello near Treviso.

Serves 6

400g (10oz) ricotta
3 egg yolks
1 tablespoon semolina
2 tablespoons grated parmesan
A good pinch of nutmeg
Salt and pepper
1 tablespoon butter
2 tablespoons double cream
100g (3½oz) gorgonzola
1 tablespoon chopped parsley

Mash the ricotta with the parmesan, egg yolks, semolina, nutmeg, salt and pepper and mix well. On a lightly oiled surface roll the paste into thin rolls about 1½cm (½in) in diameter, then cut with a sharp knife into pieces about 2cm (¾in) long.

Melt a tablespoon of butter with the cream in a pan, add the gorgonzola and cook over a very low flame, crushing and stirring the cheese until you have a homogeneous sauce.

Drop the *gnocchetti* into plenty of boiling water and let them simmer for about 2 minutes or until they rise to the surface. Serve hot with the sauce and sprinkled with parsley.

RISI E BISI

Rice with peas

This is one of Venice's great loves. They make it in the springtime with tiny, tiny young tender peas. It is moist, with a little liquid and they call it a *minestra* or soup, but it is something between a soup and a risotto. Like all *risotti* it is served as a first course. Unless you can get really tiny young peas it is best to use frozen *petits pois*.

Serves 4

1kg (2lb) tender young fresh peas in the pod or 250g (½lb) frozen petits pois
2 rashers pancetta or unsmoked bacon, chopped
1 small onion, chopped
40g (1½oz) butter
1 tablespoon olive oil
1½ litres (2½ pints) light meat or chicken stock or stock made by boiling the pods
Salt and pepper
1 teaspoon of sugar
200g (7oz) Italian risotto rice
Small bunch parsley, finely chopped
Generous quantity of grated parmesan

Shell the peas. Fry the pancetta or bacon with the onion in half the butter and the oil till the onion is soft. Add the fresh peas, cover with a little of the hot stock and simmer 5–15 minutes, depending on how tender the peas are.

Now pour in the rest of the stock and bring to the boil. Throw in the rice, season with salt and plenty of pepper and a little sugar if the peas are not sweet enough, and cook gently, stirring occasionally until the rice is tender. Then stir in the rest of the butter, the parsley and cheese and serve.

NOTE With frozen *petits pois*, cook the rice first and stir them in (defrosted) when the rice is almost cooked.

RISOTTO AI FRUTTI DI MARE

Seafood risotto

Every region of Italy has its own way of cooking rice. In the south, where rice dishes are a festive and not an everyday food, they appear in the form of little balls (*arancini*) or large cakes (*gattò* and *sartù*) while the famous risotto of the north is soft and creamy (they call it velvety) with grains remaining firm (*al dente*). Even the risotto is different in the Veneto from its neighbours. In Lombardy and Piedmont the rice is fried in butter first then stock is added gradually, as it becomes absorbed, while in the Veneto the rice is cooked from the start in plenty of stock, often with the addition of wine and sometimes of milk. And in Venice they make it almost liquid and call it a *minestra* or soup.

There are dozens of fish and seafood risottos using only one kind or, as restaurants now mostly offer, a variety of fish and seafood.

Serves 4

400g (14oz) mussels, scrubbed and beards removed
350g (12oz) Italian risotto rice
About 1 litre (1¾ pints) water or light fish or vegetable stock (optional)
200ml (7fl oz) dry white wine
1 small onion, finely chopped
50g (2oz) butter
100g (4oz) prawns, shelled
200g (7oz) scampi or king sized prawns, shelled
Salt and pepper

Place the mussels and wine in a saucepan and cook moments only with the lid on over fierce heat until they open. Strain the cooking liquid and reduce by simmering for 10 minutes to about 150ml (¼ pint). Take the mussels out of their shells.

Bring a large pan of salted water or fish or vegetable stock to the boil. Take some out which you can add later (because rice varies so much, it is impossible to know how much liquid it will need). Throw in the rice, stir and simmer for about 10 minutes. Then pour in the reduced wine (used to cook the mussels) and cook 5–10 minutes longer, adding a little stock if necessary, until the rice is tender but firm and there is still a little liquid left.

In the meantime fry the onion in a tablespoon of butter till soft, add the prawns, cook for a minute or two until they turn pink, add the mussels and mix into the rice. Stir in the rest of the butter before serving.

It is a heresy to serve parmesan with fish or seafood risotto. I saw a cook adding some in a restaurant kitchen who said with a smile, 'We are all heretics!'

VARIATION Add squid, cuttlefish or baby octopus, cut into small pieces and cooked in the wine mixture or, if you like, clams and other shellfish.

SEPPIOLINE NERE

Cuttlefish in their ink

The Veneto is famous for cuttlefish cooked in their own black ink served with creamy polenta (*risotto nero* has rice cooked in the black sauce), but the legendary Harry's Bar has been serving it with tagliatelle for some years and started a fashion. Most of the cuttlefish sold in Britain have had their ink bags

removed because they crush easily with messy results, so you will be lucky if you find some with their ink. The dish can be made without it and it will be good, though lacking in the distinctive extra flavour from the ink and in the dramatic visual effect.

Serves 4

1kg (2¼lb) cuttlefish
½ an onion, finely chopped
2 cloves garlic, finely chopped
2–3 tablespoons olive oil
125ml (4fl oz) dry white wine
1 tablespoon tomato paste (optional)
Small bunch parsley, finely chopped
Salt and black pepper

Pull off the head and tentacles, then carefully remove the ink bags from the cuttlefish without breaking them and put them aside. Wash the cuttlefish in running water and remove the soft innards and the cuttlebone from the bodies. Cut the body into small thin strips and the tentacles into pieces.

In a large saucepan fry the onion and garlic in oil till the aroma rises. Then add the cuttlefish and cook, stirring and turning them over, for a few minutes. Pour in the wine and the ink from the bags, add tomato paste and parsley, season with salt and pepper and simmer gently for 20–30 minutes, adding a little water if necessary to have enough sauce. Add the parsley.

Serve hot with soft polenta or with tagliatelle or fettuccine. Harry's Bar in Venice started the fashion for serving this as a sauce for pasta.

NOTE For *risotto nero* throw 275g (10oz) short-grain rice into the sauce when it has cooked for 20 minutes, and continue to cook, stirring and adding water or fish stock – you may need about 1 litre (1¾ pints) – until the rice is done. There should be a little liquid left at the end.

BACCALÀ ALLA VICENTINA

Creamed stockfish with olive oil and milk

It seems strange that a country which juts out into the sea and which has so much coast should adore salt cod (*baccalà*) – cod dried and preserved in salt, and stockfish (*stoccafisso*) – cod dried in the sun and the wind until it is rockhard, both imported from North Sea countries, and that sea towns should have adopted them more than towns inland. But though the variety of fish is great in the Mediterranean, it has always been scarce and expensive. And in the days when preservation was difficult and Lenten dishes were obligatory, this cod was a more certain and cheaper source of fish. Now that it is no longer cheap it is a much loved delicacy.

Every region has its special ways of making *baccalà* and *stoccafisso* and the Veneto and Liguria have the most (there are at least 150 dishes). Vicenza is especially proud of her *baccalà alla vicentina*, her local glory. It is the dish that everyone there wanted me to taste and, when I did, everyone looked at my face to see my reaction. The name is a little confusing because in the Veneto they call stockfish *baccalà*.

The best quality of stockfish is the smallest and least hard called *ragno* in Italy.

Serves 8

1kg (2lb) stockfish
½ litre (18fl oz) olive oil
½ litre (18fl oz) milk or as required
1 large onion, chopped
1 clove garlic, crushed
6 anchovy fillets, finely chopped
Salt and white pepper
Small bunch of parsley, finely chopped

Break the stockfish with a hammer, then soak in cold water for 2 days, changing the water a few times. Drain, put in a pan covered with cold water, bring to the boil and poach (the water must barely tremble) for 18 minutes, then drain. Carefully remove the skin and bones, and chop the flesh very finely in the food processor.

In a heavy-bottomed pan, over very gentle heat, fry the onion in a few tablespoons of the oil till golden. Add the garlic and anchovies and when the aroma rises, the stockfish. Add the olive oil, a little at a time, working it in very hard with a wooden spoon. Then add the milk, very gradually and, as it becomes absorbed, beat vigorously all the time as if making mayonnaise, until the *baccalà* has the consistency of creamy mashed potatoes. Add salt, pepper and parsley, pour into a baking dish and bake at 200°C (400°F, gas mark 6) for 15 minutes.

Serve with polenta or with pieces of fried or toasted bread.

VARIATION In Venice they make *baccalà mantecato* with only olive oil and no milk – although I have seen some people add cream flavoured with garlic and served with a squeeze of lemon.

MAIALE AL LATTE

Pork cooked in milk

Pork is traditional country fare here. This exquisite way of cooking it makes it an elegant dish.

Serves 4

1kg (2¼lb) leg or loin of pork
3 tablespoons white wine vinegar
300ml (½ pint) white wine
2 tablespoons oil
Salt and pepper
A few leaves sage
Sprig rosemary
600ml (1 pint) milk

Put the meat into a deep dish, cover with vinegar and white wine and leave to marinate overnight.

Next day remove the meat, dry it and brown it in a pan in oil. Season with pepper and salt, add a few leaves of sage and a sprig of rosemary and cover with milk. Put the lid on and place the pan on the heat to cook very slowly for about two hours. When the meat is very tender take the lid off, increase the heat and allow liquid to reduce.

Take out the pork, slice (not too thinly) and put on a warm plate. Strain the sauce if you like (it always curdles), putting a little on the meat and serving the rest in a sauce boat.

FEGATO ALLA VENEZIANA

Liver, Venetian style

This famous Venetian dish is always popular.

Serves 4

4 tablespoons olive oil
50g (2oz) butter
2 large onions, halved and thinly sliced and cut into pieces
600g (1lb 5oz) calves' liver, very thinly sliced
Handful of parsley, chopped
Salt

Heat a frying pan with 2 tablespoons of oil and the butter. As soon as the fat is melted, add the onion and stir. Cover the pan and cook the onion on a low heat, stirring occasionally, for about one hour until very soft and creamy.

Heat the remaining oil in a frying pan, add the liver and fry very quickly until brown on all sides, then add the onions. When the liver is cooked (it takes less than five minutes), take it off the heat, stir in the parsley, season to taste and serve at once.

POLLASTRI PINI E BONI

Roast chicken stuffed under the skin with cheese and herbs

I am not sure if this dish originated in the region, but it comes from the celebrated Ristorante Cipriani in Venice.

Serves 4

250g (1lb) fresh soft caciotta cheese
2 or more tablespoons milk
Large bunch of herbs including parsley, rosemary, sweet marjoram, basil and sage, finely chopped
Salt and pepper
1 chicken

Blend the soft cheese to a paste with the milk, then mix in the herbs (plenty of them), salt and pepper.

Starting at the neck, work your hand under the skin of the chicken, separating it with your fingers from the flesh all the way along the breast and legs (the membranes which join them are easily detached). Then stuff the pockets formed with the cheese and herb mixture, pushing it in from the neck and pressing it evenly into place from the outside. Close up the opening at the neck and sew up any tears in the skin with a needle and thread.

Roast the chicken in a 230°C (450°F, gas mark 8) oven for 10 minutes, then lower the heat to 180°C (350°F, gas mark 4) and cook another 40–50 minutes, basting occasionally with the pan juices.

OCA CON MELE E CASTAGNE

Goose with apples and chestnuts

Serves 6

1 goose, weighing about 6kg (12lb)
Salt and pepper
8 large apples, such as Cox's Orange
Pippins or Golden Delicious
4 tablespoons unsalted butter
1kg (2lb) chestnuts

Remove the giblets from the body cavity and wash the goose thoroughly inside and out. Sprinkle with salt and pepper and stuff with 2 of the apples, coarsely chopped.

Place the bird in a roasting pan (on a rack if you like) and pierce the skin all over with a fork to allow the fat to run out. Roast at 220°C (425°F, gas mark 7) for 20 minutes, then cover the bird with foil, turn the oven down to 180°C (350°F, gas mark 4) and roast for another 2¼ to 2¾ hours. Test for doneness by piercing the thigh with a pointed knife. The juices which run out should not be pink.

Peel the remaining apples and slice them thickly. Fry gently in batches in the butter in a large sauté pan until soft.

Slit the skin of the chestnuts on their flat side with a pointed knife and put them on a tray under the grill (close to the flame) for 10 minutes, turning them over once, then peel them while still hot, making sure that you remove the inside skin. They should not be allowed to brown or they will become too hard. An alternative, resulting in softer chestnuts, is to boil them for about 20 minutes. In this way peeling is slightly more difficult. (I prefer them when they are roasted and firm.) Break the chestnuts into quarters and mix with the apple slices. Put them in an oven dish and heat through in the oven when you are nearly ready to serve the goose.

POLENTA

Restaurants were once ashamed to offer polenta. After thirty years of neglect, the old heartwarming maize flour mush, rejected as 'poor food' in the fifties, has made a triumphal comeback and is now very fashionable in the north of Italy and especially in the Veneto, where it was once a staple. Restaurants serve elegant portions, often in the form of thin toasted slices, *crostoni*, which act as a bed for game birds, sausages, fish and meat stews. Some pour it on to a large board and cut it with a long thread in the old way, or press it in a mould and turn it out.

Polenta is not an easy dish to master, partly because there are so many ways of making it. There are those who like it soft and creamy, those who prefer it firm to cut with a knife, those who want a thickness of 3 or 4 fingers and those who like it as a slice no more than a centimetre thick.

There is a white maize flour as well as the more common yellow one but they taste the same, and there are different degrees of fineness. The fine ground flour is considered the best though many prefer the coarse one.

The difficulty with the traditional way of making polenta is that it must be stirred for about 45 minutes so that lumps do not form. The flour is gradually poured in with the left hand, in a thin rain, into boiling salted water while the right hand stirs vigorously, always in the same clockwise direction. As the thick mass gurgles and splatters you must be careful that the bottom does not stick and burn or the taste will be spoilt. The traditional polenta pan, *la caldiera*, is in heavy copper with a pointed cone-shaped bottom which fits into a hole in the old hearths and which has a kind of oar, *la caldina*, which makes stirring easier. Although gourmets claim that polenta made in the slow, even heat of a *caldiera* is superior to any other and has another flavour and another smell, people have successfully devised ways of making it more easily and you can even buy a special polenta pan with a built-in electric oar.

Here is a basic and easy, although heretical way of making polenta, given by Lucia Alberini, which works very well.

Serves 4

300g (10oz) polenta (maize flour or maize meal)
2 teaspoons salt
1¼ litres (2½ pints) of water

Put the maize flour with the cold water in a very large saucepan (it needs space to grow by more than a third) and stir very thoroughly. Add salt and, stirring vigorously and constantly so that lumps do not form (this is crucial), bring to the boil slowly. Cook for a few minutes, stirring, then pour into a greased baking tray or bowl. Cover with foil and bake at 200°C (400°F, gas mark 6) for at least an hour.

To make *crostoni* turn out while still hot and let it cool and become firm, then cut into slices and toast under the grill or over a fire till lightly browned on both sides.

VARIATIONS For a softer creamier polenta use 3 litres (5¼ pints) water or a half-and-half mixture of milk and water for 300g (10oz) maize flour. This too eventually becomes firm and can be sliced and grilled resulting in a lovely crisp crust and a soft inside.

For *polenta a bocconi* serve in deep bowls with plenty of butter and grated parmesan. For sweet *polenta a bocconi dolce* sprinkle with sugar and cinnamon instead of parmesan. For *polenta conzada* serve with plenty of butter, ricotta and grated parmesan. *Pasticcio di polenta* is a baked pie with layers of pigeon, chicken or veal stew with ham and mushrooms and polenta.

A dramatic traditional way of serving polenta is poured out on to the table (you can cover it with silver foil) with different foods such as fried sausages, slices of salami or cheese, quail, lightly fried mushrooms, pigeon or hare stew laid on top for people to help themselves straight from the centre. The traditional way of cutting plain polenta is with a thread.

FUNGHETTI AL VINO

Mushrooms in white wine

There are many varieties of wild mushrooms in these parts. They are fried lightly in butter with garlic and parsley, grilled, deep-fried in batter, and stewed with tomatoes or in wine. When they are in season you find them in everything – soups, tarts, risottos, gnocchi, omelettes, pancakes. I tried them in many different ways at Da Celeste in Venegazzù di Volpago del Montello, near Treviso. This recipe is good with every kind of mushroom.

Serves 4

4–5 tablespoons olive oil
1 small clove garlic
700g (1½lb) mushrooms, cut into pieces if large
1 tablespoon thyme
Salt and pepper
150ml (5fl oz) white wine
2 tablespoons fresh parsley, chopped

In a saucepan, heat oil with garlic. When the aroma rises, add the mushrooms and thyme and cook over a high heat for a minute or two. Season with salt and pepper, add wine and boil vigorously until it almost evaporates. Add parsley and serve hot or cold.

RADICCHIO CON RUCOLA

Radicchio and rocket salad

The salad leaf that has become popular all over the world because of its beautiful red colour is, in its native Veneto, grilled, fried in egg and breadcrumbs as well as braised and made into risotto. But the type available here is best simply eaten raw as a salad. A traditional radicchio salad, a speciality of Vicenza, is dressed with hot bacon fat with a sprinkling of fried bacon bits, but the following combination with rocket is now the most popular.

There are five types of their famous red *radicchio*. The most popular are the long-leafed variety of Treviso (they have a festival in November when they make everything, even puddings with it) and the round variegated kind from Castelfranco. They are used raw in salads, grilled and also cooked with onion and bacon.

Serves 4

2 heads of radicchio
Bunch of rocket leaves
3 tablespoons olive oil
1 tablespoon vinegar
Salt and pepper

Dress the salad leaves with oil, vinegar, salt and pepper just before you are ready to serve.

TIRAMISU

Cream cheese and rum pudding

There cannot be a restaurant or trattoria in Italy that does not have their stock of little individual bowls of *tiramisu* in the freezer nor a housewife that does not have a favourite recipe cut out from a magazine. This easy dessert which is only about 15 years old has many versions. The following is my own favourite.

Serves 8

4 tablespoons rum (or to taste)
100ml (4fl oz) strong black coffee
2 tablespoons brandy
16–20 sponge fingers
400g (14oz) mascarpone
2 medium eggs, separated
4 tablespoons icing sugar
75–100g (3–4oz) bitter chocolate,
pulverized in a blender

Mix 2 tablespoons rum with coffee and brandy. Dip sponge fingers in this mixture and lay in a shallow dish. Pour over any remaining coffee mixture but not so much that the sponge becomes soggy. Beat together mascarpone, egg yolks and icing sugar and add remaining rum. Whisk egg whites until stiff but not dry and fold into mascarpone. Spoon over sponge fingers. Sprinkle with chocolate; and refrigerate overnight.

SEMIFREDDO AL MIELE

Honey ice-cream

The Valle del Zoldo near the town of Belluno in northern Veneto is known for its creamy, delicately flavoured *semifreddo* which is quite different from the legendary Sicilian and Neapolitan ice-creams. The men of the region

– like Sicilians and Neapolitans before them – have brought their trade all over Italy and abroad (they go to Germany especially). They are constantly bringing out new flavours like this one.

Serves 4–6

1 whole (size 1) egg
4 large egg yolks
100g scented honey (such as acacia honey)
284ml (10fl oz) double or whipping cream

Beat the egg and yolks with the honey in a bowl over boiling water until the mixture becomes thick and pale. Then beat the cream stiff and fold it in. Pour into a serving bowl and freeze overnight.

The whipping cream gives a fluffier, lighter ice-cream.

SEMIFREDDO DI CIOCCOLATO

Chocolate ice-cream

250g (½lb) bitter or dark chocolate
3 tablespoons milk
6 eggs
4 tablespoons Cognac
300ml (½ pint) whipping cream

Melt the chocolate with the milk over boiling water. Then beat in the egg yolks vigorously, one at a time, and add the brandy. Now whip the cream and fold it in. Then whip the egg whites stiff and fold them in gently. Pour into a bowl and put into the freezer for several hours until the mixture hardens. Take it out about one hour before serving.

NOTE If you want to serve the ice-cream moulded, line a mould with clingfilm so that you can easily turn it out.

SEMIFREDDO AL VINO

Wine-flavoured ice-cream

Serves 6

2 eggs
175ml (6fl oz) sweet wine (white or red)
100g (3½oz) sugar
284ml (10fl oz) whipping or double cream

Beat the eggs with sugar in a bowl placed over boiling water; then gradually add the wine, beating well until the mixture thickens. Beat the cream till stiff and fold into the cooled egg and wine mixture. Freeze overnight.

ZABAIONE FREDDO

Cold zabaglione pudding with cream

This recipe comes from Giorgio Gioco, chef-owner of the Ristorante 12 Apostoli in Verona, who has a story, a saying or a poem about every dish.

Serves 6

6 egg yolks
150g (5oz) sugar
200ml (7fl oz) Marsala
Grated rind of ½ a lemon
1 teaspoon cinnamon
Few drops of vanilla essence
200ml (7fl oz) double or whipping cream

Put all the ingredients except the cream in the top of a double boiler or in a bowl placed in a pan of boiling water and beat vigorously until the mixture is frothy. Then put directly on the heat and beat constantly until the mixture is thick and creamy. Take off the heat and let it cool.

Now beat the cream until stiff and fold into the egg mixture. Pour into a bowl or wine-glasses and serve chilled with biscuits.

Friuli-Venezia Giulia

I was brought up in Egypt by a woman who came from a village near Gorizia on the Yugoslav border. She taught me Italian and introduced me to polenta, and because of her this eastern corner of Italy is magical for me. Friuli covers most of the region since a great part of Venezia Giulia was given to Yugoslavia after the Second World War. The Friulani are a quiet reserved people who speak a language of their own – they complain that no one knows they are there and that everyone thinks Italy stops at Venice. Life has always been harder and people poorer here than anywhere else in the north – the men go to work in Switzerland and Germany – yet it is the area which produces the best white wines in Italy (they rival those of Alto Adige) and the sweetest, most tender, pinkest raw ham at San Daniele, a little town on a hill which has fifteen *prosciuttifici* and just the right air and humidity to dry the hams without needing too much salt to preserve them.

In this modest backwater you can still find good home-made produce. In the village of Sauris in the Carnia mountains in the north, they smoke the hams of their little brown pigs by burning juniper and fruit wood in the room below, and letting the smoke come up through the floorboards. In the Carso hills above Trieste they cure hams that have hardly any fat and a great deal of flavour, and they smoke goose. Spicy sausages, *lujanis* and *muset* (this one is meat from the head of the pig flavoured with cinnamon, coriander and other spices) are also produced. Mountain cheeses called *formaggio di malga*, made in the alpine huts they use when they bring the cows up to graze in the mountains in the summer are montasio, pendolon, tegolino and fresh smoked ricotta, blackened, pear-shaped and with herbs. Tolmezzo in Carnia is famous for these and for a much-prized breed of veal called *Pezzata Rossa*.

Friuli-Venezia Giulia has a fascinating and complex gastronomy because it was a zone of passage, invaded by '*tutti, tutti, tutti*', where three cultures meet – Venetian, Austro-Hungarian and Yugoslav. And the cuisine is further divided into primitive mountain food, homely cooking of the plain, sophisticated city dishes and the cooking of the sea.

In the mountains, the heart of the cooking is polenta which 'sings, snores, blows and smokes' on the fire. It is white here from the special white maize that grows in the Friuli plain. The people pour out the cooked polenta on to a board, cut a cross on it with the ladle and eat it with salami (hot and sprinkled with vinegar), spit-roasted birds, pork, game, fish and *frico* – grated cheese cooked in a pan until it is crisp and crackling. In the autumn they live on game such as hare, partridge, pheasant, wild boar and deer, and on trout, mushrooms and wild salad leaves like rocket and lamb's lettuce.

In the plain, they eat roast chicken, duck, goose, turkey stuffed with chestnuts and tiny pork chops, a legacy from the days when small farmyard animals, *animali di cortile*, were considered a woman's job and raised for the family table – the men took care of cows and sheep.

Pork cooked in milk and *bollito misto* (boiled meats) are eaten in town with *brovada*, a kind of relish of turnips fermented in marc which is the most typical food of the area. Like the grand villas in Udine (the last Doge, Manin, had his just outside), many dishes are a testimony to the long domination of Venice.

Soups are as important here in the north as spaghetti is in the south, made with root vegetables, barley and rice and, the most popular, with beans. They have *risotti* with herbs and vegetables, pumpkin and sausage, chicken livers and quails, frogs and snails. Gnocchi are part of the Austrian heritage. Other Germanic touches are fruit and horseradish sauces and combinations of fruit and meat such as apples, prunes and bilberries with pork.

Near the border towards Gorizia and Trieste where they speak Slovene (the towns were annexed to Italy in 1918), the Austro-Hungarian influence is strongest. *Gulasch* and sauerkraut are served in beer cellars. Hare with sweet and sour sauce is another Bohemian dish. And, because Trieste was a great centre for trade with the Levant (and southern Yugoslavia was part of the Ottoman Empire), it has dishes like the Greek rice with egg and lemon sauce and pastries stuffed with dried fruit and nuts, spices and honey.

By the sea in Trieste and Grado the cooking is very Venetian. These towns are famous especially for scampi, oysters, eels, sole, turbot and crab and their fishermen's stews. Grado's *broeto* (fish stew) is turbot and eel cooked in wine.

For dessert they like pastries, Austrian in style and made with apples and cherries. The most famous are *gubana*, a crusty strudel, and *putizza*, a yeasty roll – both stuffed with walnuts, pine nuts, raisins and chocolate. And to end the meal one of the oldest traditions in this country of fine wine, where everyone seems to make grappa (an alcohol distilled from grape seeds and skins) at home, is to dunk little hard biscuits called *pandaluts* in your drink.

FRITTATA

Omelette

Frittate are common throughout Italy, except for Sicily and Sardinia. Piedmont is famous for its truffle omelette, Trentino for its mushrooms and artichoke ones; in Trieste they make them sweet, filled with fruit or jam and cream, but they are especially popular in Friuli where they make great use of eggs. There, *frittate* are taken to work for lunch and served as a snack in *osterie*. In most regions they are thin and pliable like a French omelette, but in Friuli they make them two fingers thick, crusty and brown outside and creamy inside. And whereas in central Italy they cook them in oil, here they use butter and sometimes still pork or goose fat.

Onion frittata with herbs
Serves 4–6

2 large onions, coarsely chopped
3 tablespoons oil
Salt and pepper
4 eggs
Bunch of herbs such as oregano, marjoram,
thyme, sage, parsley, mint, and basil
(choose 2–3)
1 tablespoon butter

Fry the onion gently in 2 tablespoons of oil for 20 minutes, adding salt and pepper and stirring often, until very soft and golden. Then put it in a bowl with the eggs and herbs (in Friuli they also use every kind of edible plant that grows wild in the fields including nasturtium and poppy) and a little more salt and pepper, and beat well.

Pour the mixture into a large non-stick frying pan with the sizzling butter and 1 tablespoon of oil. Cook until the bottom is set and browned and then turn over or put under the grill to do the other side.

VARIATIONS Use vegetables such as spinach, spinach beets, leeks, courgettes, asparagus, peas and cabbage, previously boiled, or fried bacon, salame or pork sausage cut into pieces. Fold into the eggs with herbs and seasoning and cook in the same way.

Potato frittata
Serves 4–6

500g (1lb) potatoes
4 eggs
Salt and pepper
1 large beef tomato, peeled and chopped
Bunch of mint, finely chopped
1 tablespoon butter
1 tablespoon oil

Boil the potatoes till tender; peel and mash them, then beat in the eggs, tomato, salt, pepper and mint.

Heat a mixture of butter and oil in a large non-stick frying pan and pour in the potato and egg mixture. Cook until the bottom of the omelette is set and lightly browned. Then do the other side by slipping the omelette on to a plate with a spatula and slipping it back into the pan upside down. Or put it under the grill to brown.

ZUPPA DI FUNGHI

Cream of mushroom soup

This is the way they make mushroom soup with wild porcini and ovoli up in the hills around Gorizia. A few dried porcini (which need to be soaked) give a special flavour. Out of season the soup is made entirely with dried mushrooms. I find that here shiitake ones give the best results.

300g (10oz) porcini or shiitake mushrooms
250g (8oz) potatoes
25g (1oz) butter
2–3 tablespoons olive oil
Salt and pepper
1 clove garlic, crushed
1 tablespoon flour
150ml (¼ pint) white wine
1½ litres (2½ pints) light chicken stock (you
can use water and 2 stock cubes)
Sprig of marjoram, finely chopped
2–3 tablespoons brandy (optional)
Small bunch of parsley, finely chopped
350ml (12fl oz) sour cream

Chop the mushrooms and potatoes very finely (I put them separately through the food processor). Sweat the mushrooms in a large pan in a mixture of butter and oil for 5–10 minutes, adding salt and pepper. Then add the garlic and, when the aroma rises, stir in the flour. Add the wine, potatoes and stock and stir in the marjoram. Simmer for 25 minutes or until it is creamy and tastes cooked, adding more salt and pepper and brandy towards the end. Serve sprinkled with parsley and pass the sour cream to be stirred into each serving to taste.

TAGLIOLINI DI ZUCCA

Thin tagiatelle made with pumpkin

Pumpkin has never found favour in Italian gastronomy until today. In the past culinary writers always seemed to deprecate this vegetable, commenting that the flavour was insipid and that it upset the humours.

It has now been 'discovered' and it is very popular and fashionable in Venezia Giulia, the Veneto and Lombardy and also in Sicily.

There are many varieties of pumpkin, with different shapes and colours, and their flavour varies enormously so it is important to find a good one.

The toasted seeds are eaten as *passatempi*, 'to pass the time'.

This recipe comes from the Trattoria 'Da Toni' at Gradiscutta di Varmo outside Udine.

500g (1lb) slice of pumpkin (weighed with
the seeds and skin removed)
Salt and pepper
250g (8oz) flour plus a little more
4 egg yolks
½ onion, chopped
1 tablespoon butter
Smoked or salted ricotta, grated

Wrap 100g (3½oz) of the pumpkin in foil and bake in a 200°C (400°F, gas mark 6) oven for 1 hour. Mash to a purée and season.

Put the flour in a bowl with the egg yolks and pumpkin purée. Mix well and knead for about 10 minutes until the dough is soft and elastic, adding flour if it is too sticky (the amount will depend on how moist the pumpkin is).

Wrap in clingfilm and leave to rest for half an hour. Then roll out as thinly as you can on a well-floured surface with a generously floured rolling pin and proceed as indicated on page 84, cutting the sheet into very thin ribbons.

For the sauce: dice the remaining pumpkin and simmer in a little salted water to cover for about 5 minutes, until just tender, then drain. Fry the onion in butter till soft and add the diced cooked pumpkin.

Boil the tagliolini in plenty of boiling salted water until *al dente*. Drain, mix with the sauce and serve with grated smoked or salted ricotta.

GNOCCHI DI PATATE

Potato dumplings

Potato gnocchi are a speciality of the north of Italy and they are especially popular in Friuli where they make them in all shapes and sizes – in little balls the size of peas or large walnuts, and also in squares, ovals and fingers. Having failed more than once to make them years ago – they either fell apart in the cooking water or tasted of uncooked flour – I asked everyone on my recent trips for their secret of success, and after much experimenting I found that baking, not boiling the potatoes results in the perfect gnocchi which never fail. Because there is less moisture they need less flour and taste purely of potato.

Serves 4

800g (1½lb) baked potatoes, weighed
skinned (I use King Edwards)
Salt
2 egg yolks
100g (3½oz) plain flour

For the dressing

50g (2oz) melted butter
Grated parmesan or grana

Choose mature baking potatoes which have a flaky quality. They should be of the same size. Wash them and bake them in their jackets (not in foil as it makes them retain too much moisture) in a 200°C (400°F, gas mark 6) oven for an hour or until tender.

Peel, weigh and mash them while still hot so that they are very smooth, without any lumps. Add salt, work in the yolks and flour, and knead well to a smooth, elastic doughy paste.

Now shape the paste into little balls: the usual way is to make long rolls the thickness of a thumb and cut them into 2cm (¾in) segments. Press these against a grater or the prongs of a fork to mark them, so that they hold the dressing better. Place them, so that they do not touch, on a floured cloth.

Cook the gnocchi in batches in barely simmering, slightly salted water (take into account they are already salted) for at least 10 minutes. Lift them out of the water with a slotted spoon, drain well and serve with melted butter and a sprinkling of cheese.

VARIATIONS 1 teaspoon of cinnamon is sometimes dusted on.

Gnocchi are often served with the sauce from a meat or a duck stew.

Veneto-style gnocchi are served with 500g (1lb) peeled and chopped tomatoes heated in a pan with 2 tablespoons of butter, seasoned with salt and pepper, and finished with a sprinkling of chopped parsley – and of course grated cheese is passed around.

For Piedmontese *gnocchi alla bava* put the cooked gnocchi in a very hot oven with butter and fontina cheese, cut in thin slices, until the cheese melts.

GNOCCHETTI DI ZUCCA

Pumpkin dumplings

It is best to buy pumpkin cut up, by the piece, so that you can taste it before you buy, as they vary quite a bit in flavour. You will know, even without experience, if it is not a very good one.

Serves 4

800g (1¾lb) pumpkin flesh, weighed with
the skin, seeds and stringy bits removed
1 egg
200g (7oz) flour
Salt and pepper
75g (3oz) butter, melted
Grated hard salty ricotta, grana or
parmesan cheese

Wrap the pumpkin flesh in foil and bake it in a 220°C (425°F, gas mark 7) oven for 1 hour or until it is very tender. Then mash it to a paste, or blend briefly in a food processor (do not over-blend). Add the egg, salt (it needs plenty) and pepper, and work in enough flour to have a firm paste.

Make dumplings by dropping the paste by the tablespoon (using another tablespoon to push it off) into barely simmering salted water. When the dumplings rise to the top, let them cook a few minutes longer, then lift them out carefully with a slotted spoon.

Drain well and serve with melted butter and grated cheese.

made below the head and the skin is pulled off like a stocking), but all those I have seen at fishmonger's here have been small.

Roll the eels in flour. Fry the onion till soft in a mixture of butter and oil then add the garlic and the pieces of eel. Turn the eel to brown it all over and add the rest of the ingredients except the parsley. Simmer for about 20 minutes or until the eel is tender, add the parsley and serve hot.

This is usually served with a creamy polenta.

ANGUILLA IN TEGAME

Stewed eel with wine and vinegar

Eels abound in the lakes and rivers and lagunas around the coast in Friuli (they are less fatty and at their best in the winter months). They are also grilled on charcoal, fried dipped in egg and breadcrumbs and stewed with tomatoes.

Serves 4

4 small eels weighing about 750g (1½lb) cut into 5cm (2in) pieces
Flour
1 onion, chopped
1 tablespoon butter
1 tablespoon olive oil
2 cloves garlic, finely chopped
3 tablespoons white wine vinegar
600ml (1 pint) dry white wine
Salt and pepper
2 bay leaves
Sprig of fresh sage leaves
Small bunch of parsley

Buy the eels live. The fishmonger will gut and clean them for you and cut them into pieces. Only large eels need to be skinned (a cut is

ANATRA ARROSTO

Roast duck

The herbs and grappa give this simple way of cooking duck an Italian flavour.

Serves 4

1 duckling
Salt and pepper
Juice of 1 lemon
1 onion, peeled
3 bay leaves, cut into pieces
Sprig of sage
2 sprigs rosemary
4 tablespoons brandy or grappa

Sprinkle the duck inside and out with salt, pepper and lemon juice. Put the onion inside the cavity with a bay leaf and a few sage and rosemary leaves and sprinkle the rest of the herbs outside.

Bake breast side down in a 200°C (400°F, gas mark 6) oven for half an hour. Then take it out, turn it over, and prick the skin all over with a fork to allow the melting fat to escape, and bake for half an hour longer. Now pour out all the fat, sprinkle with brandy or grappa and return to the oven until done.

'PITA' DI MELE

Apple slice

I ate this at Gianni Gosetti's Ristorante Roma at Tolmezzo in the mountains.

For the biscuity pastry

250g (8oz) flour
50g (2oz) sugar
Grated peel of ½ a lemon
150g (5oz) unsalted butter
1 tablespoon rum
1–2 tablespoons milk (if necessary)

For the filling

750g (1½lb) sweet dessert apples (such as
Golden Delicious), coarsely grated
75g (3oz) sugar
50g (2oz) raisins
4 tablespoons rum or 3 of grappa
2 teaspoons cinnamon
Juice of 1 small lemon
100g (3½oz) walnuts, hazelnuts or
almonds, coarsely ground
Icing sugar to garnish

To make the pastry: mix the flour, sugar and grated lemon peel, cut the butter into small pieces and rub it into the flour until you have a crumb texture. Add the rum and work briefly with your hands into a soft dough, adding the extra milk only if necessary. Wrap the pastry in clingfilm and let it rest for half an hour.

Mix all the filling ingredients together.

Divide the pastry into 2 and make each into a ball, one of them slightly larger. Roll the larger one out on a generously floured board with a floured rolling pin and line the base and sides of a 25–30cm (10–12in) tart pan or flan mould. Spread the filling on top and cover with the rest of the pastry rolled out thinly. Prick a few holes with a fork and bake in a 180°C (350°F, gas mark 4) oven for about 45 minutes until it is a light biscuity colour. It will firm as it cools. Serve sprinkled with icing sugar.

TORTA DI CASTAGNE

Chestnut cake

I found many chestnut cake recipes in different regions and liked this one best.

500g (1lb) chestnuts or tinned chestnut purée
300ml (½ pint) milk
250g (8oz) sugar
100g (3½oz) blanched almonds or walnuts,
finely chopped
5 eggs
100g (3½oz) butter, softened
Grated peel of 1 lemon
100g (4oz) bitter or dark chocolate, grated
2–3 tablespoons of Strega or cognac
A little flour

For the fresh chestnuts, make a long slit on the flat side of each and put them under the grill, turning them over to brown both sides. Peel them while still hot. Simmer chestnuts in enough milk to cover for about 15 minutes till soft. Drain and mash to a pulp in a food processor. Use the purée as it is.

Beat the egg yolks with the sugar. Add the butter (keep aside a knob to grease the cake tin), chestnuts and almonds or walnuts, grated lemon peel, chocolate and Strega or cognac, and stir thoroughly. Then fold in the stiffly beaten egg whites and pour into a buttered and floured 27cm (10in) cake tin.

Bake in a 180°C (350°F, gas mark 4) oven for about 50–60 minutes. Turn out and serve cold.

Emilia-Romagna

The people of Emilia-Romagna eat more, care more and talk more about food than anyone else in Italy. They like nothing better than to get together, eat, drink, tell jokes, sing and discuss the merits of dishes. Other regions describe this feel for the good life as *il culto del ben essere*, needing a strong stomach and a delicate palate. Bologna became famous for gastronomy when the university, the first in Europe, opened in the twelfth century and the city became known as Bologna *la grassa e la dotta* (the fat and the learned). Her reputation as gastronomic capital of Italy has flourished ever since.

Rich, abundant, robust, even opulent, but also elaborate and refined, the cooking of Emilia-Romagna came to represent the ideal Italian cuisine through Pellegrino Artusi's *La Scienza in Cucina e l'Arte di Mangiare Bene* (Science in the Kitchen and the Art of Good Eating), Italy's most famous cookery book, published in 1891 and reprinted more than 100 times. Now simply called *l'Artusi*, it was the first book to deal with the cooking of Italy as a whole. The author, fired by patriotic fervour and the desire 'to create a national cuisine that would achieve cultural unity', developed a 'common national cuisine' from the multitude of regional ones, 'so that Italians could understand each other at table'. But Artusi came from Forlimpopoli; Emilia was his model and her dishes, which he describes with special enthusiasm, form the bulk of his recipes. (Romagna is a separate entity from Emilia with a different character.) As for the Italian south, Artusi transformed their dishes by reducing or eliminating garlic, onion, spices and peppers and increasing the quantities of meat (he wrote for an emerging middle class who could afford it) and by adding butter and velvety sauces. He told his readers to 'make a deep bow when you meet Bolognese cooking, it deserves it'.

In the Fifties and Sixties Bolognese cooks won international prizes, but today some Bolognese gastronomes feel their cooking should be less famous. In this age of health and cholesterol awareness and dieting, there is too much emphasis on meat, charcuterie and cheese, with pork fat, butter and oil and too few vegetables. Today in Emilia they are pulling out from the past dishes that Artusi would have ignored.

Emilia, with her long plain in the valley of the river Po and rich alluvial soil, has always been the greatest food-producing centre of Italy. She grows huge quantities of soft wheat and tomatoes, and also sugar beet, rice and maize, onions, apples and pears, plums, quince, sweet melons, watermelons and cherries. Emilia too is the home of the biggest pasta-making, tomato-preserving and fruit and vegetable canning plants. But her reputation as the great gastronomic centre of Italy is based mainly on *prosciutto di Parma* – Parma ham, the most popular antipasto in Italy, whose special tenderness, sweet delicate flavour, enticing perfume and pale pink shades marbled with pure white fat have made it famous all over the world; and on parmesan cheese, the most essential ingredient in Italian cooking.

According to legend, Hannibal, on his way to fight the Romans, was served raw cured ham at a banquet in Parma in 217 BC. Now it is a large industry involving about 250 firms, but the old artisan methods of treating and curing continue. The pigs are a cross between an English and a Danish breed which grow voluminous legs in eleven months on a mixture of whey and maize, barley and soya flour. By law, hams can only be branded with the ducal crown of Parma if they are taken from this variety of pig raised in northern Italy and fed on controlled foods; and if they are cured in the traditional manner in a strictly defined zone.

The hams are trimmed, brushed and polished; a few, especially those for export, are also boned. Otherwise, retailers do this before they can slice very thin by machine. The hams are salted and left for a few weeks in a very cool atmosphere while much of their water drains away, then they are washed and allowed to dry out and mature for ten to twelve months. Only just enough salt to draw out the water and prevent fermentation is used, so the hams are only slightly salty. At a certain height, the hills of Langhirano outside Parma have the ideal climate, neither too dry nor too humid, with cool winters and breezy, perfumed air. The cool ventilated environment, once controlled by the opening and closing of special long thin windows, is now technologically reinforced.

Apart from prosciutto, there is a whole world of cured meats and salamis to be discovered in Emilia. Zibello and Busseto make the highly prized culatello from the best part of the buttock, matured in the bladder of the animal, and fiocco or fiocchetto from the top of the leg, and also *spalla cotta* – boiled shoulder. Coppa, the fillet encased in sausage skins, and pancetta, unsmoked bacon used for cooking, are a speciality of the region around Piacenza. Bologna is known for mortadella. *Zampone* – stuffed pigs' trotters, *cappello da prete*, the lower part of the leg, treated with salt, garlic and spices and sewn up in the shape of a triangle and cotechino, a strongly-flavoured boiling sausage, are specialities of Modena. One of the best salamis comes from Felino. Ferrara is known for *salame da sugo* made with minced pork, liver and tongue, enriched with spices and red wine. It was thought to have aphrodisiac qualities and it is still served at wedding parties. A selection of salamis and cured meats served with bread or grissini or a plate of prosciutto accompanied by slices of melon or ripe figs are the usual way to start a meal.

For years Parma and Reggio, the two great centres of parmesan cheese, battled over the name. (In reality the cheese was born in the Val d'Enza in the province of Reggio but it was first sold through Parma.) The controversy was finally settled with the official, double-barrelled *Parmigiano Reggiano*. The king of the hard grana-type cheeses, it holds its lofty position by keeping the highest possible standards. Here, too, there is a defined and jealously protected production zone, with requirements specified by law and a consortium to control and guarantee quality.

The method has not changed for seven centuries. The cheese is made from a mixture of morning and evening milk from cows fed on fresh green grass and clover between mid-April and November. (The rest of the year, when the cows eat hay, they produce a paler cheese of slightly lesser quality called *vernengo*.) The evening milk is left in shallow basins overnight to allow the cream to rise. This is removed (it will be used for making butter) and the skimmed milk is mixed with the full-fat morning milk (that is why parmesan is a semi-fat cheese) and boiled in huge copper vats with rennet from a kid as the curdling agent. No preservative or anti-fermenting substance is used. When it separates, the whey is sent off to the pigs and the curds are broken, then drained in large cloths and pressed into great rounds. As soon as it is firm the cheese is left to float in brine until it has absorbed the right amount of salt. Then the huge drums of cheese, up to 40kg (88lb) in weight, are aged for two or three years. They are regularly turned and cleaned so that each side is properly aired.

The cheese can be eaten after a year when it is *nuovo*. It is 'opened', not cut, so as not to spoil the grainy texture, and it is chipped at with a small knife. It is golden with a delicate fragrance and a rich delicious flavour. Only recently parmesan has been discovered as a dessert cheese and appetizer – one of the best in the world. For its traditional role of grating over pasta, soups and rice (its special quality is that it melts and does not produce threads), and for lovers of a more piquant flavour, it must wait another year when it is *vecchio* – old, or a third year when it is *stravecchio*. At Peck, the Milan food shop, they have aged some parmesan for seven years, but in Emilia they don't approve and believe the cheese goes downhill after the third year. Grated parmesan is used so much that it has been called the vice as well as the backbone of Italian cooking.

One of Emilia's great strengths is a vast range of first courses of pasta. It is the land of fresh egg pasta. The stuffed pasta is a world in itself with different shapes: little hats, scarves, rings, sweet-wrapping twists, butterflies, little squares, big squares, triangles, rounds, half moons, different names and an astonishing variety of fillings.

For Bolognese tortellini, the king of this world, a square is folded into a triangle, then the triangle is wound into a ring on the end of a little finger and the points stuck together like a tiny headscarf. The filling is a mixture of veal and pork cooked in white wine with added ham and mortadella, garlic, rosemary and pepper, all minced fine and worked into a paste with a little egg, grated parmesan and a pinch of nutmeg. I have watched women prepare millions of these in restaurants – it is always women, standing up, laughing and gossiping, making an art of each one. The tortellini are served *in brodo* – in a meat or chicken broth or with meat sauce, the famous bolognese *ragù* (the origin of our Bolognese sauce which is never, ever served there with spaghetti).

Another triumph of Emilian cooking is the *fritto misto*, a grandiose assortment of breaded and deep-fried morsels, which is served as an antipasto in winter. There can be sweetbreads, liver, brains, veal, chicken pieces, chicken livers, slices of cheese and prosciutto sandwiches soaked in milk and called *bocconcini*; extraordinary mixtures of liver, ham and cheese with truffles, bound together with a thick bechamel sauce, rolled into balls and threaded on to skewers; and vegetables such as artichokes and cardoon fritters, courgettes cut into sticks, and sweet things like apple slices, macaroons, and cream croquettes. After this there can be little room for anything else.

But traditionally an hors d'oeuvre is followed by a soup, then by a pasta. There may also be a risotto. Then come the meats. *Stracotto* is in the great tradition of Italian stews where the meat is cooked for up to five hours until it practically falls apart, rich with the flavours of gentle spices such as cinnamon, cloves and nutmeg and constantly replenished because evaporated red wine. *Arrosti* are roasts and may be pheasant, duck, chicken, rabbit and hare, wild boar and veal or baby pig, flavoured with garlic and rosemary and doused with white wine. Some meats are cooked *in due tempi*, which means first boiled then roasted. *Bollito misto* – mixed boiled meats, a speciality of Modena, is a great dish served with pomp.

A usual way of cooking vegetables is *alla parmigiana*, baked with parmesan and sometimes with prosciutto. There are more tomatoes here than anywhere else in Italy. This is mushroom and white truffle country and, in season, their delicate perfume pervades many of the dishes. In the Apennine hills they have some of the best mushrooms in Italy. Porcini, cèpes or boletus and the egg-shaped ovulo, which is white outside and red inside, are the local favourites.

In the old days there was never much fish cooked despite the rivers. I was told, 'And who had time to fish?' The really poor ate polenta with melted pork fat, salted herrings, snails, frogs, chestnut cakes and fritters.

Gargantuan banquets which lasted days with songs, dances, music and games are constantly featured in tales of Bologna's past. Great feasts, with thirty different dishes and an extraordinary, even bizarre presentation (game birds dressed to look alive, beaks set alight, suckling pigs) were at their peak during the Renaissance and in the baroque period, when table setting and table manners were a refined art. The table remained a symbol of power and status and there was always a ceremonial dimension to Bolognese cooking.

Now, most people want to make life easy for themselves and to lighten things, and they go out to the trattorias to eat what they can no longer be bothered to make. Restaurants have a double menu, one for 'creative cooking' and one for Bolognese dishes. There are 100 confraternities of people whose purpose, apart from conviviality, is to uphold the standards of one particular food such as *fritto misto* or tortellini. Members go on group tastings and complain if, for example, the broth in which the tortellini are cooked does not have golden globules of fat swimming on the surface (some restaurants remove fat).

In today's Communist-governed Emilia-Romagna, the great old dishes are offered at a subsidized price at the annual communist *festa dell'Unita*. The feasts are held by all the political parties for a week each summer in the parks and streets of every district and are as much gastronomic as political events. Members donate their skills and their produce and, so they say, the same people can be spotted at the Christian Democrat *festa dell'Amicizia*, the Socialists' *Avanti* and the Fascists' *Tricolore* as well as the *festa dell'Unità*, savouring the cappellini and tortellini, lasagne, *bolliti misti* and *arrosti* which are dished out from moveable kitchens or roasted on open fires.

The provincial cities – apart from Ferrara and Ravenna, they are all on the Via Emilia which was built by the Romans and runs through Bologna, Modena, Reggio Emilia and Parma, all the way to Piacenza – have kept their own traditions, a mixture of grand style and simple farmhouse cooking. Their history was one of Roman and Byzantine domination, rule by Longobards and Franks, episcopal domination and a long period of free communes until these gave way, in the fourteenth century, to the *signorie*, when each was governed by a single family. They were not all-powerful families as in Tuscany and Lombardy, but small local nobility. The most important were the Este and the Farnese. In this period of Renaissance splendour cooking also reached great heights of magnificence and dishes were recorded by Cristoforo de Messisburgo, who was in charge of the Este household, in his sixteenth century treatise: '*Banchetto, composizione di vivande e apparecchio generale*' (banquets, composition of dishes and general utensils).

Ferrara has many elegant, delicate dishes which originated in the princely court of the Este family: one such is a *pasticcio* – a pasta pie filled with meat sauce, wild mushrooms and white truffles. They say Ferrara's bread, *coppietta*, is the best in Italy. But what really makes Ferrara's cuisine distinctive is a range of dishes originating from her once-important Jewish community: *prosciutto d'oca*, smoked goose; *buricco*, a large raviolo stuffed with minced chicken and rabbit (without the usual pork); *ciccioli d'oca*, deep-fried goose scraps; and *l'hamin*, egg noodles dressed with goose fat, raisins and pine nuts; *polpettone di tacchino*, turkey loaf; and a vast range of marzipan and deep-fried 'holiday sweets' such as *coppette* and *pignolate*. From the Jews the Ferrarese also learnt how to make sturgeon's caviar.

Parma, capital of a duchy under the Farnese family lordship, briefly under Bourbon princes with Spanish and French connections; and given to Maria Luigia (Marie Louise), the estranged second wife of Napoleon, after the Congress of Vienna (1815), is a noble city, an artistic city (they had Antelami and Correggio), a musical city (they had Verdi and Toscanini) and an industrious city. Its culinary traditions are born of its produce, butter, ham and cheese. Cooking *alla parmigiana* means with cheese, a manner that has been adopted all over Italy. The pig is almost sacred. Pork is grilled, roasted, boiled, stewed with tomatoes and cooked in milk. Everything is used – feet, ears, liver, bladder, guts. There is a saying in Parma, 'The pig is like Verdi's music, there is nothing to throw away'.

A great number of game dishes such as hare in salmi, quails cooked in rice, pheasant, woodcock, partridge, thrushes – roasted, stewed or cooked with cream – are part of Parma's court traditions. The nobility had turned the hills into a game reserve. Many dishes such as turkey breasts *della duchessa* and *tagliatelle della duchessa*, with fried chicken livers and beaten eggs and cheese stirred in at the end, are in homage to Maria Luigia who is said to have been as fond of food as she was of men. The Duchess, who was Austrian (her father was the Austrian Emperor Francis I) brought chefs from France and pastry cooks from Austria so now Parma has pastries such as *bigne*, *millefoglie*, '*St Honoré*', *bavarese*, *charlotta* and *Krapfen*.

Parma's most famous dish, *tortelli alle erbette*, is special to the night of June 24 – a midsummer feast which commemorates witches, called *rugiada di San Giovanni*, night dew of John the Baptist. The great liqueur of the Po valley, *nocino*, dark brown, slightly bitter made with green walnuts, is also linked with the *rugiada*. By tradition the nuts are picked on June 24 at dawn, when they are still damp with dew. They are macerated in pure alcohol with cinnamon, cloves and lemon peel for forty days. Then the liquid is filtered, mixed with sugar syrup and left to age for a year.

Modena is famous for her zampone sausage, the emblem of her cooking; her *amaretti* – almond macaroons; the cherries in alcohol made in nearby Vignole, and for her *aceto balsamico*, balsamic vinegar. In the past balsamic vinegar was made at home by wealthy landed families who had vineyards, people to boil up the grape must, attics to keep the barrels (they need to be in an airy ventilated place, not a wine cellar, so that the vinegar can reduce by evaporation) and who could sit on their capital. It took at least twelve years to produce a good vinegar and it was the kind of thing you passed on to your children and grandchildren and started as a dowry for your daughter when she was born. The habit was almost lost when the system of *mezzadria* (share-cropping) was abolished and country life was transformed. But a competition for the best balsamic vinegar at the fair of San Giovanni in the village of Spilamberto in 1966 reawoke the passion which the people of Modena still kept in their hearts. Now it has become an important industry, with exports all over the world, especially to America.

To make it, grape juice with crushed skins and seeds is allowed to ferment just long enough for the right amount of alcohol, sugar and acidity to develop, then the juice is filtered and boiled down in huge copper vats to one third or half its original volume. A little caramel is produced in the process, which gives a bitter-sweet flavour and an amber colour. Then the boiled-down grape must (*vin cotto*) is mixed with strong wine vinegar and starts a long ageing process (I tasted some that were thirty and eighty years old) and a voyage from one wooden barrel to another. There should be at least five barrels of different woods, the more the better, so that each can give its own special aroma. They use oak, chestnut, juniper, ash, locust, acacia and fruit woods such as cherry, apple, pear and mulberry. Some people who are starting an *acetaia* look for old Marsala or cognac barrels. Every year a part of the vinegar from each barrel is transferred to another and gradually it becomes more concentrated, darker (the dark luminous brown can get almost black), denser – like a syrup, and develops a rich sweet-and-sour flavour and seductive perfume.

It is said that balsamic vinegar was made in Roman times and that the Court of the Estensi raised it to the level of an art. It was thought to have medicinal properties – that is why it is called *balsamico*. A drop goes in an olive oil dressing; on strawberries; with fried liver, kidneys or pork, or veal or duck and into *frittate* (omelettes). What you find cheaply on the market is a very far cry from the real thing. There is not yet a consortium to guarantee standards.

Romagna is very different from Emilia: the people even speak differently.

On a train journey some Romagnols explained to me that it was because they had been part of the Papal States from 1278. They were poor while Emilia was rich. The popes in the old days had been tyrants, so traditionally the people of Romagna are anticlerical. Everyone in the carriage revealed they had not baptized their children. In contrast, the predominantly Communist Emilians are said to be ecstatic when the Pope visits. Culturally Romagna is more like the neighbouring Marches.

It is a small world of wooded mountains, fertile plain and seacoast where foothills gradually give place to harsh rocky mountains. Villages sit on top of hills. Towns – Rimini, Cesena, Forli and Faenza – stand on the Via Emilia where five rivers flow down the mountains to meet them. There is a sense of lost greatness and ancient glory about them and Ravenna, port of entry for the Eastern Roman Empire. Gleaming mosaics, mausoleums, basilicas and convents testify to the Greek, Roman and Byzantine presence. The words of Boccaccio and Dante echo about the place. Romagna made a special impression on Dante and his poems have kept the petty nobles, the brigands of the Apennine passes and the corrupt *signori* alive.

Now the tourist industry on the coast has brought prosperity, but Romagnols remember working hard in the fields only thirty years ago, and they know the harsh life of the mountains. Where the Emilians are peaceful, the Romagnols are rebellious, fiery, prickly. Their traits are reflected in their cooking. Emilia's dishes are buttery and velvety, with delicate flavours. Romagna's are rough and simple with strong earthy flavours: they use plenty of onion and garlic, masses of herbs and hot red pepper, and olive oil, not butter.

But theirs is really poor peasant food – unleavened bread, *piadina*, made of flour, water and lard, baked on a metal sheet over a fire; beans with *maltagliati*, 'badly cut' pasta; hand-made flour-and-water pasta and *minestre*, soups. *Garganelli* are squares of pasta rolled around a stick and patiently pressed one by one *sul pettine*, on a 'comb' which gives them a ribbed surface. *Passatelli* is a dough made with fine breadcrumbs, eggs and cheese worked to a paste, passed through a mincer, turned into curly, thickish vermicelli and cooked in broth.

They have made an art of the grill – everything goes on it: fish, chicken, veal chops, rabbit, game, meat, sausages and *castrato* (castrated mutton whose flesh becomes extraordinarily fat and tender). *Porchetta*, roast baby pig, has come from the other papal states.

And there is the cooking of the sea. They have a great variety of fish and they are famous for their *mistigriglia*, mixed grills, and fish soups which contain just about everything from the sea. Romagnol dishes, like flour-and-water pasta and cakes and fritters made with mountain chestnuts, which people stopped eating in the Sixties because they were considered too poor, are now back in fashion.

ANTIPASTO DI SALUMI

A plate of raw ham and salami

Emilians are not keen on *antipasti* generally. Old sayings condemn them as *la morte del pranzo* (the death of the meal) and *la malizia degli osti* (the host's trick) implying that a host who fills his guests with *antipasti* may not have much to offer in the way of main courses. But a few slices of their prosciutto or local salami are a must.

For a party, have a well chosen selection of two or three arranged on a large plate, accompanied by bread and butter and grissini.

PROSCIUTTO CON FICHI O MELONE

Parma ham with figs or melon

Serves 4

12 slices Parma ham
1 ripe melon, cut into wedges and seeds removed, or 4 ripe figs

Lay the paper-thin slices of prosciutto out on a large platter and arrange the figs or melon beside it. Serve with grissini or bread.

POMODORI RIPIENI ALLA CIPOLLA

Tomatoes stuffed with herbs and onions

Emilia is the greatest producer of tomatoes in Italy. Most of them go into cans. This antipasto is one way they use them in the countryside to make the most of their sweet, fresh flavour.

Serves 4

8 small tomatoes
2 medium-sized sweet, mild onions (red or white) or a bunch of spring onions, very finely chopped
1 clove garlic, crushed
3 tablespoons parsley, finely chopped
3 tablespoons basil, finely chopped
2 tablespoons or more olive oil
Salt and pepper

Wash the tomatoes, cut a slice off the top of each to form lids, scoop out the seeds with a teaspoon and discard.

Mix together the onions, garlic, parsley, basil and olive oil, seasoning to taste, fill the tomatoes with the mixture and cover them with their lids.

Serve two tomatoes per person.

FUNGHI CRUDI

Mushroom salad

This salad is made with different types of wild mushrooms such as porcini and ovoli but you can try it with other mushrooms.

Serves 4

400g (14oz) mushrooms
5 tablespoons olive oil
Juice of 1 lemon
Salt and pepper

Clean the mushrooms, and slice them thinly. Beat the oil with the lemon juice, salt and pepper, pour over the mushrooms, mix well and let them macerate in the dressing for half an hour before serving.

VARIATIONS Sprinkle with finely chopped parsley or with truffles or parmesan shavings.

In Piedmont they add crushed garlic and finely chopped anchovies to the dressing.

MINESTRA DI SPINACI ALLA MODENESE

Spinach soup

Serves 6

700g (1½lb) spinach or 350g (12oz) frozen spinach, thawed
50g (2oz) butter
Salt
Pinch nutmeg
4 eggs
5 tablespoons grated parmesan
1¾ litres (3 pints) stock

Wash the spinach and remove the hard stems. Cook the leaves in the butter in a saucepan with the lid on, adding a little salt and nutmeg and turning them over occasionally, until they crumple. Chop finely by hand or in a food processor.

Beat the eggs together with the grated parmesan and add to the spinach.

Bring a well-flavoured stock to the boil, turn down the heat and, just before serving, beat in the spinach and egg mixture. Leave the soup on the heat for a minute or two, beating in the mixture vigorously until the soup turns creamy: the eggs must not be allowed to curdle and spoil the texture.

Serve accompanied by toast.

PASTA FRESCA ALL'UOVO

Fresh egg pasta

Fresh pasta, rolled out by hand or made industrially, called *pasta sfoglia* or 'sheet' pasta, belongs traditionally to Emilia-Romagna, Tuscany, Liguria, Piedmont and Lombardy. Despite the industrial production of fresh and dry pasta, and although young women will not do it now, the tradition of rolling it out by hand continues – and nowhere more than in Emilia which is the true home of egg pasta. It is so appreciated there that most restaurants employ a *sfoglina* – a woman who rolls out the pasta and makes tagliatelle, tagliolini, lasagne, tortellini and pappardelle once, even twice a day.

Until recently all the regions had different ways of making pasta dough with a varying ratio of flour and eggs, more or less water, and a little oil or milk. Piedmont used egg yolks only with the flour and Romagna in the south used only flour and water. In Alto Adige they add milk instead of water. Although the old differences persist in some places and the old 'poor way' of making dough with only flour and water has come back into fashion, the richer flour-and-egg dough, in the manner of Emilia, has been adopted all over Italy.

Their old cookery books give the quantity of dough by the number of eggs, adding 'as much flour as it takes'. Nowadays the quantity given per egg is 100g (3oz) of flour, but in reality this varies according to the type of flour, the size of the eggs and their freshness.

The manner of rolling out and cutting the dough also differs. In Mantua they use a rolling pin 1m 20cm (4ft) long called *materello mantovano*. Around Alba and the Langhe in Piedmont, they cut their sheet of dough ever so thinly with a knife to make tajarin, while in Tuscany they cut it into wide strips to make pappardelle. Apulians cut it with a *ferro da maccheroni* – a metal roller with cutting discs. In the Abruzzi they cut the sheet by rolling it on top of a kind of loom with wire threads – the *chitarra*. Apulia, Basilicata and Calabria all make the same triangular lagane but maltagliatti (badly cut) vary from place to place. They are long, thin lozenges in Mantua, while in Emilia, Lombardy and Veneto they are small and rhomboid. In the manner of cutting too, Emilian ways have won over the country because Emilia is considered mistress in the field.

Many now roll the dough out with a machine. Rough rollers are preferred so that the pasta does not come out too smooth and holds the sauce better.

There are many kinds of manual and electric pasta machines that roll out and also cut pasta very well which you might like to try.

Serves 4–6

400g (14oz) flour
Pinch of salt (optional)
4 large eggs

Put the flour and salt in a bowl (traditionally it is piled in a mountain on a marble slab but it is easier to use a bowl). Make a well in the centre and break in the eggs. Work the flour into the eggs with a fork and continue with your hands until the ingredients are well mixed, adding a tablespoon or more of flour if necessary, so that the mass holds well together.

Knead for 10–15 minutes until the dough is smooth and elastic, adding a little more flour if it is too sticky. Wrap in clingfilm and leave to rest for 15–30 minutes at room temperature before rolling out.

Divide the dough into 2 balls for easier handling. Roll each out as thinly as possible on a lightly floured surface with a lightly floured rolling pin, working from the centre outwards. With experience you should be able to roll it out evenly, almost paper-thin, without breaking it.

Leave to dry for 20 minutes before cutting.

PASTA VERDE

Green pasta

Serves 6

200g (7oz) fresh spinach or 100g (3½oz)
frozen
400g (14oz) flour
Pinch of salt
3 eggs

Wash the fresh spinach and cook in the water that clings to the leaves, turning them over until they are limp and crumple in a soft mass. Drain and squeeze as dry as you can, then reduce to a purée in a food processor.

Put the flour in a bowl with a pinch of salt and make a well in the centre. Drop the eggs in and the spinach and work the flour in with your hands until you have a soft dough that holds together well. Knead for 10–15 minutes, leave it to rest wrapped in clingfilm for 30 minutes, then roll out thinly as for *pasta fresca* (page 84).

To prepare noodles such as tagliatelle, tagliolini, fettucine and pappardelle

Fold the sheets of pasta over and over. With a sharp knife cut into ribbons about ½cm (¼in) wide for tagliatelle, narrower for tagliolini and fettucine and wider for pappardelle. Open out the rolls of noodles and let them air for 5–10 minutes.

Cook in plenty of boiling salted water (see page 208).

To prepare ravioli and other stuffed pasta

In various recipes for stuffed pasta you'll find throughout my book, I have given different methods for making them, but the following are the most common and you can use them for all the recipes.

Roll out two fairly thin sheets of dough. Dot one with evenly spaced mounds of filling. The amount of filling is a matter of preference – these days people like to make rather large stuffed pasta with plenty of filling. Brush the spaces in between with egg yolk beaten with a drop of water, and cover with the second sheet. Press with your fingers around the mounds of filling to stick the dough together and cut the pasta into squares with a pastry wheel by cutting parallel lines between the mounds. If you want to make 'rounds' of pasta, space the mounds of filling a little further apart and cut around them with a round biscuit or pastry cutter.

You can also use a ravioli tray which is like a baking sheet with square hollows. The first sheet of pasta is placed over it and pushed gently into the hollows. The filling goes into these hollows and egg yolk is brushed in between. The second sheet of pasta is placed on top and rolled firmly up and down with a rolling pin. The whole thing is turned out of the tray and cut into squares with a pastry wheel.

Let the stuffed pasta rest for an hour or so and cook, a few at a time, in boiling salted water for 3–4 minutes.

TORTELLI ALLE ERBETTE

Ravioli with cheese and spinach beet or chard

This is my favourite Parma dish. A type of ravioli, it is made quite large with plenty of *code* (tails) – that is, with a large fringe of dough, so they do not take long to make and do not open. The name *erbette*, which means herbs, is mystifying and restaurateurs like to be mysterious about the filling. Actually, it is made with spinach beet and the name comes from the dialect *arbetta* derived from the latin *herba beta* (spinach beet) and not from *erba*. We sometimes get spinach beet here but you can use the different kinds of spinach which are in our supermarkets. You will understand at once the difference between a great dish and industrial ravioli sold by the metre.

Serves 4–6

Fresh egg pasta made with 3 eggs and 300g (7oz) flour (see page 84)
400g (14oz) Swiss chard, or 225g (8oz) frozen spinach, defrosted
250g (9oz) ricotta cheese
1 egg
Pinch of nutmeg
Salt and pepper
50g (2oz) grated parmesan
50g (2oz) butter

Roll the dough out thinly.

To make the filling: boil the chard or spinach for four to five minutes until tender, drain thoroughly and squeeze all the water out. Chop finely, then blend with the ricotta, egg, nutmeg and seasoning.

Roll out the dough into strips about 10cm (4in) wide. Place small balls of filling on half the strips of dough about 5cm (2in) apart, cover with the rest of the strips, press the edges to seal them and cut into separate squares or rectangles using a pasta wheel. Or use the method for ravioli on page 86 and make them large.

Cook the tortelli in boiling salted water for five minutes until *al dente*, drain and serve with melted butter and grated parmesan.

LASAGNE AL FORNO

Baked lasagne with meat sauce

Serves 8

*1 onion, finely chopped
1 carrot, finely chopped
1 celery stalk, finely chopped
50g (2oz) unsmoked bacon, chopped
75g (3oz) butter
100g (3½oz) beef, minced
100g (3½oz) pork, minced
500g (1lb) tomatoes, peeled and chopped
300ml (½ pint) dry white wine
Salt and pepper
100g (3½oz) chicken livers, coarsely
chopped
75g (3oz) prosciutto, minced
Fresh egg pasta dough (recipe page 84)
using 200g (7oz) of flour and 2 eggs
75g (3oz) grated parmesan
Béchamel sauce (recipe page 102) with 3
tablespoons of butter, 3 tablespoons flour
and 600ml (1 pint) milk*

Make a *ragù* (meat sauce): fry the onion, carrot and celery (they can all be chopped together in a food processor) and bacon in half the amount of butter until the onion begins to colour. Add the minced meats and fry, stirring for 3 minutes. Add the tomatoes and cover with wine, then season with salt and pepper, and simmer for at least an hour, adding water if necessary so as not to let it become too dry. The sauce should be just moist but there should not be any liquid left. Then mix in the chopped livers and prosciutto.

Prepare the pasta. Make 3 balls of dough and roll them out thinly, then cut them into 3 rounds or rectangles the size of your oven dish. Boil the sheets of pasta one at a time in plenty of salted water and lift out when still very firm. As each is done, drain and lay out on a cloth.

Butter the oven dish, arrange a sheet of pasta at the bottom, spread with a layer of meat sauce, cover with a few tablespoons of béchamel sauce and sprinkle with a little grated parmesan. Repeat with the second sheet of pasta, sauces and grated parmesan and finish with the third sheet covered with béchamel and dotted with butter shavings. Bake in a 200°C (400°F, gas mark 6) oven for half an hour until browned and serve very hot.

VARIATION For green *lasagne verdi* use the green pasta recipe with spinach on page 85.

SALSA AL GORGONZOLA

Gorgonzola sauce for pasta

This is not a traditional sauce but it is very good and very easily made. For four: melt 1 tablespoon of butter in a pan, add 200g (7oz) gorgonzola and crush it with a fork. Add 200ml (7fl oz) double cream or milk and stir until well blended, adding pepper and a touch of nutmeg. Serve well mixed with pasta.

RAGÙ DI CARNE ALLA BOLOGNESE

Bolognese meat sauce

Serves 6

50g (2oz) butter
2 tablespoons olive oil
1 medium onion, finely chopped
1 medium carrot, finely chopped
1 stick celery, finely chopped
25g (1oz) diced mushrooms (optional)
75g (3oz) pancetta (or unsalted bacon) finely chopped
400g (14oz) minced beef, pork or veal, or a mixture
300ml (10fl oz) dry red wine
Salt and pepper
4 tablespoons tomato purée
300ml (10fl oz) meat stock
150ml (5fl oz) double cream

Heat the butter and oil in a deep pan, add the vegetables and fry until they soften and brown lightly. Add the *pancetta* and minced meat and fry until the meat changes colour. Moisten with wine, simmer until it evaporates, add seasoning, tomato purée and a little stock. Cook slowly, covered, stirring occasionally and gradually stirring in all the stock.

After one and a half hours, stir in the cream and cook, uncovered, until reduced. Serve with tagliatelle.

FETTUCCINE CON PROSCIUTTO DI PARMA E PANNA

Fettuccine with Parma ham and cream

Serves 4

750g (1½lb) fresh egg pasta, bought or home-made (see page 84)
400ml (14fl oz) double cream
100g (4oz) Parma ham, cut into thin strips
100g (4oz) parmesan, grated
2 egg yolks
Pepper, freshly ground

Place the cream, ham, half the parmesan and egg yolks in a large bowl, season and stir until thoroughly blended. Warm it by standing the bowl in a pan of boiling water.

Cook the fettuccine in salted boiling water until *al dente*, drain, add to sauce and mix well. Serve with the rest of the parmesan.

ANGUILLA IN UMIDO

Eels in tomato sauce

Serves 4

4 small eels weighing about 750g (1½lb)
1 small onion, chopped
1 tablespoon butter
1 tablespoon olive oil
1 clove garlic, crushed
500g (1lb) tomatoes, peeled and chopped
300ml (½ pint) dry white wine
Salt and pepper
Pinch of nutmeg
1 teaspoon sugar
1 bay leaf
Few sage leaves
Few celery leaves, chopped
Few sprigs of parsley, finely chopped

The fishmonger will clean and gut the eels for you and cut them into pieces. All you need to do is wash them in cold running water.

Fry the onion in a mixture of butter and oil till soft and golden then add the garlic, tomatoes and white wine. Season with salt, pepper, sugar and nutmeg, add the bay leaf, sage and celery and simmer for about 10 minutes. Then put in the eel and cook gently for about 10 minutes longer or until the fish is done.

Serve hot sprinkled with parsley, accompanied if you like by polenta.

LOMBATA DI VITELLO

Veal escalopes

Serves 4

4 × 175g (6oz) veal escalopes
Seasoned flour
1 egg, beaten
175g (6oz) fresh or dry breadcrumbs
50g (2oz) butter
4 slices prosciutto (Parma ham)
25–50g (1–2oz) parmesan, roughly grated
or shaved with a potato peeler
4 tablespoons double cream
Chopped parsley, to garnish

Lay each escalope between sheets of damp greaseproof paper or clingfilm and flatten with a rolling pin until very thin. Dip in seasoned flour, then in egg, and coat with breadcrumbs. Melt butter in a frying pan. When foaming, add escalopes and cook for one minute each side until brown.

Put the escalopes on a baking tray. Top each one with a slice of *prosciutto*, cover with parmesan, and pour one tablespoon of cream over each one. Put under the grill until the cheese is melted and golden. Serve sprinkled with parsley.

ZAMPONE CON LENTICCHIE

Stuffed pig's trotter with lentils

Stuffed pig's trotters are a speciality of Modena. They are like a coarse boiling sausage and need at least 2 hours' cooking. But those obtainable in this country are pre-cooked and vacuum-packed and need to be boiled for only 20 minutes.

Serves 4

1 zampone (stuffed pig's trotter)
350g (12oz) brown or green lentils soaked
for an hour
1 onion, finely chopped
2 cloves garlic, finely chopped
Few sage leaves, finely chopped
1 slice of bacon, chopped
1 stick celery, finely chopped
2 tablespoons olive oil
Salt and pepper

Drain and rinse the lentils. You can finely chop the vegetables in a food processor. Fry the onion, garlic, celery and bacon in the oil till the onion begins to colour, then add the drained lentils and sage leaves, cover with water, and simmer until the lentils are tender – the time varies but it generally takes about 20–25 minutes – adding water as it becomes absorbed. Add salt and pepper when the lentils have begun to soften.

Cook the *zampone* and serve very hot, cut into slices, on a bed of lentils.

VARIATIONS *Zampone* is also served with spinach and mashed potatoes or with a savoury *zabaione* sauce (see asparagus recipe page 56) with a touch of balsamic vinegar.

CAPPONE LESSO

Boiled chicken

Put a chicken in a large saucepan, cover with water and bring to the boil. Remove the scum, add salt and pepper, 1 celery stick, 1 carrot and 1 onion, and simmer for about an hour until very tender. Keep the chicken covered in broth. Serve hot or cold with the green or red sauce or with both.

SALSA VERDE EMILIANA

Green sauce Emilian-style

Serves 4

1 large bunch (about 350g/12oz) fresh parsley, chopped
1 bunch fresh basil (optional)
1 tin anchovies
3 tablespoons capers
2 cloves garlic, peeled and crushed
1 tablespoon shallots or onions, finely chopped
25g (1oz) white breadcrumbs
3–4 tablespoons white wine vinegar
100ml (4fl oz), or more, olive oil

Process all but the oil in a blender, then slowly trickle in the oil to make a smooth green sauce. If it is too thick you can dilute it with a little more oil.

Salsa verde is very flexible: you can use lemon juice instead of vinegar; add a teaspoon of prepared mustard; omit the breadcrumbs to make a thinner sauce; add tiny pickled onions or a finely chopped gherkin or two after the sauce is blended.

SALSA ROSSA EMILIANA

Red sauce Emilian-style

Serves 4

1 onion, chopped thin
1 red pepper, chopped
2 tablespoons olive oil
4 tomatoes, peeled and cut into pieces
Salt
Good pinch of chilli pepper, to taste

Fry the onions and peppers in the oil in a saucepan until very soft but not coloured. Add the tomatoes, salt and chilli pepper (it should be quite peppery) and simmer for 30 minutes, or until reduced to a thick sauce. Serve cold.

FINOCCHI GRATINATI

Baked fennel with cream and parmesan

Serves 4

1kg (2lb) heads of fennel
Salt
Butter to grease the dish
Pepper
2–3 tablespoons grated parmesan
300ml (½ pint) double cream

Remove the tough outer leaves of the fennel, quarter them and simmer in salted water until very tender but not floppy. Drain well and arrange the pieces in one layer in a generously buttered oven dish. Sprinkle with salt, pepper and parmesan and pour over the cream.

Bake in a 200°C (400°F, gas mark 6) oven for 15–20 minutes until golden brown. Serve sizzling hot.

12. Genoese specialities: trenette with pesto (basil and pine nut sauce) (p30), and pansoti with herb stuffing and walnut sauce (p30)

13. *Butchers in Venice specialise in offal – liver is the most popular – and local sausages*
14. *Curing ham in Parma. Their sweet prosciutto is the most popular antipasto in Italy*
15. *A grocer's in Bologna, Italy's capital of gastronomy*

16. *Bread making*
17. *Bread shop in Trento – a variety of sweet regional breads and pastries are on display: raisin bread; fan or shell-like Neopolitan sfogliatelle; ring-shaped Bolognese ciambelle*

18 *(overleaf). Pasta with aubergines and courgettes (p185), pasta with olive and mushroom sauce (p113), and spaghetti with mussels (p147)*

19. Home-made pasta in Bologna
20. Making pasta in Cortona
21. Sicily. Palermo market – selling parmesan and sheep's milk pecorino for grating
22. Ricotta made from the boiled whey of cow's or sheep's milk (the creamy granules which float to the top are skimmed off and put into baskets) is much used for cooking both savoury and sweet dishes

23. Rice dishes are a speciality of northern Italy: rice and spinach cake (p31), pumpkin risotto (p39), and risotto with Barolo wine with truffle shavings (p17)

TORTA DI RISO
Rice cake

1 litre (1¾ pints) milk
175g (6oz) arborio rice
Pinch salt
150g (5oz) sugar
50g (2oz) blanched almonds
3–4 bitter almonds (optional)
2 eggs, separated
Grated rind of 1 lemon
50g (2oz) candied citron and orange peel, diced
25g (1oz) pine nuts
1 teaspoon vanilla essence
Butter to grease the cake tin
Fine dry breadcrumbs
4 tablespoons maraschino (optional)
Icing sugar (optional)

Boil the milk in a heavy pan, add the rice, salt and half the sugar and simmer gently for 20 to 30 minutes, stirring occasionally, until the rice is tender and the milk absorbed. Let it cool. Toast the almonds under the grill and chop them finely. Beat together the egg yolks and the rest of the sugar, add the rice, lemon rind, candied peel, pine nuts, almonds and vanilla. Beat the egg whites until stiff and fold in.

Pour the whole mixture into a 25cm (10in) springform tin, buttered and coated with breadcrumbs. Bake in a pre-heated oven at 170°C (325°F, gas mark 3) for about an hour, until brown on top. Let the cake cool, then prick it all over and pour on the maraschino. Leave for 24 hours then turn out and dust all over with icing sugar.

FRITTELLE DI MELE
Apple fritters

Serves 6

6 large dessert apples, peeled, cored and sliced
200g (7oz) flour
2 eggs
175ml (6fl oz) milk
4–6 tablespoons grappa or rum
Grated peel of ½ a lemon
Sugar
Sunflower oil for frying

Make a batter: blend the flour, eggs, milk, grappa or rum, grated peel and 2 tablespoons of sugar. Leave to rest, covered, for 1 hour.

Dip the apple slices in the batter and deep-fry till brown, turning them over once. Drain on kitchen paper and serve hot, with sugar.

NOTE You can macerate the apple slices in a mixture of grappa and sugar for 10 minutes before cooking.

PANNA COTTA
Cream custard

Serves 4

300ml (10fl oz) double cream
2 tablespoons sugar or more to taste
About 8 drops vanilla essence
1 teaspoon powdered gelatine

Simmer the cream with the sugar and vanilla for 2–3 minutes. Dissolve the gelatine (do not use more or the cream will be rubbery) in 2 tablespoons of cold water and beat well into the cream. Pour into a little serving bowl or 4 small ramekins. As the cream is very rich portions are best small. Chill for a few hours.

Tuscany

The British fell in love with Florence and Tuscany before any other part of Italy. We were the first to discover, as tourists, her splendid cities and churches, her art and her countryside and our appreciation of her cooking has something to do with this long-standing love affair. Tuscan dishes evoke the tender climate and brilliant light, the gentle harmony of contrasting hills and valleys, vineyard and rock, squat silver olives and slender dark cypresses and the pastel hill towns we see in the background of paintings by artists like Masaccio, Uccello, Fra' Angelico, Fra' Filippo Lippi and Piero della Francesca.

Milan and the north of Italy also got to know Tuscan cooking early, when they were inundated with *trattorie toscane* offering fresh, light dishes quite different from their own rich, heavy foods. The greatness of Tuscan cooking is an idea deep in Italian minds, bound up with the reverence they feel for the region that produced so many of their geniuses, that generated so many of their ideas about art, literature, science, politics, individual liberty and love, and whose vernacular became their standard language.

In the fifteenth century Tuscany glittered with splendour. Florence dominated the region and stood above all the capitals in other Italian states. She was one of the wealthiest cities: a mercantile city of artisans, traders and bankers (they dyed silk, minted coins, traded in wool cloth, incense, pearls and gems), and also a city of intellect and passions, the powerhouse of the Renaissance, whose influence was felt all over Europe.

The wealth and splendour of the ruling Medici family, the goings-on at the Palazzo di Via Larga and the Palazzi Vecchio and Pitti fascinated Europe. When the French came to Florence for the nuptial celebrations of their king Henry IV's marriage to Maria de' Medici in 1599 they were stunned by the embroidered tablecloths, ornate china, sparkling Murano glasses and glittering silver settings, the flowers and golden vines and the sugar sculptures which decorated the table. On the great day, twenty-four different cold dishes were served as a first course, eighteen hot ones as a second, ten more as a third, and as a fourth there were fourteen plates of raw vegetables, cheese and fruit, followed by nine sweets.

It is part of Italian folklore that France learned most of her dishes from the Italians when their future king Henry II married Catherine de' Medici in 1535. The queen took a retinue of cooks with her to France and they are supposed to have revolutionized the cooking of the Parisian courts. Tuscans are among those who are dubious about such claims. Catherine was only fourteen when she married and her mother was French and partly German. The cooking at the Florentine court and in the noble houses in the Middle Ages was international and by the sixteenth and seventeenth centuries French cooking became the standard and most of the cooks were French. They wrote their menus in French, and were called *monsieur*.

The Italians did have *some* influence in the French kitchen. They brought sorbets and ice-creams and fruits preserved in syrup, ideas for pastry-making, like frangipane cream, rice cake and macaroons (pastry-making had just arrived in Florence and Catherine sent for pastry cooks) and also pasta. Platina of Cremona's cookery book, *De Honesta Voluptate* (which contained many French recipes), was translated into French. Forks were introduced, glasses replaced goblets, sugar sculptures (an art developed in Venice which was inspired by the glass blowers) appeared on tables.

The Florentines also brought manners and refinement to the French court. A sonnet writer, Giovanni della Casa, set out rules of courtesy and good manners in his book *Il Galateo*: 'When you are eating do not masticate noisily or crouch gluttonously over the food without raising your head. That is not eating but devouring, and then you soil your hands and even your elbows and dirty the cloth'. He exhorted people to avoid spitting, not to offer a neighbour a morsel already bitten, not to sniff another person's food or point with a fork or put a leg on the table, not to get drunk. The French considered the Italians too refined (King Louis XIV still ate with his hands while the Florentines had started observing table manners in the twelfth century).

But the most important impact the Florentines had was to bring simplicity and frugality to the gothic opulence and disorder of the French court. Tuscans liked natural food undisguised by sauces and elaborate artifice. They hated excess. The Medicis might have offered spectacular banquets and hospitality, but for themselves they were frugal. Dante had described Florence as sober and modest, and that is what she was. There was always a streak of austerity in Florence, even during the pleasure-loving and sumptuous fifteenth century when there had been sumptuary legislation forbidding people to have more than forty guests for dinner and more than three courses. The Florentines never liked extravagance and always liked their own good food. When eventually there was no money and no place for the French cooks in their kitchens the *monsieurs* went away leaving little behind but *besciamella* and *maionese*.

As far back as the eighth century BC, the Tuscans' Etruscan ancestors were known for their sobriety. But Etruscan paintings show banquets and revellers with happy smiles; men and women sitting together on beds, eating; game hanging in the kitchen, figures cooking steaks and chickens opened out flat on the fire (Tuscans still do this today). You can see they valued the good life.

Because it was enclosed, bounded in the east, north and west by the Apennines and the Tyrrhenian sea, the region formed some kind of political entity since Etruscan days. In the fourth century BC the Etruscans were subdued by the Romans. Christianity came in the fourth century and in the fifth the Roman Empire crumbled. Convents and monasteries, despite the strict rules and asceticism, contributed to a flowering of the culinary arts as cultivators and animal farmers and formed a nucleus of cooks and artisans around them. Later Tuscany became part of the Holy Roman Empire which had transferred to the Germans. After that there were continual wars fought by the cities for their independence from the German Emperor and the Popes. By the eleventh century the cities had become very industrious and also prosperous. Communes came into being and for a time there was inter-city rivalry and wars involving Pisa, Lucca, Pistoia, Siena, Volterra, Florence and Arezzo. Cooking started to become interesting after the twelfth century and between 1300 and 1600 it reached its golden age.

Tuscany was different from other Italian states in that a kind of equality prevailed. All the people – noblemen, merchants and even peasants – were citizens with political rights and all more or less shared in public life. The land-owning nobility did not live in castles. As soon as a merchant became well-off he invested some of his money in farmland, often with a small villa where his family spent the hot summer months. The slopes of the surrounding hills were dotted with such villas and there was a perpetual two-way traffic between town and country. Everyone was tied to the land. The farms were run according to the *mezzadria* system whereby proprietor and cultivator shared the profits. The first contract of *mezzadria* was made between a landed bishop and a peasant in 759 at Lucca and this system survived until the 1960s, by which time the produce was shared half and half.

The estates produced olive oil and wine, wheat, maize and forage, all kinds of vegetables and fruit trees and small farm animals such as chickens, ducks, rabbits and pigs. There were sheep and in the two large valleys, the Val di Chiana and the Maremma, they raised cows – native breeds, massively built and pure white. Sixteen families, numbering as many as 300 people (there were several generations) lived as *mezzadri* in some of the large estates.

In the Sixties farm workers began to work regular hours and were paid a regular wage, but most still abandoned the land for the factories. Landowners, finding themselves without workers, sold their properties cheap. People from Milan and Rome, and foreigners, mostly British and American, bought farmhouses as holiday homes. Entrepreneurs from the north came to farm in a modern intensive way. A few cottage industries producing tomato juice, vegetables in oil, jams and fruit preserves developed. Sardinian shepherds purchased a large part of the pasture lands and brought their sheep over from the island on boats. They produce their own pecorino and ricotta, maintain their traditions and their way of life and keep very much to themselves.

Tractors and machinery were introduced and changed the landscape. The old agriculture of intermingled vines, mulberry, and olive trees on the hill slopes (it is called 'promiscuous' agriculture), the little patches of wheat, maize, cereals, legumes and forage, where the large *mezzadri* families had spent their days fighting their way through the entanglements to pick everything by hand, were replaced by a more specialized agriculture. Trees were cut down, different fields were made into one, bushes were separated, to allow machines through. A few small farmers continue in the old archaic way of varied mixed cultivation, and their bit of landscape has remained like the bits of background in Renaissance paintings, but the rest has changed.

Country life has changed dramatically but the old dishes never disappeared and now they are very much in fashion; even the creative innovative cooking is based on them. Tuscan cooking is entirely rustic. The landowners and nobility were always frugal, even austere and parsimonious (many jokes are told about their meanness), and farmhouse cooking is what they always liked.

The *fattoressa* – farm manageress – cooked for the labourers (usually about twenty-five) who walked for up to one and a half hours to get to the farm each day. During olive and grape picking time they slept at the farmhouse. The landowners lived in town but they would only eat their own produce. Twice a week the farm manager brought them home-grown produce and when they went to the country they ate what the *fattoressa* made: soups, pasta, beans, salad, vegetables, grilled or roast meats.

Tuscan cooking is the simplest in the whole of Italy but it is not poor, and at its best it can be exceptional. What makes it so good is the presence of wine and olive oil, the use of herbs, especially sage, rosemary and basil, and the cooking methods: grilling over chestnut and vine embers and deep frying in olive oil. Writers describe it as sincere and serene. It is also refined. Everything is produced locally and is of superb quality and the ingredients are always fresh.

Local hams are small, lean and salty, larded with the fat that lies under the skin. They also make wild boar hams which have a strong flavour, and *coppiette* (courting couples) made of beef, pork or wild boar cut into strips, seasoned with salt, ginger and plenty of pepper, dried and smoked, then tied in pairs. A favourite salami is finocchiona, flavoured with fennel seeds. They are cut by hand into thick slices and served with Tuscan bread, made without salt.

Little cheese is made (the cows produce hardly any milk) other than sheep's milk pecorino. The most famous is the oval shaped marzolino produced in the heart of the Chianti region which is eaten fresh or ripened and can be grated. Tomato paste is rubbed on the surface of those that are ripened (once sheep's blood was used) so they have a reddish tinge. The woodland produces a few truffles, both black and white, and plenty of mushrooms. Cutigliano has a market for porcini, ovoli and the rare prugnoli (spring mushrooms).

Chestnuts growing wild have been a staple of Tuscan cooking for centuries and there is a whole tradition of specialities based on fresh and dried chestnuts and chestnut flour. Like polenta in the north they once provided the food for the very poor and, because of the memories they evoked, they have not been popular in the recent past. But they have made a comeback. Since huge numbers of chestnut trees have been cut down or killed by what is called the 'American disease', chestnuts have acquired the status of a delicacy. In the old days peasants made their own flour with which they made a kind of thick mush like polenta and a whole variety of foods from waffles and fritters to cakes and the centuries-old *castagnaccio*.

The most important ingredient of the region is olive oil, which is used as much for cooking as raw and comes into almost every dish. It is lighter, more delicate and paler than in the south and it can be yellow, gold or green. The spicier, more pronounced piquant flavour is sought when it is to be eaten raw. This flavour should be intense but mellow and should not grate the throat (it seems too strong for many in Britain who prefer a blander taste). For cooking, a blander flavour, which will not dominate the dish, is preferred.

Tuscany produces very little in comparison to Apulia but it is of very high quality, partly because the olive trees are situated on hillsides and get the full benefit of the sun. In 1985 a great frost and a freezing north-easterly wind, which blew for a week, killed 50–75 per cent of the olive trees – on the hilltops up to 90 per cent. The snow protected the vines but the olives were more exposed. Now many of the large producers have had to become blenders, using oils from other parts of Italy (and sometimes other countries), striving to find the combination which will reproduce the characteristics of their own lost oil.

Olive oil varies like wine. Its character is determined by the type of tree, the soil on which it grows, the position (on hill, plain or coast), the weather, when and how the olives are harvested and how quickly they are pressed and by which means. Many of the commercial oils are chemically refined and rectified and some are mixed with seed oils. To be sure of their oil Tuscans go to the grower-producers for their supplies. Olive picking begins around November when the olives are not yet ripe (they are green at first and gradually turn purple-black) and harvesting continues for several weeks. The best oil comes from less ripe olives. It is pea-green but turns paler after three months and is more piquant than oil made from riper olives where the yield is greater.

The best way is to pull the olives off by hand. Tuscan trees have huge branches pruned inside so you can climb in. Great nets are sewn together and held up with stakes to catch the falling olives. The branches are sometimes beaten with sticks, and machines like combs, which rip off leaves and twigs, then separate them, are also used (though it is not easy to use machines on slopes). In these last methods the olives get bruised, and as they spoil quickly (oxidization brings acidity) they must be cleaned and washed and pressed within twenty-four hours. Growers take their olives to a local press where they are sure to get their own oil back (at the communal press you wait to make sure you do not get someone else's). Mills used to be stone, now they are steel rollers. The olives (including stones) are ground to a paste which is then processed hydraulically to extract the oil and liquids. These are then separated centrifugally and the pure oil which comes out is what is called a 'first pressing, cold pressed olive oil'. Factories buy the pulp and press it again using heat and boiling water: this is called 'second pressing' and the result is fattier and more acid. Big oil merchants blend this with virgin oils to make branded oils. They can remove the acidity by a chemical process and produce a standard flavour.

The finest oil is Cold Pressed Extra Virgin. There is a consortium to protect the standard of the Extra Virgin label, but they classify only by acidity and do not specify how the oil was made or whether it was rectified. Extra Virgin must have less than 1 per cent acidity (the best has 0.5 per cent acidity). Then in descending order of quality come Soprafino Virgin, Fine Virgin and Virgin. The last can have up to 4 per cent acidity. Tuscans are so concerned with quality that they are prepared to pay very high prices for the best, believing that it makes the dish.

The main influence in the Tuscan kitchen is the cooking of her chief city. The most famous and most important Florentine dish is *bistecca* (steak) or (another cut) *costata alla fiorentina*. It is a thick T-bone steak, weighing about a pound, grilled over charcoal. Cooking over wood embers here is an art. There are those who believe the meat must be salted and peppered and brushed with a drop of olive oil before it is cooked and those who think all that should be done after, but they all like it rare, *al sangue*. The meat comes from the Chianina breed of cows, native to the Val di Chiana, which is considered the best in the world. It is tender and flavoursome *vitellone* – red meat somewhere between beef and veal, from an animal slaughtered between sixteen months and two and a half years. Another, though less highly prized meat, used outside Florence is of the Maremmana breed. Contrary to other regions that are fond of white meat, here the ideal is red.

Favourite pasta dishes are *pappardelle con la lepre*, wide ribbon noodles topped with boned hare cooked in wine with fried bacon and tomatoes, and *pappardelle aretine* with duck. *Pasticcio alla fiorentina* is a Renaissance-style pie filled with short macaroni and meat sauce, sometimes perfumed with truffles and encased in a sweet crust.

In the past, game was reserved for the landlord. The *mezzadri* and labourers were forbidden to catch or eat game (at a trattoria in Florence older men remembered how poachers used to be whipped in the square). When hare went to the master's table, the peasants collected the blood from it and made a sauce for their pasta. *Lepre in dolce e forte* is another Renaissance dish – hare cooked in wine and tomatoes with raisins, pine nuts, candied orange peel and a long list of aromatics. Game birds are cooked *in salmi* – stewed in broth with Marsala and juniper berries. The many tripe dishes such as *trippa e zampa*, with calf's foot, onions and tomatoes, white wine, garlic and nutmeg, are peasant foods.

Vegetables are cooked in oil with tomatoes or with bits of raw ham or bacon or dipped in batter and deep-fried or made into omelettes. Spinach makes a bed for poached egg and for sole.

Apart from the usual seafood which you find all around Italy, the Tyrrhenian coast has its own cooking traditions: they say it is because, unlike other parts of the coast, there were colonies of fishermen who had not been frightened away by pirates. The coastline was too straight and the land then too marshy (it was reclaimed in the eighteenth century) for pirates, and the Tuscans were capable of defending themselves. There are also specialities of the lagoon and fresh-water fish, especially trout and eel, in the Arno. One is the curious dish of baby eels called *cieche* which means 'blind' because they are caught at night in the winter with lamps that blind them as they enter Pisa at the mouth of the River Arno when they start swimming up river.

Fruit comes after the meal with the usual hard biscuits to dip in to the sweet *Vin Santo*. There are only a few desserts.

What gives eating in Tuscany a particular charm is the central Italian habit of eating and chatting together, elbow to elbow, at long tables. I had a taste of it in Florence when I was there one August and all the grand restaurants were closed. I was directed to 'da il Latini', via dei Palchetti, 6, a *trattoria fiaschetteria* where everyone knows everyone and where so many of the regulars are poets, that every year they give a poetry prize of a meal and a whole ham to take home.

CROSTINI DI FEGATINI

Chicken liver on toast

Everywhere, I have been offered little deli-cacies – chopped mushrooms, mashed auber-gines and other vegetables (they call them *salsine*) on toast as appetisers. This one is the most popular in Tuscany.

Serves 8

*1 medium French bread cut into slices
diagonally
250g (8oz) chicken livers
3 tablespoons olive oil
2 cloves garlic, crushed
4 tablespoons Vin Santo or Marsala or more
to taste
5–6 small anchovy fillets
2 tablespoons capers
4–5 tiny (midget) pickled cucumbers or
1 medium one*

Lay the bread out on a tray and toast in a 190°C (375°F, gas mark 5) oven until golden. Fry the chicken livers gently in the oil with the garlic for about 4–5 minutes until they are brown outside and still pink and juicy inside. Add the rest of the ingredients and blend all together to a paste in a food processor. Spread on the toast and serve at once.

PANZANELLA

Tomato and bread salad

This very popular country salad needs a firm, coarse textured, good tasting country bread to be good. I found it in many versions. An elegant one has the moist bread mashed fine in a blender, then mixed with very finely chopped raw vegetables and presented like a ball of ice-cream on the plate. I prefer the following which I ate in a Florentine *trattoria*.

Serves 6

*200g (7oz) coarse white bread, crusts
removed
6 ripe tomatoes
1 red onion
½ cucumber
2 sticks celery
½ bunch basil, shredded
75ml (3fl oz) olive oil
25ml (1fl oz) vinegar
Salt and pepper*

Cut the bread into small pieces. Put in a salad bowl and sprinkle with cold water so it is well moistened but not soggy. Add all the veget-ables, cut into pieces or slices, and the basil. Dress with oil, vinegar, salt and pepper, stir well and leave for half an hour for the bread to absorb the dressing.

VERDURE IN PINZIMONIO

Raw vegetables dipped in olive oil

This is a most delightful central Italian (from Rome to Romagna) way of serving vegetables raw.

Serves 4

*2 fennel bulbs
1 celery bulb
2 large carrots
2 cucumbers of the very small variety
8 spring onions
150ml (¼ pint) extra virgin olive oil
Salt and pepper*

Quarter the fennel and celery and halve the carrots and cucumbers lengthwise. Arrange them on a plate or serve in a deep bowl so that they stand up, accompanied by a bowl of oil with a little salt and pepper beaten in to dip in, and some bread.

FIORI FRITTI

Courgette flowers fried in batter

This is the simplest and most popular version of one of the most delightful of dishes.

Courgettes have male and female flowers, and it is the long male ones which are best used for this dish. They must be fresh and firm; very large ones can be cut in half lengthwise.

Serves 4

150g (5oz) flour
Salt and pepper
Pinch nutmeg
2 tablespoons olive oil
2 eggs separated
6 tablespoons white wine
6 tablespoons water
16 courgette flowers

To make the batter, put the flour, salt, pepper, nutmeg, oil and two egg yolks in a bowl and beat well. Then beat in the wine and water gradually until it has a light creamy consistency (you might need a little extra liquid). Leave to rest about half an hour and, just before using, fold in egg whites, beaten stiff. Detach the stem and green leaves from the flowers, remove the inner pistils or stamens, dip the flowers in batter and deep fry in hot oil. Serve hot and crisp.

NOTE Fresh sage leaves are used in the same way as the flowers – dipped in batter and deep-fried. They are served as an appetizer.

VARIATIONS A Ligurian version has the flowers stuffed before frying with a purée of mashed boiled potatoes, green beans and courgettes with grated parmesan, chopped basil and marjoram, garlic and pepper, a little melted butter and beaten egg.

A Piedmontese filling for *fiori farciti* is a mixture of minced veal, breadcrumbs dipped in milk and squeezed dry, parmesan, garlic, parsley and basil.

PAPPA AL POMODORO

Bread and tomato soup

Only make this mushy rustic soup (*pappa* means 'mush') if you can use really good country bread, flavoursome ripe tomatoes and fruity olive oil.

Serves 4

200g (7oz) stale coarse country bread, sliced
and crusts removed
3 cloves garlic, crushed
4–5 tablespoons olive oil
750g (1½lb) very ripe tomatoes, peeled and
cut into pieces
1 litre (1¾ pints) light chicken stock
(use 1 stock cube)
Salt and pepper
Good bunch of basil, shredded

Toast the bread very lightly in the oven so that it dries out but does not colour, then break into pieces. Fry the garlic in 1 tablespoon of oil till it just begins to colour, add the tomatoes and toasted bread and cook, stirring, until the bread falls apart and blends with the tomatoes. Now stir in enough hot stock – a little at a time – to get a thick mushy consistency. Season with salt and plenty of pepper, add basil, and simmer gently for about 20 minutes, stirring occasionally.

Serve hot with a little raw olive oil dribbled over each serving.

TEGAME DI CONCHIGLIACCI CON BRUSCHETTA ALL' AGLIO

Shellfish soup with garlic toast

In this country mussels are the best choice, but if other shellfish are available it is good to have an assortment.

Serves 6

2kg (4lb) shellfish such as mussels, clams and sea dates
2 cloves garlic, crushed, plus 2 for the garlic toast
5–6 tablespoons olive oil
3 tomatoes, peeled and chopped (optional)
Salt and pepper
150ml (¼ pint) dry white wine
Bunch of parsley, finely chopped
6 large slices of toasted bread

Clean and wash the shellfish and steam them open in a large pan as described on page 206. Take them out of the pan and filter their liquor to remove any sand.

In the same (washed) pan fry the crushed garlic in 3 tablespoons of olive oil and when it begins to colour, add the tomatoes, salt and pepper, the wine and the filtered liquor from the shells. Simmer 15–20 minutes then put the shells in or, for easy serving, turn the sauce and shells into a very large oven dish and heat through. Sprinkle with chopped parsley and serve with garlic toast.

To make it, crush the garlic but keep whole and rub all over one side of each slice, then dip the same side of the toast in what is left of the olive oil and sprinkle with salt and pepper.

SPAGHETTI CON GAMBERETTI

Spaghetti with prawns

This recipe comes from the Ristorante 'La Barca' in Forte dei Marmi, Versilia.

Serves 4

1kg (2lb) prawns in their shells
1 carrot, sliced
1 stick of celery, sliced
1 small onion, cut into pieces
Salt and pepper
2 cloves of garlic, crushed
1 small hot chilli pepper
2 tablespoons olive oil
4 tomatoes, peeled, seeded and chopped
Few basil leaves (optional)
Small bunch of parsley, finely chopped
400g (14oz) spaghetti

Boil the prawns in water very briefly until they turn red. Drain and save the cooking water. Shell the prawns and return the shells to the broth. If the prawns are already cooked (the way they are normally sold here) shell them and boil the shells alone. Add the carrot, celery, onion, salt and pepper and simmer for half an hour to get a good stock. Then strain.

To make the sauce, fry the garlic with the chilli pepper (leave it whole or if you want the sauce a little fiery, take the seeds out and chop it up) in the oil until the aroma rises. Add the tomatoes and cook for 10 minutes, then add the herbs and a little of the fish broth and cook a few minutes more. Put in the cooked prawns and turn off the heat.

Cook the spaghetti in the strained fish stock, adding boiling water if necessary and salt, until *al dente* and drain.

Serve with the sauce heated through poured on top.

NOTE You can buy shelled prawns and boil the pasta in salted water.

SOGLIOLE ALLA FIORENTINA

Sole, Florentine style

Cooking with spinach is a style long associated with Florence. For this dish you could also use other kinds of white fish.

Serves 4

1kg (2lb 4oz) spinach, or 450g (1lb) frozen
spinach, thawed
Salt and pepper
125g (4½oz) butter
Nutmeg
8 fillets of sole
1 glass white wine
50g (2oz) flour
500ml (17fl oz) milk, heated
Freshly grated parmesan

Wash the spinach, place in a pan, cover and cook for a few minutes with a little salt and only the water that clings to the leaves, turning them over until they crumple. Drain well, return to the pan with 25g (1oz) butter and sauté briefly. Season with salt, pepper and a pinch of nutmeg and set aside.

Heat the wine with 25g (1oz) butter, salt and pepper in a frying pan. Poach the sole fillets for ½ a minute, then remove the fish and let the sauce reduce to about three tablespoons.

Now make the béchamel sauce: melt 50g (2oz) butter, add the flour and stir well. Add the milk gradually, stirring all the time until the sauce thickens. Season with the salt and pepper and a pinch of nutmeg and stir in the reduced wine.

Grease an ovenproof dish with the remaining butter, line the bottom of the dish with the spinach, lay the sole on top and coat with the sauce. Sprinkle with parmesan and bake at 200°C (400°F, gas mark 6) for 15 minutes until a crust has formed on top.

UOVA ALLA FIORENTINA

Eggs Florentine

Serves 4

1kg (2lb) fresh spinach or 500g (1lb) frozen
5 tablespoons butter
Salt
4 eggs
Pepper
3 tablespoons flour
½ litre (18fl oz) warmed milk
50g (2oz) grated parmesan
Good pinch of nutmeg
Salt and pepper

Wash the spinach, remove the stems and put it in a large pan with 2 tablespoons of butter. Season with salt and steam with the lid on until the leaves crumple to a soft mass, turning them over a few times. With frozen spinach, defrost, drain then stir in salt and butter. Spread the spinach in a shallow, ovenproof dish, make four depressions with the back of a tablespoon and drop in the eggs. Sprinkle with salt and pepper.

Now make a béchamel sauce: melt the butter in a saucepan, stir in the flour and very gradually add the milk, stirring constantly, and waiting until it boils, before adding more. Then cook very gently, stirring often, until the sauce thickens. Add salt and pepper, nutmeg and half the grated parmesan and pour evenly over the spinach and the eggs. Sprinkle with the rest of the parmesan and bake in a 200°C (400°F, gas mark 6) oven for 10 minutes or until the egg whites have set.

GRIGLIATA MISTA DI CARNE E SELVAGGINA

Grilled meat and game

Cooking *alla brace* or *ai ferri*, over a wood or charcoal fire, is popular in central and southern Italy. It imparts a uniquely appetizing smoky flavour and a most alluring perfume, so good that all you need is bread and salad to accompany and fruit to follow. They say that even an old shoe tastes good if it is cooked in this manner.

For a special occasion offer a *gran misto griglia* – a selection of different meats and young tender game. Choose a few from the following: veal, lamb or pork chops, rabbit (cut into 3 or 4 pieces), chicken or spring chicken, jointed or split open along the breastbone, pulled out and pounded as flat as possible (see page 106 *pollo alla diavola*). Game birds such as quail, guinea hen, partridge and woodcock, pigeon, duck and grouse, providing they are young and tender are all excellent cooked over embers. They are sometimes flavoured by stuffing with a small onion or juniper berries and with herbs such as rosemary or sage. Pork sausages are often part of a mixed grill as are *spiedini*, kebab-type skewered meats.

Some do marinate their meats in olive oil with rosemary or sage and perhaps wine or lemon juice and garlic, but most find it sufficient to rub the meat with oil, salt and pepper before cooking and to brush it with olive oil or melted butter as it cooks to prevent it from drying out.

It is usual but not always necessary to bard the breasts of game with thin strips of bacon or pork fat tied with string. As the birds are turned over (for 10–40 minutes depending on their size) the fat melts away, keeping the meat moist and tender and lending it a distinctive flavour. But more simply you can split the game birds in half and flatten them (they require much less time).

Start to cook only when the fire has burned down and the smoke has gone and a light powdery grey ash covers the glowing embers. Place the meats on a well-oiled grill and turn them at least once, brushing them with oil or butter or a marinade occasionally. The cooking time will depend on the thickness and type of food, its distance from the fire, the type of embers, the size of the firebed and even on the weather. The best way to find out if it is done is to cut into the meat with a sharp knife.

Serve on a thick slice of bread or toast to capture the juices.

AGNELLO ARROSTO

Roast lamb

Serves 6

1.35kg (3lb) boned leg of lamb (weight after boning)
2 cloves garlic, crushed
4 tablespoons olive oil
3 sprigs rosemary
Salt and pepper
200ml (7fl oz) white wine

Lay the boned leg out flat and rub with the garlic and half the olive oil. Sprinkle with rosemary, salt and pepper. Roll up the leg neatly and tie with string. Place in a roasting tin with the rest of the oil and the wine and roast in a pre-heated oven at 230°C (450°F, gas mark 8) for 20 minutes to seal it. Turn the oven down to 190°C (375°F, gas mark 5) and cook a further ¾ hour, basting occasionally. This will produce lamb with a slightly pink tinge. Allow an extra 20 minutes if you prefer it well done.

ARISTA ALLA FIORENTINA

Crown roast of pork

According to a legend, this ancient dish acquired its name when Greek bishops, attending an ecumenical council in Florence in 1430, were served the roast and exclaimed *àristos!* which, they say, means 'very good!'

Serves 6

*1½kg (3lb) loin of pork with rib bones
(chine or crown roast)
6 cloves of garlic, crushed
Salt and pepper
2 sprigs of rosemary
3 tablespoons olive oil*

Ask your butcher to cut the joint almost but not entirely away from the bone and to break the bones so as to make carving easier.

With a sharp pointed knife make several incisions all around into the meat.

Make a paste with the garlic, salt, pepper, rosemary and the olive oil (put them through the food processor if you like). Press a little into each incision and rub the rest all over the surface of meat (including where it had been attached to the bone). Tie the meat back onto the bone with string or with skewers and put it in a roasting pan. Bake in a 200°C (400°F, gas mark 6) oven, for 1½ hours, or until done to your taste, turning the roast over at least once and basting frequently with the melted fat.

To carve, untie the meat and cut between the rib bones. Serve each person a chop.

NOTE 1 hour before the end of the cooking time, you can put potatoes, cut into small cubes, to cook in the fat.

PORCHETTA

Roast suckling pig

You can buy suckling pigs weighing between 7kg (15lb) and 9kg (20lb) all the year round, both fresh and frozen. They are very expensive but their delicate flesh makes a real event of a meal. In Sardinia, where *porchetta* (*porceddu* in Sard) is the favourite food, they will not use any flavouring other than salt and pepper and cook it on the spit at a distance of 40–50cm (16–20in) from the fire, for about 3 hours until crusty and brown, greasing it occasionally with a lump of pork fat (melted in the fire) held at the end of a skewer. Sardinians also eat it cold, in which case they wrap the sizzling roast in myrtle leaves so that the aroma penetrates the flesh as it cools.

Roast piglet is also a speciality of Lazio, Umbria, the Marches and Tuscany. For special occasions it is cooked on the spit or in a baker's oven with burning aromatic wood but people still make it at home. This is the way they make it in Arezzo in Tuscany.

Serves 6–8

*1 suckling pig weighing about 7kg (15lb)
4 cloves garlic, crushed
2 sprigs rosemary
3 bay leaves
A bunch of wild fennel (or use the feathery
leaves of a fennel bulb or fennel seeds)
4 cloves, crushed
¼ teaspoon nutmeg
Salt and pepper
2 tablespoons olive oil
300ml (½ pint) dry white or red wine*

Clean the pig. Stuff with a mixture of garlic, herbs, cloves and nutmeg, salt and pepper and rub all over with salt, pepper and olive oil. Roast at 150°C (300°F, gas mark 2) for 3–4 hours until brown and crusty, basting every half hour with the pan drippings and some wine.

TRIPPA ALLA FIORENTINA

Tripe with tomatoes and parmesan

Tripe is very popular all over Italy and there are many ways of cooking it. This one may please even those who are squeamish.

Serves 4

1kg (2lb) tripe
1 onion, finely chopped
1 carrot, finely chopped
1 celery stalk and leaves, finely chopped
4 tablespoons olive oil
1–2 cloves of garlic, chopped
2 bay leaves
1 sprig rosemary
400g (14oz) tomatoes, peeled and chopped
300ml (½ pint) dry white wine
Salt and pepper
Few basil leaves, chopped
Few sprigs of parsley, chopped
4 tablespoons parmesan

Tripe is now sold cleaned, bleached, washed and boiled in supermarkets as it is in many Italian markets and needs hardly any cooking. Cut it into thin ribbons.

In a large pan fry the onion, carrot and celery in 2 tablespoons of oil till very soft and the onion golden. Add the garlic, bay leaves and rosemary and fry until the aroma rises. Then add the tomatoes, pour in the white wine, season with salt and pepper and simmer until the sauce is reduced by almost half. Now put in the tripe and cook gently for 15 minutes longer, adding basil and parsley at the end. Then stir in the rest of the oil and the cheese and serve hot.

POLLO FRITTO

Fried chicken pieces in batter

I ate this in Florence with a whole *fritto misto* which included fried brains, sweetbreads, chicken croquettes, tiny lamb chops and rabbit pieces as well as artichoke hearts, courgette slices, pumpkin flowers and tomatoes.

Whereas in Piedmont they dip their little morsels in egg, flour and breadcrumbs, here they use only flour and egg.

Serves 4

1 chicken or boned chicken pieces
3 tablespoons olive oil
Juice of 1 lemon
2 cloves garlic, crushed
Salt and pepper
Flour
2 eggs, beaten
Olive oil for frying
1 lemon cut into wedges

Cut the chicken into small pieces with the bones or use boned chicken (the thighs are particularly good for this). Marinate for an hour in a mixture of olive oil and lemon juice, garlic, salt and pepper. When you are ready to serve, roll the drained chicken pieces in flour then soak them in beaten egg seasoned with a little salt, and deep-fry in not very hot oil till crisp and golden, turning them over once. Drain on kitchen paper and serve very hot accompanied by lemon wedges.

VARIATION Rabbit treated in the same way is also very good.

POLLO AI FUNGHI

Chicken with mushrooms

Italian dried mushrooms have a strong flavour and firm texture when they are cooked.

Serves 4

---

1 chicken cut into boned pieces
1 tablespoon butter
2 tablespoons olive oil
120ml (4fl oz) dry white wine
Handful of dried mushrooms, soaked in
water for ½ an hour or 500g (1lb) fresh
mushrooms
4 tomatoes, peeled and chopped
Salt and pepper

Quickly fry the chicken pieces in a mixture of butter and oil till coloured all over. Add the wine, drained mushrooms and tomatoes, season with salt and pepper, and cook for about 25 minutes or until tender.

POLLO ALLA DIAVOLA

Grilled chicken

This is a very good way of cooking a whole chicken in the summer on the barbecue.

Serves 4

1½kg (3lb) chicken
5 tablespoons olive oil
Juice of 1 lemon
2–3 sprigs rosemary
Salt and pepper
1 lemon, sliced, for garnish

Cut the chicken open along the breast and pull it out as flat as you can so that it cooks evenly. Cut the wing and leg joints just enough to spread them flat and pound the chicken as flat as you can. Marinate in a mixture of olive oil, lemon juice, rosemary, salt and pepper for an hour.

Place on an oiled grill set 10–13cm (4–5in) above the embers, skin side towards the fire. Grill until the skin has turned golden brown, brushing with the marinade from time to time, turning it over more than once, and leaving it longer on the bone side, until the juice coming out of the thigh is no longer pink – usually about 30 to 40 minutes.

Serve garnished with lemon wedges.

POLPETTE ALLA FIORENTINA

Meat or chicken cutlets

Every region of Italy has its own special cutlets which they make with left-over boiled meats. These are soft and creamy inside.

Makes about 12 and serves 4 as a main dish

250g (½lb) potatoes
300g (10oz) boiled meat or chicken
2 eggs, lightly beaten
Good bunch of parsley, finely chopped
1 clove garlic, crushed
1 slice of bread, crust removed, dipped in
milk and squeezed dry
Salt and pepper
Breadcrumbs
Oil for frying
1 lemon cut into wedges

Boil the potatoes in their skins then peel and mash them. Finely chop the meat or chicken (you can do it in a food processor). Put both in a bowl with the eggs, parsley, garlic and soaked and crumbled bread. Add salt and pepper and mix well. Shape the paste (it will be very soft) into little round cakes or fingers, dip them in breadcrumbs and fry them in oil, turning to brown them all over. Drain on kitchen paper and serve very hot.

CROCHETTE DI POLLO

Chicken croquettes

Serve as part of a *fritto misto* or with fried potatoes.

Serves 4 or more

10oz (300g) boiled boned chicken
Stiff béchamel (page 102) made with 25g
(1oz) butter, 2 tablespoons flour and 300ml
(½ pint) milk
1 egg
3 tablespoons parmesan
Pinch of nutmeg
Salt and pepper
Breadcrumbs
Oil for frying

Finely chop the chicken (you may use a food processor) and put it in a bowl with the bechamel, egg, parmesan, nutmeg, salt and pepper. Mix well, shape into little round cakes, dip in breadcrumbs and deep-fry in oil till golden. Drain and serve hot.

CONIGLIO IN CASSERUOLA NEL PEPERONE

Peppers stuffed with rabbit

This recipe from the beautiful Locanda dell'Amorosa, which is part of a fourteenth century village farm estate outside Sinalunga near Siena, is an example of how old traditional recipes are glamorized today. Rabbit cooked with peppers is turned into peppers stuffed with rabbit.

Serves 4

4 medium peppers, washed
600g (1lb 5oz) rabbit, boned and chopped
small
50g (2oz) butter
200g (7oz) mushrooms, sliced
½ glass dry white wine
100ml (4fl oz) chicken stock
1 tablespoon tomato concentrate
Salt and pepper

Cut the tops off the peppers a third of the way down to make lids, and scrape out the seeds. Bake in a pre-heated oven at 180°C (350°F, gas mark 4) for about 20 minutes until tender, but take care they remain fairly firm.

Meanwhile, fry the rabbit pieces in the butter, add the mushrooms and then the wine, allowing it to evaporate slowly. Pour in the stock, add the tomato concentrate, season to taste and cook slowly for about 15 minutes. Fill the peppers with the rabbit, cover with their lids and bake for 10 or 20 minutes until the peppers are tender. Serve hot.

FAGIOLINI ALL'AGRO

Green beans with oil and lemon

Serves 4

500g (1lb) French beans
Salt
2–3 tablespoons olive oil
Juice of ½ a lemon
Pepper

String the beans and boil in salted water for about 6 minutes till tender but still crisp, then drain and serve hot or cold, dressed with oil and lemon, salt and pepper.

FAGIOLI ALL'UCCELLETTO

Beans in tomato sauce

This is perhaps Florence's most famous dish.

Serves 6

500g (1lb) small white cannellini beans,
soaked overnight
2 sprigs of sage
6 tablespoons olive oil
Salt
2 whole cloves of garlic
5 ripe tomatoes, peeled and chopped
Pepper

Drain the beans and simmer in fresh water to cover, with a sprig of sage and a tablespoon of olive oil, for about 1½ hours or until tender, adding salt when the beans begin to soften.

Heat the oil on low heat with the garlic and the rest of the sage so that the flavours infuse, but do not fry. Add the tomatoes and simmer for 10 minutes, then add the drained beans, season with salt and pepper, and cook for another 15 minutes or so. There should be a good amount of sauce.

INSALATA VERDE

Green salad

Green salad is the salad which accompanies or follows the second course. Lettuce leaves are served alone or mixed with other salad leaves such as endive, chicory, lamb's lettuce and rocket. Rocket, a native of Apulia where it grows wild in vast quantities, is so fashionable now that it is offered by itself in restaurants throughout the country. The dressing is simply olive oil and salt, with a drop of vinegar.

In the spring, wild leaves and herbs may go in.

PISELLI AL PROSCIUTTO

Peas with ham

Serves 4

1.2kg (2lb 10oz) small fresh peas, or 500g
(1lb 2oz) frozen petits pois
1 small onion, finely chopped
100g (3–4oz) raw ham or bacon, cut into
cubes or strips
4 tablespoons olive oil
Salt
Bunch parsley, finely chopped
1 teaspoon sugar
150ml (5fl oz) stock

Shell the peas or defrost them. Fry the onion and ham or bacon in the oil. When the onion is golden, add the peas, salt, parsley and sugar and continue to cook slowly, moistening with a little hot stock, for about 15 minutes or until the peas are tender (frozen ones take only a few minutes).

PATATE AL FORNO

Baked potatoes with rosemary and garlic

A simple and most delicious way of preparing potatoes.

Serves 4

900g (1¾lb) new potatoes
Salt
3–4 cloves garlic, crushed
5 tablespoons olive oil
Salt and pepper
Leaves from 2 or more sprigs of rosemary

Scrub and wash the potatoes well and boil in salted water till tender. Drain, cut them in half if they are large and put with the rest of the ingredients in a baking dish, turning them to cover them well with oil and the aromatics. Bake at 200°C (400°F, gas mark 6) for 20 minutes or until golden.

CASTAGNACCIO

Chestnut flour cake

This very ancient cake, which has no sugar, only the sweetness of the chestnut flour, was born in Lucca. The taste is one that you acquire.

The cake is now on sale in Italian supermarkets.

300g (11oz) chestnut flour
4 tablespoons olive oil
Salt
75g (3oz) raisins, soaked in water
75g (3oz) pine nuts
Sprig of rosemary, chopped

Put the chestnut flour into a blender and gradually blend in about 500ml (17fl oz) water, enough to make a smooth batter. Add two tablespoons of oil, a pinch of salt, the drained raisins, 50g (2oz) of pine nuts and the rosemary. Stir well and pour into an oiled cake tin about 28cm (11in) in diameter: it is usual to use a rectangular one, large enough so the mixture is less than 2cm (¾in) high. Sprinkle the top with the remaining pine nuts and a few rosemary leaves and bake at 230°C (450°F, gas mark 8) for about 30 to 40 minutes or until the top is crisp and golden and cracked.

Serve warm – it is soft and creamy inside.

SCHIACCIATA CON L'UVA

Florentine flat bread with grapes

This lovely grape bread recipe was given by Lorenza de'Medici who for a few weeks a year is hostess and cooking instructor at her 11th-century villa at Badia a Coltibuono, the prestigious family wine estate. Lorenza has written several cookery books.

Serves 6

2 tablespoons fresh yeast, or 2 packets active dried yeast
150ml (5fl oz) milk
300g (11oz) flour
130g (5oz) sugar
Pinch salt
500g (1lb 2oz) black grapes, pitted, skin left on
200g (7oz) raisins soaked in Vin Santo or other sweet dessert wine

Dissolve yeast in lukewarm milk. If using dried yeast, add to dry ingredients, leaving milk to the end. Mound the flour in a bowl and make a well in the centre. Add 100g (4oz) sugar, salt and stir in the yeast/milk mixture. Knead for five minutes then cover with a clean cloth and leave in a warm place to rise until double the original size.

Punch down and shape into two rounds about 20cm (8in) across. Place one on a floured baking sheet, cover with half the grapes and half the drained raisins. Cover with the second round of dough and on top put the rest of the grapes and raisins. Leave, covered, to rise again until double. Sprinkle with the rest of the sugar and bake in a pre-heated oven at 180°C (350°F, gas mark 4) for about 45 minutes.

Umbria

The little 'green heart' of Italy is so beautiful, so spiritual, so artistic that one feels that perhaps the people here are less interested in the needs of the body.

Umbria is the only region in central and southern Italy entirely surrounded by land and the soft, hilly landscape is particularly seductive and familiar, like the background in a Renaissance painting. It is full of history, with Etruscan arches in Perugia, Etruscan tombs in Orvieto, Roman remains in Spoleto, Spello, Gubbio and Norcia, and it feels intensely holy. They say 20,000 saints were born here. St Francis was. In Assisi I spotted several well-built, even fat, priests, and waited for the right moment to ask about church cooking and the Vatican kitchen, but it never came.

Umbria is full of splendid churches and stunning religious paintings and frescoes. Every little hill town with its narrow, twisting streets, grips you and pulls you straight into the Middle Ages. It is an incredible feeling but it does not take away your appetite.

The food here is simple, sober and homely, but it also has great elegance. It is the incredible abundance of truffles that gives it style. The black truffles of Norcia are the most characteristic produce of Umbria and the most highly prized are found in the Val Nerina, in the Spoleto area, with their main market centre at Scheggino.

Apart from the black knobbly ones (they are black all the way through), truffles also come in lighter colours, which the Umbrians call *il bianchetto*, and white. Truffles are so prolific that they are put into everything – spaghetti, omelettes, scrambled eggs, salads; served with fish, cheese, as a garnish for grilled meats; spread on toast and in the sauce of almost all the roasts and stews. Great handfuls are used grated, chopped up and in shavings, and not treated too well – as though the *funghi* were parsley or, as someone remarked, potatoes – mashed up with garlic and anchovies or with black olive paste or chopped mushrooms.

There is none of the respectful attitude of the other regions which have truffles: Piedmont and Emilia, for instance. There, black truffles are not generally as prized as white ones because they have less perfume, but in Umbria they claim that black ones have a better taste. People use them all the year round, keeping them frozen, vacuum-packed, or preserved in jars and tins. But in the autumn, in the truffle season, when the dogs and pigs are taken to sniff them out and they are pulled out of the ground, it is a time for celebration and festivities.

The seasons are very noticeable in Umbrian cooking, especially the seasons for mushrooms and game – there are hare, pheasant, partridge and guinea hen, quail and pigeons (Assisi is famous for them). The people also catch migratory birds that, twice a year, stop for a month to feed on olives and juniper berries.

One thing that distinguishes the taste of Umbrian food is the extraordinarily fine olive oil from the silver trees that hang on to the rocky hills. Green, light, full of flavour and highly scented, the oil is used in all the cooking, while the black olives, marinated in oil with orange peel, garlic and herbs, are served with wine.

There are beans at Trasimeno, cardoons and celery at Trevi, peas at Bettona, marvellous tiny lentils (the best in Italy) in Castelluccio. The characteristic, strongly perfumed honey is made by nuns: the bees have hundreds of wild flowers to feed on.

But the most important and interesting feature of the local gastronomy is the pork products of Norcia. Norcia is the gastronomic capital of the region, as much for her cured hams, sausages and salamis as for her truffles. In this little medieval town the most brilliant tradition of pork processing in Italy was born. Vittorio Battilocchi, who specializes in local dishes at his trattoria Dal Francese, thinks it may be because Norcia had the oldest school of surgery (surgeons from Norcia operated at the court of the king of France) and this knowledge of anatomy may have helped them deal with the anatomy of the pig. Norcia's men are artists in the art of preparing the pig. For centuries they have been going to Rome and all over the country, seasonally, to do this work, and *norcino* has come to be the general term used for a pork butcher. Shops selling charcuterie in Rome and Tuscany are called *norcineria*. The *prosciutti* (hams) are lean and compact, made with the meat of small black pigs fed on acorns and chestnuts (though now they do not have enough pigs of their own, they bring them in from other regions) and their ham is stronger, more peppery and garlicky than most.

Other towns have their own specialities and use other breeds of pigs. Recently wild boar has come on to the scene – Umbrians say some escaped from the reserves in Tuscany and reproduced so quickly that they have become a nuisance. The butchers leave a little fur on the hams made with wild boar meat so that they are easily recognized.

Umbria is famous, too, for *porchetta*. It is sold in the streets from large vans: you get slices of pork and a bit of crisp skin sprinkled with salt and wrapped in a bit of paper.

One of the main characteristics of Umbrian cooking is the use of the grill and the spit. The use of wood embers gives meat an incomparable flavour. The people do steaks of beef and veal and also grill chicken, rabbit, guinea hen, pheasant, partridge and other kinds of game.

Lamb is another speciality. There are villages, like Capelluccio, an old hill village, that are inhabited entirely by shepherds. The shepherds sell their cheeses to the men of Norcia, who age them alongside their sausages. They also exchange them with peasants for wine, olive oil and salami (barter is still a common practice).

Fresh-water fish – trout from the rivers Nera, Noro and Clitunno, and tench, grey mullet, pike, perch from Lake Trasimeno – is usually grilled. And of course there is home-made pasta – a rough tagliatelle called *strascinati* and *umbricci* which are fat spaghetti pulled out by hand.

Bakeries sell only *tozzetti* and *ciambelloni*, biscuits to dip in sweet wine. Their pastries, many of them of Longobard and German origin (the old nobility was of Frank origin from the time of Charlemagne, and Longobard) and some of which go as far back as the Etruscans, are reserved for festive occasions. Every feast has its speciality.

Christmas has *pinocchiatte* – biscuits with pine nuts, and sweet tagliatelle with sugar, walnuts, raisins and chopped dried figs. At Easter time there is *la crescia di Pasqua*, a savoury brioche baked in a conical earthenware pot and eaten for breakfast with hard-boiled eggs and raw ham. For the Day of the Dead they make *le fave dei morti* and *ossi dei morti*. (These sweets with macabre names and shapes were originally made in convents). *La castagnione*, a carnival speciality, is a mass of round, biscuity fritters (*gli strufoli*) in the shape of little chestnuts (*castagne*), hence the name, made with leavened dough and wine, dipped in honey with a few drops of Alchermes liqueur.

Il roccio is a brioche with raisins and orange peel. *La rocciata* is a very rich winter speciality of Assisi, Spello and the towns around. It is a shortcrust strudel-type roll filled with dried figs and prunes, almonds, pine nuts and hazelnuts, as well as fresh apples and pears (now they add bananas and crystallized orange peel), perfumed with nutmeg and cocoa, which is eaten either hot or cold. A chocolate and apple strudel in the shape of a coil is called *torciolata* because it is like the rolled cloth women put on their heads when they carried heavy things. *Torciglione* is a marzipan pastry shaped and painted like an eel.

CROSTINI DI OLIVE

Olive toast

There is a fashion for *crostini* in restaurants. This olive spread is easy to make now that you can buy good quality, tasty, pitted olives in the supermarkets. It is really worth making and keeping in a pot as a ready appetizer.

150g (5oz) pitted black olives
4 anchovies, chopped
2 tablespoons capers, the vinegar
squeezed out
1–2 cloves garlic, crushed
2 tablespoons rum (optional)
5 tablespoons olive oil
1 French bread, sliced and toasted

Put everything except the bread in the food processor and blend only briefly so that the first three ingredients are finely chopped and not turned into a paste. Spread on toast.

TAGLIATELLE ALLE OLIVE

Pasta with olive and mushroom sauce

Olive paste and mushroom paste are used so much in Umbrian dishes that they are sold already prepared, and are often mixed together. You can sometimes find them in Italian shops here. This recipe for the sauce is from the Ristorante Umbra in Assisi.

Serves 4

250g (8oz) field mushrooms, thinly sliced
2 tablespoons olive oil
1 clove garlic, crushed
175g (6oz) pitted black olives
3 tablespoons parsley, chopped
Salt
¼ teaspoon or more chilli pepper (optional)
500g (1lb) tagliatelle
120ml (4fl oz) whipped double cream
50g (2oz) fresh parmesan, grated

Lightly fry the mushrooms in oil till tender, then blend with the garlic, olives and parsley in a food processor.

Cook the tagliatelle *al dente*.

Meanwhile, heat the olive mixture adding salt and chilli pepper. Mix with the tagliatelle and serve with a bowl of cream and parmesan.

VERDURE ASSORTITE ALL'AGRO

An assortment of vegetables with an oil and lemon dressing

Vegetables steamed or boiled to a crisp tenderness, left whole if very small or cut into largish pieces, simply dressed with olive oil and lemon juice, salt and pepper, make a good first course and an accompaniment to most dishes.

For a party choose a variety of vegetables, from new potatoes, carrots, green beans and cauliflower, fennel, artichokes, chicory and courgettes, broad beans, celery, radicchio and asparagus. Cook them in a large pan of boiling salted water, first putting in those, like potatoes and carrots, which take longer and those, like radicchio and asparagus tips, which take hardly any time at the end, for the last minute or two. Serve hot or cold and be generous with the dressing.

TROTA CON SALSA VERDE

Trout with green sauce

Green sauces based on parsley are very popular in northern and central Italy. This one is good with trout.

Serves 4

4 trout, cleaned and the heads left on
Salt and pepper
2 tablespoons olive oil
200ml (⅓ pint) dry white wine

For the sauce

1 large bunch of parsley
1 tablespoon capers
2 midget pickled gherkins
3 anchovies
6 tablespoons olive oil
Juice of 1 large lemon
Salt and pepper

Wash the trout, season with salt and pepper and place in an oiled oven dish. Pour over the wine and bake in a 230°C (450°F, gas mark 8) oven for 7–10 minutes or until the flesh is opaque and flakes when pierced with a pointed knife.

To make the sauce, finely chop and blend all the ingredients in a food processor. Thin, if you like, with a few tablespoons of the cooking wine.

Serve the fish hot with the sauce.

SALSICCIA CON LENTICCHIE

Sausages with lentils

This is one of Vittorio Battilocchi's specialities at the Trattoria Dal Francese, Norcia. He uses the famous tiny brown lentils of Castelluccio and the equally famous sausages of Norcia.

Serves 4

300g (11oz) brown or green lentils
50g (2oz) pancetta or bacon, chopped
1 small onion, chopped
2 cloves garlic, crushed
2 sticks celery, finely diced
Salt and pepper
4 to 8 pure pork sausages such as luganega,
Cumberland or any best butcher's sausages

Soak the lentils for an hour.

Fry the pancetta or bacon until the fat melts, then add the onion, garlic and celery and fry until soft and coloured. Add the drained lentils, cover with water and simmer for 25 minutes until tender, adding water as necessary. Season to taste during cooking.

In the meantime fry the sausages. Serve the sausages on a bed of lentils.

FARAONA ALLE ERBE AL CARTOCCIO

Guinea hen with herbs in foil

Serves 2–4

A guinea hen
Salt and pepper
Juice of ½–1 lemon
2 tablespoons olive oil
1 clove garlic, crushed
Sprig of rosemary
Few sage leaves
2 bay leaves

Season the guinea hen with salt and pepper and lay it on a large sheet of foil. Sprinkle with lemon juice and olive oil, crushed garlic and herbs and wrap it up in the foil. Bake in a 200°C (400°F, gas mark 6) oven for about an hour, opening out the foil for the last 15 minutes to let it brown.

CROSTATE

Fruit tarts

For the pastry shell

125g (4oz) unsalted butter
250g (9oz) flour
2 tablespoons caster sugar
2 egg yolks
2–4 tablespoons water or milk
1 egg white

For the custard (crema pasticcera)

175g (6oz) sugar
5 egg yolks
70g (3oz) flour
450ml (17fl oz) milk
4 tablespoons kirsch, rum, Maraschino or
Cognac (optional)
100g (3½oz) finely chopped blanched
almonds or amaretti (optional)

For the filling

Choose from cherries, plums, greengages,
peaches and nectarines, apricots,
strawberries, raspberries, grapes, figs,
bananas, tangerines, oranges and kiwis
Half a jar or more apricot jelly for the glaze

Cut the butter into pieces and rub into the mixed flour and sugar. Add the egg yolks and just enough water or milk to bind it into a soft dough, stirring with a knife, then briefly mixing with your hands. Wrap in clingfilm and leave in a cool place for an hour.

Roll out the dough on a floured board with a floured rolling pin. Lift it up with the rolling pin and lay it gently into a 33cm (13in) tart pan or flan mould, pat it into place, and press it into the sides. Trim the edges and prick all over with a fork to prevent puffing. Bake the shell in a preheated 200°C (400°F, gas mark 6) oven for 10 minutes. Then take out of the oven and brush with egg white to seal the crust and prevent it from becoming soggy. Return to the oven for 5–10 minutes longer, until it is a light biscuity colour. It will become firm and crusty as it cools.

For the custard, beat the sugar into the egg yolks until light and pale, then beat in the flour. Bring the milk to the boil and pour on to the egg mixture gradually, beating vigorously until well blended. Then pour into a heavy-bottomed saucepan and bring to the boil, stirring constantly. Simmer for 3 minutes longer, stirring occasionally so that the cream does not burn at the bottom of the pan. Stir in the alcohol and the almonds or macaroons and let the custard cool before spreading it in the pastry shell.

Pack as much fruit, peeled, seeded, pitted or sliced and skinned where necessary, as you can on top, mixing them if you like and making an attractive pattern.

To coat the fruit with a light glaze, melt the apricot jelly in a saucepan with a few tablespoons of water and spoon it over the fruit.

NOTE Poach fruits that tarnish in sugar syrup for 5–10 minutes, then drain. For the syrup, boil ½ litre (18fl oz) water with ½kg (1lb) sugar and 2 tablespoons lemon juice.

VARIATION Instead of the custard use a jam or a fresh fruit purée: blend very ripe sweet fruits such as strawberries, raspberries and black-currants with a little sugar.

RICOTTA AL CAFFE

Ricotta with coffee

For four to six people, serve a mound of about 1lb (500g) ricotta, sprinkled with 6 table-spoons caster sugar and 4 tablespoons ground or pulverized coffee (preferably a dark roast). Or better still serve individual portions of ricotta and pass round bowls of caster sugar and ground coffee and a bottle of rum for everyone to help themselves and stir them in.

The Marches

This part of the Adriatic coast, all high slopes and torrents rushing into the sea, is one of the most sparsely populated regions in Italy and also one of the most beautiful. Neglected by tourists, it has remained serene, with its animal and arable farming (there is good pasturage for cattle, sheep and pigs and they have wheat, maize and sugarbeet), fishing, and a few industries. It has kept the rhythm of the old rural civilization and of the sea, and its people are still involved in the countryside and close to the land, even if they live and work in the city.

This is Etruscan and Roman territory. Feudalism and the ecclesiastical authority were powerful until the thirteenth century; then came a period of free communes followed by the *signorie*, rule by families. From the middle of the fifteenth century to 1860 when the region became part of the Kingdom of Italy, the Marches were ruled by the Church. It is a peaceful history compared to that of some of the other regions.

The people of the Marches live entirely on what they produce, which is rare now in Italy. The tradition of keeping the pig and making salami and cured ham at home has been kept up.

Here cheese is made from sheep's milk. *Pecorino di Monterinaldo* is perfumed with a wild herb called *serpillo*. At San Leo they wrap their pecorini in chestnut leaves and leave it to ripen in terracotta jars.

The Marches are important gastronomically as the greatest producers of truffles in Italy. They come in every kind of colour – white, black, grey, brown and hazelnut, and Acqualanga in the province of Pesaro is the market centre. The white truffles, the most strongly perfumed and most prized, compare with the famous ones of Alba.

The giant green olives of Ascoli are also famous. They have a wonderful flavour and are so huge they can be stuffed, deep fried and eaten hot.

The cooking of the Marches is simple and like that of Tuscany and the other regions of central Italy.

BRODETTO ALLA MARCHIGIANA

Fish soup of the Marches

The many different dialect names for fish soup – *zuppa di pesce, brodo di pesce, ciuppin, brodeto, broeto, cacciucco, burrida, sburita* – are an example of just how complex and perlexing the world of food in Italy can be. Fish soups are also an example of what Italians call their gastronomic *campanilismo*, because every port and every beach claims that theirs is the best. A large assortment of fish cooked together in the simplest possible manner, they are basically very similar.

The difference lies in the varieties of fish, shellfish and molluscs used (in Trieste they put in crabs and in Sardinia, lobster) and in little touches, such as whether they use onions or garlic, vinegar or white wine, both together or neither and whether they use tomatoes. The Tuscan *cacciuco* has ginger (*zenzero*), in the Marches there may be a touch of saffron, in Romagna they put in masses of garlic, in the Abruzzi and in much of the south hot red pepper. Very rarely, you detect a new note like a few mashed anchovies, pieces of potatoes or sweet red peppers. And that is all.

Fish soups can be served as a first or a second course or as a one dish meal.

On the Adriatic coast where they call fish soup *brodetto*, they normally cook it with vinegar and '*in bianco*', that is without tomatoes.

The greater the variety of fish, the better the soup. In the Marches they put in a scorpion fish (unobtainable here at the moment) at the start, cook it with the tomatoes for added flavour and take it out before serving.

Buy whole fish, steaks or fillet. It is more sensational to see a whole fish in the soup but more practical to serve when it is already cut into pieces. You may prefer to use the cheaper white fish available here such as cod, cut in steaks. The result will be just as good.

Serves 8

1½kg (3lb) mixed fish and seafood chosen from: turbot, monkfish, hake, flounder, cod, sole, red mullet, gurnard, scorpion fish, small eel, mantis shrimp, king prawns, squid, cuttlefish
500g (1lb) mussels
2 onions, chopped
120ml (4fl oz) olive oil
3 cloves garlic, finely chopped
1kg (2lb) tomatoes, peeled and chopped or tinned ones
1 teaspoon sugar
Salt and pepper
6 tablespoons white wine vinegar
Good bunch of parsley, finely chopped
8 slices bread, toasted

Scale and clean the fish and seafood (see page 207.

In a large and shallow pan or casserole from which you can serve the soup (a terracotta dish which will go on the fire can be used), fry the onion in the oil till soft, then add the garlic and fry till the aroma rises. Add the tomatoes and a touch of sugar (as they are not usually sweet enough here). Season, add ½ litre (18fl oz) water and simmer for 10 minutes.

Put in all the fish and seafood in the order of the cooking time they need – first the mantis shrimp and the monkfish, then the squid and cuttlefish and so on. Hake and sole go in last. Add vinegar and a little more water if necessary to half cover the fish, and simmer gently for about 15–25 minutes until the fish is done. Open the mussels separately in another pan and arrange them on top (see page 206). Add the parsley and serve with slices of toasted bread.

VARIATION Leave out the vinegar and stir in half a teaspoon of saffron pistils or 1–2 envelopes of saffron powder (in the Marches they use wild saffron – *zafferanella*) towards the end.

MINESTRA DI CECI

Chickpea soup

Serves 6

1 onion, finely chopped
1 carrot, finely chopped
1 stick celery, chopped
1 clove garlic, chopped
3 tablespoons olive oil
300g (10oz) chickpeas soaked for a few hours
2 litres (3½ pints) of stock
4 tomatoes, peeled and chopped
Salt and pepper
500g (1lb) spinach

Soften the chopped vegetables in oil.

Add the drained chickpeas, the stock and the tomatoes and simmer for about 1½ hours until the chickpeas are tender. Add salt and plenty of pepper when they begin to soften.

Wash the spinach leaves and remove the hard stems. Put them into the soup and simmer for a few minutes until they are soft.

PICCIONE RIPIENO

Stuffed pigeon

Our pigeons haven't the flavour of Italian ones, so use the *pigeonneaux* available here.

Serves 4

4 pigeons or poussins
2 tablespoons rosemary
Few leaves sage
1 clove garlic, crushed
4 tablespoons olive oil
Salt and pepper
8 slices pancetta or streaky bacon
1 glass white wine
2 tablespoons cognac (optional)

For the stuffing
(make double quantity for poussins)

225g (8oz) minced meat (pork, veal or chicken)
2 chicken livers, cleaned and chopped
4 slices bread, made into crumbs and moistened with 2 tablespoons milk
1 small egg
Salt and pepper
Nutmeg
2–3 tablespoons cognac

Mix the minced meat, chicken livers, breadcrumbs and egg together, season well with salt, pepper and nutmeg, add cognac and stuff the birds. Do not overfill.

Spread rosemary, sage, garlic, oil and seasoning over birds, wrap each one in pancetta or bacon and place in a roasting pan. Pour in wine and roast at 200°C (400°F, gas mark 6) for 30–40 minutes, basting occasionally and adding more wine or a little stock if needed, until tender but still pink on the breast.

Before serving pour cognac over the birds and flame.

FRUTTI DI BOSCO

Wild woodland fruit

Serve one fruit only or a mixture of strawberries (*fragole*), raspberries (*lamponi*), blackberries (*more*) and bilberries (*mirtille*). Pick over the fruit and rinse briefly or, better still, avoid washing them. Serve them on a bed of leaves in a shallow basket or platter, to be eaten with sugar and whipped cream or with mascarpone, ice-cream or *panna cotta* (page 91).

An unusual way of preparing berries which I discovered is *gratinati* – under the grill, with mascarpone poured over and a sprinkling of sugar.

Lazio

Only Rome counts in Lazio. It dominates the region and eighty per cent of the inhabitants live there: the rest are spread out in very small provincial centres like Viterbo, Rieti and Frosinone. Rome's inhabitants come from all over Italy, especially from the south, Tuscany and Sardinia, to work in the ministries (it is the Mecca of civil servants). But the true cooking of Lazio is the cooking of Rome, and it can be found in the taverns and *trattorie* of the city and in the restaurants in the hills around the city known as the *Castelli*, where Romans escape in the evenings and weekends to enjoy the cool fresh air of the lakes and forests.

Romans have always liked to eat out, a tradition which does not exist to the same extent in most of the rest of Italy. Years ago they went to *osterie 'fuori porta'* (taverns outside the city gates) which sold wine. Groups of friends met up, whole families went, many of them taking their own food, cooked at home and still hot in the saucepan. In the taverns they were given bottles of wine and a sheet of paper to put on the table. They sang, laughed and fought, and the wine flowed until everyone was drunk – at least that is how they remember it. *Trattorie* were one step up from the taverns. They sold wine and *paniotelle* (bread and butter with anchovies) and one or two homely pastas. The first restaurant serving French food and dishes from other parts of Italy, Il Fagiano, opened in Rome in 1937 and until after the war there were only two or three.

I cannot think of a more pleasant and convivial eating place than a Roman one, especially when the weather and the traffic make it possible to sit outside. People go out to restaurants to enjoy themselves, to express themselves and to look at others. It is like going to the theatre. There is an atmosphere of noisy cordiality and joyfulness.

The capital and heart of Italy, once centre of the Roman Empire and capital of the Papal States, Rome is not the capital of Italian cooking. Roman cooking has few elements and all of them are cheap, simply prepared and without frills: a matter of making a virtue out of necessity. It is their very simplicity which is attractive and there is something about the way the Romans mix garlic, rosemary and white wine, the way they roast, simmer and deep-fry in a mixture of lard and olive oil which makes everything taste good.

In the past, pork fat was used in great quantities (every family in Lazio had a pig which kept them supplied for a year). Now, in line with modern ideas about healthy eating, its place has gradually been taken by olive oil. Many rich vegetable soups, which once gained flavour from pork fat, now have a dribble of raw olive oil poured on at the end. Roman dishes are all homely and rooted in popular tradition but the food is really sensual. A popular saying, '*più se spenne, peggio se magna*', which means 'the more you spend the less well you eat', is strongly felt. Romans really love their simple food and don't like fancy dishes.

It seems strange that the only cooking anyone knows of in this city of triumphal arches, grandiose monuments, frescoed basilicas and extravagant Renaissance villas is poor food. No dishes, it seems, have come out of the palaces of the aristocracy nor from the kitchens of the cardinals other than roast baby lamb (*abbacchio arrosto*) – so young that 'it has not yet eaten grass', 'more full of its mother's milk than of blood', flavoured with garlic and rosemary; sucking pig (*porchetta*), boned and stuffed with garlic and fennel; and *saltimbocca*, thin slices of veal fried with raw ham and a sage leaf, so-called because they are said to be so good they 'jump in the mouth'.

Roman cooking is based on pasta, pulses and offal. This is part of peasant cooking everywhere in Italy, but nowhere more than here. Great quantities were always available in Rome because the nobles and churchmen ate so much meat and would only eat the best cuts. Popes were notoriously interested in food and they entertained and were entertained lavishly. How the priests liked their food remains a secret but what the princes of the church rejected is the basis of the dishes the Romans love. Many favourite dishes were born in the Testaccio district in the trattorias near the slaughterhouse where the rejects – in slaughterhouse jargon '*il quinto quarto*', the 'fifth quarter' of the animal – were used up.

Among them is the popular *coda alla vaccinara*, a rich oxtail stew (*vaccinari* are butchers). *Zampetti all' agro* are calf's feet served with green sauce made from anchovies, capers, sweet onions, pickled gherkins and garlic, all finely chopped, bound with potato and thinned with olive oil and vinegar. *Rigatoni alla pajata* (or *pagliata*) is pasta topped with the intestines of new born veal still full of milk (don't squirm, they are delicious) cooked with onions, white wine and tomatoes and flavoured with cloves and garlic. They are now hard to get and have become expensive delicacies.

In Lazio the meat used is mostly lamb (the provinces are shepherd's territory and are second only to Sardinia in the number of sheep) and pork. Young milk-fed animals and *castrato* – castrated lamb, which has a fatty tender flesh – are specially prized. Baby lamb is cooked hunter's style – *abbacchio alla cacciatora*, simmered with oil, vinegar, garlic, sage and rosemary, or *brodettato*, with an egg and lemon sauce.

Here, in the centre of Italy, where the fresh egg pasta of Emilia meets the dry hard pasta of the south, both kinds are eaten. The most famous Roman pasta (they call it 'the immortal') is bucatini or *spaghetti all'amatriciana*. It originates in Amatrice, a small town which was once part of the Abruzzi, whose men went to work as cooks in Rome. The sauce is made with *guanciale*, cured meat from the pig's cheek (purists claim that it must be from this part, but you could try bacon) fried in olive oil with a piece of chilli pepper, a few tomatoes and grated *pecorino romano*. The common belief is that another famous dish, *spaghetti alla carbonara*, is Umbrian and was brought to Lazio by the *carbonari* (coal men), but actually it is a relatively new dish and some say it was inspired by the American GIs with their egg and bacon rations.

Other first courses are *calascioni*, huge ravioli filled with ricotta, spinach and egg, baked in the oven like pies; *fregnacce*, a speciality of Viterbo, thin pancakes quickly poached (it makes them lovely and soft) and served with fresh cheese; and the famous *gnocchi alla romana*. It is a Thursday dish: no one has told me why.

There is splendid fish and seafood – in the restaurants along the coast and in Rome, but there are no authentic, local fish dishes. The people of Lazio started cooking seafood only thirty years ago. In the past fish, like meat, was only for the tables of cardinals and princes.

The countryside above Rome is rich with volcanic soil and provides an abundance of vegetables. Artichokes are the most popular and most important. There are several qualities – one, variously called *romagnolo*, *romanesco* and *mammolo*, is round, sweet and so tender you can eat it raw. There are so many ways of serving them: raw dipped in olive oil or in a vinaigrette dressing; preserved in oil, *sott'olio*; *alla matticella*, brushed with oil flavoured with chopped mint and grilled over burning vine prunings; and, in the springtime, with onion, peas and ham. *Alla romana* means stuffed with garlic and mint and cooked in a mixture of oil and water. The most famous, *alla giudea*, Jewish style, was popularized by restaurants in the old ghetto where there was once a large Jewish community. The choke is removed, the hard ends of the leaves trimmed and they are opened out like the petals of a flower. Then the artichokes are deep-fried, head down, in not very hot oil. They are cooked slowly for half an hour, then fried a minute or two in very hot oil in another pan until they are slightly brown and crisp, sprayed with salted water and served immediately with pepper. They are heavenly, but this can only be done with the entirely edible *romaneschi*.

Central Italians have adopted the marvellous habit, started in Rome, of bringing out a dish full of different raw vegetables to be eaten dipped in olive oil with only salt and pepper, which is called *pinzimonio*. They also do *misticanza*, a mixture of lettuce and wild salad leaves which include *rucola*, *rughetta* and *puntarelle*, a type of wild, rather bitter chicory, dressed with olive oil, vinegar, garlic and anchovy.

Deep-frying is a typically Roman way of cooking: it used to be done outdoors to tempt passers-by and is said to have been started in the Jewish ghetto. The Romans deep-fry everything: tiny lamb chops, brains, sweetbreads, liver, artichokes, courgettes, ricotta, apples, pears, pieces of bread, provatura cheese, salt cod. The vegetables are dipped in batter, the rest are egg-and-breadcrumbed. Their classic *fritto misto* is made up of brains, sweetbreads, liver, artichokes, courgettes, apples, pears and bread dipped in milk.

Hors d'oeuvres are not an old tradition: restaurants only started offering them twenty years ago, but now they have a huge selection to choose from. Some are old peasant snacks like *crostini di provatura*, skewered cubes of soft cheese alternating with pieces of bread spread with melted butter and a touch of mashed anchovy, heated in the oven.

The meal ends with fresh or seasoned sheep's milk cheeses made in the same provincial centres as salami and cured ham (the whey, mixed with cereals, is fed to the pigs), or local buffalo milk mozzarella and other southern cheeses like provolone, smoked provola and caciocavallo, followed by sweet wine and alcohols with almond and hazelnut biscuits (*tozzetti*) and little round *ciambellini* to dunk in the wine. And many meals end with the anise-flavoured sweet liqueur Sambuca, which the Romans drink after dinner with *mosche* (flies) in the shape of roasted coffee beans floating on top, and also pour into their coffee in the morning.

Inspired by the present mood of the country and the Italians' wish to rediscover their roots, food writers in Rome are looking for their heritage in the Roman Empire, studying in particular the treatise on food by Apicius, the only food writer we know of from that period. Apicius was an apostle of complication and extravagance. He describes interminable banquets with every conceivable victual from fish cooked alive at the table to peacocks and flamingoes cooked then re-covered in their plumage. Each dish required ten spices and several cooking processes. The gastronomic reputation of ancient Rome rests on accounts of its spectacular feasting, but banquets were an exceptional feature of Roman life and only 200 families could afford to give them. The feeling of those who cook in Rome today is that nothing much has been inherited from the times of Lucullus except for the talent of being *mangioni*, good eaters.

24. Grilled meat and game (p17): spatchcocked pigeon, lamb chop with rosemary, pork chop with juniper berries, slices of polenta – served with focaccia (flat bread). Cooking over embers is popular all over Italy.

25. Shepherd in Molise
26. Truffle hunter in Piedmont with giant white truffles
27. Tuscan landscape

28 (overleaf). Piedmontese cooking, once ignored, is now acclaimed as one of the great cuisines – pheasant in red wine (p22) and quails on grilled polenta (p22) are shown here with a mixture of wild mushrooms. Funghi trifolati – fried with garlic (p127) – are popular all over Italy.

29. Olive harvest
30. Olive oil poured into demijohns

Most Italians are very concerned with getting the best quality olive oil. The great oil-producing regions are Tuscany and Apulia (which produces huge quantities).

31. A country habit is to toast bread on the fire, to rub it with garlic and to pour a trickle of olive oil on top

32. Sausages with lentils (p114), a speciality of Norcia in Umbria

CROSTINI DI MIDOLLO

Toasted bread with beef marrow

This is very delicious but very rich and fat – a delicacy which was once upon a time given to children to make them strong.

Buy large beef marrow bones and remove the marrow (you can ask the butcher to split them to make it easier). Toast small rounds of bread, cut the marrow into 1cm (½in) slices, lay it on the toast and put it under the grill until the marrow begins to melt.

ZUCCHINE RIPIENE

Baked courgette boats

Most regions have their own way of stuffing courgettes. I particularly liked this one.

Serves 4

4 medium courgettes
100g (4oz) veal
1 slice of ham
1 tablespoon tomato paste
2 tablespoons parmesan
1 small tomato, finely chopped
2 tablespoons of breadcrumbs
1 egg
Small bunch of parsley
Few sprigs marjoram or oregano
Good pinch of nutmeg
Salt and pepper

Trim the ends of the courgettes and boil in salted water till you can pierce them with a sharp pointed knife. Then drain and cut them lengthwise. Remove some of the pulp with an apple corer (use in soup or salad) and place the courgette shells in an oiled baking dish.

For the filling, mince the veal and ham or blend in the food processor. Then mix and work to a paste with the rest of the ingredients except the oil. The mixture, like all fill-ings, should be strongly flavoured. Stuff the hollowed-out courgette shells – a heaped tablespoon of filling per half courgette, brush the tops with oil and bake in a 200°C (400°F, gas mark 6) oven for about 35 minutes. Serve hot.

FRITTATA DI PATATE

Potato cake

This recipe was given by Filippo Porcelli who serves it as an antipasto at his restaurant, Checco el Carretiere, in the Trastevere district of Rome. His mother made this popular Roman dish when the restaurant first opened.

Serves 4

1 large onion, chopped
2 tablespoons olive oil
350g (12oz) tomatoes, peeled and cut into pieces
150ml (¼ pint) dry white wine
Salt and pepper
450g (1lb) potatoes in their skins

Fry the onion in olive oil on a very low flame until very soft but hardly coloured, stirring often. Add the tomatoes and wine, season with salt and pepper and simmer for half an hour or until reduced to a thick sauce.

In the meantime, boil the potatoes until soft, then peel and mash them and add gradually to the tomato sauce, letting each spoonful become absorbed, until you have a firm, slightly moist texture. Serve hot or cold, shaped into a cake.

SPAGHETTI ALLA CARBONARA

Spaghetti with eggs and bacon

Serves 4

175g (6oz) unsmoked streaky bacon or
pancetta, cubed
1 clove garlic, lightly crushed
3 eggs
400g (14oz) spaghetti
Salt and black pepper
2 tablespoons parmesan, grated
2 tablespoons pecorino, grated

Fry the bacon in a wide pan in its own fat; add the garlic and remove it when well browned. Break the eggs into a bowl and beat well.

Cook the spaghetti in plenty of boiling salted water until *al dente*.

Put the spaghetti in the pan with the bacon, stir well and take the pan off the heat. Add the beaten eggs, a pinch of salt, plenty of pepper and a tablespoon each of parmesan and pecorino cheese.

Stir *spaghetti alla carbonara* until the eggs form a fluid yellow cream. Then add the remaining cheese, stir and serve on hot plates.

SALTIMBOCCA ALLA ROMANA

Veal cooked with ham and sage

This recipe is Severino's of Da Severino in Rome. He entertains his clients with Roman jokes and his piano playing when he feels in the mood. One morning, he produced one Roman dish after another so that I could taste while he explained the culinary past and recited a little poem he had written celebrating *saltimbocca*.

Serves 4

Salt
Pepper (optional)
1 tablespoon flour
8 slices of veal, weighing about 75–100g
(3–4oz) each
8 slices of ham, the same size as the veal
8 fresh sage leaves
4 tablespoons olive oil
200ml (7fl oz) white wine
50g (2oz) butter

Salt, pepper and flour the slices of veal. On top of each place a slice of ham and then a sage leaf. Hold them together with a toothpick.

Heat the oil in a large frying pan and fry the *saltimbocca* on a high flame for about two minutes on each side. Drain off the oil and pour in the white wine. Allow it to evaporate quickly.

Serve the *saltimbocca* on heated plates. Melt the butter quickly in the pan with the cooking juices and pour this sauce over the meat.

CODA ALLA VACCINARA

Oxtail stew with celery

This takes time but in the end you are more than rewarded.

Serves 8

2kg (4lb) oxtail, cut into pieces
1 carrot
1 leek
1 stick celery
Sprig of thyme
2 bay leaves
Salt and pepper
125g (4oz) streaky bacon, chopped
1 onion, finely chopped
2 cloves garlic, finely chopped
3–4 tablespoons olive oil
2 sprigs of marjoram, chopped
250ml (9fl oz) dry white wine
1kg (2lb) tomatoes, peeled and chopped
Good pinch of nutmeg
1 teaspoon cinnamon
1kg (2lb) celery hearts, cut into pieces
2 tablespoons raisins
2 tablespoons pine nuts

Trim the fat and wash the oxtail. Cover with water in a large pan, bring to the boil, simmer for 10 minutes, then drain and throw the water out. Return the oxtail to the pan, cover with water, bring to the boil and remove all the scum. Add the carrot, leek and celery, thyme and bay leaf. Season and simmer for 3 hours. Lift out the oxtail with a slotted spoon and keep the stock for later.

In another pan, fry the bacon, onion and garlic in oil till the fat has melted, and the onion is golden. Add the marjoram and put in the oxtail pieces. Turn them over, then pour in the wine. Add the tomatoes, salt, pepper, nutmeg and cinnamon and simmer for an hour or until the meat is so tender that it comes off the bone, adding a little of the stock when necessary.

In the meantime cut the celery hearts into large pieces and cook in salted boiling water until tender but still crisp. Drain and put them in with the oxtail. Add raisins and pine nuts and cook 10 minutes more. Serve hot.

PADELLATA DI POLLO E PEPERONI

Chicken with peppers

A very old and very good Roman dish.

Serves 4

1 onion, chopped
2 cloves garlic, finely chopped
4 tablespoons olive oil
4 chicken quarters, skinned and cut into smaller pieces
3 yellow and red peppers, cut into 1½cm (½in) strips lengthwise
Salt and pepper
Small bunch of basil, or a few sprigs of marjoram, chopped (optional)

In a large pan fry the onion in oil till soft; add the garlic and, when the aroma rises, put in the chicken and turn to brown all over.

Add the peppers, season with salt and pepper and cook gently with the lid on, stirring occasionally and moistening with a little water if it seems too dry, for about 25 minutes or until the chicken is done and the peppers are soft. Sprinkle in the basil or marjoram towards the end.

STRACCIATELLA ALLA ROMANA

Broth with egg

Stracciatella makes a very pleasant light soup if the broth is good.

Serves 4

4 eggs
4 tablespoons parmesan, freshly grated
Salt
Pinch nutmeg
1 litre (1¾ pints) meat stock or consommé

Beat the eggs with a fork, add the cheese, a pinch of salt and a pinch of nutmeg.

Heat the stock and, when it comes to the boil, take it off the heat and pour in the eggs, beating all the time. Simmer for five minutes on a moderate heat and serve.

ZUPPA DI CASTAGNE

Chestnut soup

Serves 6

300g (11oz) fresh or dried chestnuts, soaked overnight
200g (7oz) chickpeas, soaked overnight
100g (4oz) pancetta or bacon, finely chopped
1 onion, finely chopped
2 cloves garlic, finely chopped
2 tablespoons olive oil
200g (7oz) tomatoes, peeled and chopped (or 1 small can plum tomatoes)
3 tablespoons parsley, finely chopped
1 meat stock cube
1 small dried chilli pepper, crushed
Salt

Fry the pancetta, onion and garlic in a large pan in the oil until lightly coloured. Add the tomatoes and parsley and stir for one or two minutes, then add the drained chickpeas and chestnuts. Cover with water, add a stock cube, salt and the chilli pepper and simmer gently, covered, for about two hours. If using fresh chestnuts, slit the skin, roast under the grill and peel. Add them after one hour.

GNOCCHI ALLA ROMANA

Semolina gnocchi

Serves 4

1 litre (1¾ pints) milk
Salt
100g (4oz) butter
250g (9oz) semolina
75g (3oz) grated parmesan cheese
2 egg yolks
Good pinch of nutmeg

Heat the milk with a pinch of salt and a knob of butter. When it boils, sprinkle on the semolina and keep stirring vigorously to avoid lumps forming. When it is smoothly blended in, simmer for 15–20 minutes, stirring from time to time.

Take the pan off the heat, add half the cheese and the egg yolks and nutmeg and stir well. Pour the mixture on to a smooth, wetted surface and spread to about 1cm (½in) thick. Level off the surface using a wet palette knife. When cool and set, cut out circles about 5cm (2in) in diameter using a small glass or a pastry cutter.

Butter an ovenproof dish and arrange the gnocchi, slightly overlapping, in a single layer. Sprinkle with the remaining melted butter and cook for about 25 minutes at 200°C (400°F, gas mark 6) until the surface of the gnocchi forms a golden crust. Serve it hot.

VARIATION Serve the gnocchi with a tomato and basil sauce such as the one on page 150.

CERVELLA AL LIMONE

Brains with butter and lemon

Serves 4

*4 lamb's or 2 calf's brains, soaked in a few
changes of cold water
1 tablespoon vinegar
100g (4oz) butter
Juice of 1–2 lemons
2 tablespoons chopped parsley*

Remove as much of the covering membrane
as possible without tearing the delicate flesh.
Blanch the brains in water with a dash of
vinegar for moments only until firm. Lift out
with a slotted spoon and cut into pieces.

Heat butter until foaming and hazelnut-
coloured, add the brains and the lemon juice
and cook gently for 5 minutes until golden
brown. Sprinkle with parsley and serve.

VARIATION Add 2 tablespoons of black olives
and 1 tablespoon of capers, chopped.

FUNGHI TRIFOLATI

Mushrooms with garlic

Serves 4

*300g (10oz) porcini, shiitake or other
mushrooms
2 tablespoons butter
2–3 tablespoons olive oil
2 cloves garlic, finely chopped
Salt and pepper
2–3 tablespoons chopped parsley*

Wash the mushrooms and slice them thickly
or leave them whole if very small.

Heat the butter and oil in a pan and add the
garlic and mushrooms. Sprinkle with salt and
pepper and cook very gently, stirring every
now and then, until the mushrooms are done,
adding a few tablespoons of water if too
dry.

Add the chopped parsley and serve hot as
an antipasto or side dish.

NOTE In the north of Italy these mushrooms
are often served on a slice of grilled polenta or
as a sauce for tagliatelle.

CIPOLLINE IN AGRODOLCE

Sweet and sour onions

Serves 4

*750g (1lb 11oz) small pickling onions
50g (2oz) butter
1 tablespoon olive oil
1–3 tablespoons sugar
75ml (3fl oz) white wine vinegar
Salt and pepper*

Boil the onions for a minute and peel them
while they are still warm.

Melt the butter and oil in a pan and add one
tablespoon of sugar, then the vinegar. Put in
the onions, sprinkle with salt and pepper and
a little water to cover. Stir well, cover and
cook very slowly for 1½–2 hours, checking
every so often and adding more water if
necessary and shaking the pan so that the
onions do not stick. Taste. Add more sugar if
you like after an hour.

Serve hot or warm.

VARIATION In some families in Lazio they add
a little potato flour to the cooking juices and a
little stock and serve the onions with croûtons
toasted in the oven. Others add a tablespoon
of tomato purée to the juices.

In Sicily they make sweet and sour onions
with raisins and pine nuts which you can eat
cold. They colour the dish with a spoonful of
tomato paste and they don't use butter.

ENDIVIA BELGA LESSA

Poached chicory

Serves 4

4 large heads of chicory
Salt
About 1 litre (1³/4 pints) water or chicken
stock
3–4 tablespoons olive oil

Trim the chicory and poach in salted water or stock until it is just tender.

Drain and arrange in a small oven dish. Pour in the oil and turn the chicory to cover them well. Serve as they are, or bake in a 200°C (400°F, gas mark 6) oven for 15 minutes until very slightly coloured.

INSALATA MISTA

Mixed salad

With this salad you can improvise.

Serves 6

1 head of endive
1 bunch of radishes, sliced
¹/2 cucumber, sliced
4 tomatoes, cut in wedges
1 fennel bulb, sliced
1 celery heart, sliced
1 green or yellow pepper, cut into strips
1 mild onion or a bunch of spring onions,
thinly sliced

For the dressing

2 anchovy fillets, finely chopped
1 tablespoon capers, finely chopped
1 clove garlic, crushed
4 tablespoons olive oil
1 tablespoon wine vinegar
Salt and pepper

Wash and dry the lettuce and discard the outer wilted leaves. Cut the leaves into pieces and put them in a bowl with the rest of the ingredients.

Mix the dressing ingredients or blend them in a food processor and toss into the salad when you are ready to serve.

FRAGOLE AL LIMONE

Strawberries with lemon and sugar

For 750g (1¹/2lb) strawberries: leave small wild ones whole and cut larger ones into 2 or 4. Macerate for 20 minutes in the juice of 1¹/2 lemons and 3 or more tablespoons of sugar.

Or use orange juice or red wine or serve with whipped cream.

BUDINO DI RICOTTA

Ricotta cake

Serves 6

500g (1lb) ricotta
4 eggs
3 tablespoons plain flour
250g (¹/2lb) sugar
1 teaspoon ground cinnamon
Grated rind of 2 lemons
5 tablespoons rum
Icing sugar

Mash the ricotta and beat well with the egg yolks. Then stir in the flour, sugar, cinnamon, lemon zest and the rum and mix well. Fold in the stiffly beaten egg whites and pour into a buttered and floured 25cm (10in) cake tin. Bake at 180°C (350°F, gas mark 4) for about 40 minutes or until it is firm.

Serve hot or cold dusted with icing sugar.

Abruzzi and Molise

These two mountain regions, which until recently were united as one, are very much alike – silent and empty, with high peaks, hills covered with forests, valleys dotted with sheep, and limpid rivers cutting into the mountainsides.

Their rural and pastoral cooking traditions are similar – simple and old. *Maccheroni alla chitarra*, made by rolling out strips of egg dough over a row of thin wire threads stretched on a wooden frame like a guitar, dates from the fourteenth century. It is eaten with the sauce from hare or lamb stew. They cook lamb and *castrato* (castrated mutton is very tender with plenty of fat), the wild foods of their hills and mountains: mushrooms, asparagus, endives, chard and *cipollacci*, bitter tubers (the *lampasciuni* of Apulia) which look like a small onion, and the potatoes, cardoons, celery, fennel, tomatoes and black cabbage which they grow. They have cannellini beans and the lentils of Capracotta vie with those of Castelluccio in Umbria for the title of best in Italy. They also grow wheat (the excellence of their pasta, considered the best in Italy, is attributed to the quality of their water), maize, vines and olives which produce oil of exceptional quality, and they have fruit trees. At Piano di Navelli in the Abruzzi they cultivate saffron (a priest is said to have brought the crocuses back from Persia). Most characteristic of the cooking is the little hot red peppers, lovingly called *diavolilli* (little devils), which go into everything, fresh or dried or in powder form. *Olio santo*, olive oil in which a *diavolillo* has been macerating, is always at hand.

A meal starts with cheese or with hams and salamis. *Mortadella di Campotosto* is an oval salami which has a stick of lard running through the centre and *soppressata* has insertions of streaks of fat. Ventricina is a peppery salami flavoured with fennel and orange peel. The smoked hams of Rionero Sannitico are famous as are *mulette* of Macchiagodena. *Fegato dolce* (sweet liver) – liver and other offal mixed with honey, crystallized citrus peel and pistachio nuts, and *fegato pazzo* (mad liver), very hot with *diavolilli*, are both curious Abruzzi sausages. *Nirvi e musse* is pickled baby veal's head.

129

The fish and seafood dishes of the coast – raw shellfish and raw baby squid with lemon; grills, mixed fry, *scapece* (fried fish marinated in vinegar) – are the usual ones of the south, with the difference that the fish soups and sauces to accompany pasta and risotto are always cooked without tomatoes, '*in bianco*', and that they are peppered with a very generous amount of *diavolillo*.

Abruzzi has a special connection with cooking. If you ask any Italian cook in Italy or abroad where they come from, it is likely to be from Villa Santa Maria, a village squeezed between two great rocks on a hillside on the banks of the river Sangro among the highest Apennine peaks. Villa Santa Maria's tradition of dedication to cooking dates back to the sixteenth century when it was owned by the princes Caracciolo, who kept it as a hunting retreat for the summer months. The princes and their friends liked the way the local boys cooked game, and brought them back to cook for them at their palaces in Naples. Since then every young man of Villa Santa Maria has become a cook. First they cooked for families in Naples and eventually they went all over the world to cook in restaurants and for kings and presidents (Mussolini, Emperor Hirohito, King Gustav of Sweden, Marconi, the Shah of Iran). Already in 1607 a record in the kitchens of the Gonzagas in Mantua noted that a certain Vincenzo Pavia from Villa Santa Maria had an exclusive patent for making pasta by hand in all the lands owned by the Gonzagas. In 1939 a cookery school was started in the village and, in 1962, it was transformed into a state hotel and catering institute where young boys from neighbouring villages and from all over Italy come to be taught by the famous dynasties of chefs – the Stanzianis, Marchitellis, Spevantas, Nardizzis, Sabatinis and di Lellos – and where chefs from countries such as Japan, Russia and Gabon enlist for week-long courses.

There is a *Sagra dei Cuochi del Sangro* (festival of the cooks of the river Sangro) every year in Villa Santa Maria, which they call the 'land of international cooking'. While the chefs teach classic French and international as well as Italian cooking, their wives' simple dishes owe much to Naples and also to Apulia where, for centuries, generations of Abruzzi and Molise shepherds have spent winters with their sheep.

BRUSCHETTA

Garlic toast

Bruschetta is found from Tuscany, where it is called *fett'unta* (oiled slice), all the way down to Apulia, where very ripe tomato is rubbed into it.

Toast slices of rough country bread on the grill on both sides until golden brown. While still hot, rub one side all over with crushed whole cloves of garlic (you need half a clove for each slice). Arrange them on a plate and sprinkle with salt, pepper and olive oil (about a tablespoon for each slice). Serve hot.

CACIOCAVALLO O SCAMORZA ALLA BRACE

Grilled cheese

Grill thick slices of caciocavallo or scamorza cheese (the last is similar to mozzarella) near or under a fire until they start to brown. Serve bubbling hot sprinkled with pepper and accompanied by country bread.

ZUPPA DI CICORIA

Curly endive soup

This soup is usually made with wild endive which is quite bitter.

Serves 6

750g (1½lb) curly endive
Salt
1½ litres (2½ pints) light chicken or meat stock
Pepper
3 tablespoons olive oil
50g (2oz) grated pecorino or parmesan
6 slices of toasted bread

Wash the curly endive and boil in salted water for a few minutes until soft, then drain (this gets rid of some of the bitterness). Chop it finely – in a food processor if you like – and add to the boiling stock. Add pepper and serve with a dribble of olive oil and plenty of parmesan, accompanied by toasted bread.

VARIATION Another way is to beat the cheese with the eggs and to beat this mixture into the soup off the heat, just before serving so that the soup becomes creamy.

CICORIA E FAGIOLI

Curly endive and cannellini bean soup

Serves 6

350g (12oz) curly endive
Salt
250g (8oz) tin of small white cannellini beans
3 cloves garlic
4–5 tablespoons olive oil
1 small red chilli pepper
6 slices of bread, toasted

Wash and drain the endives and boil them in salted water for 3–4 minutes, then drain and chop them. Bruise the garlic and heat it in 3 tablespoons olive oil till slightly coloured. Add the endive and chilli pepper and stir well. Then add the beans, drained of some of their water and cook for a few minutes, remove the garlic and chilli and serve with a dribble of raw olive oil and toasted bread.

SPAGHETTI AL CACIO E PEPE

Spaghetti with cheese and pepper

This very simple spaghetti seems to be the favourite of professional cooks. After a day of preparing rich food, this is what they eat.

Serves 4

400g (14oz) spaghetti
Salt
100g (3½oz) grated pecorino or parmesan cheese
Teaspoon black peppercorns, crushed with a pestle and mortar or coarsely ground

Boil the spaghetti in plenty of salted water until cooked *al dente* and drain, reserving a little of the cooking water. Moisten with a few tablespoons of this water, sprinkle with grated cheese and black peppercorns, stir well and serve very hot.

PASTA COI CECI

Pasta with chickpeas

This comforting, rustic winter dish is served as a pasta or as a soup. What lifts it out of the ordinary is the use of good olive oil and chilli at the end, just before serving.

Serves 4–6

225g (8oz) chickpeas
225g (8oz) pasta (tagliatelle broken into small lengths, or cavatieddi – little shells)

For the stock

450g (1lb) chicken wings (about 6)
1 large onion
1 stick of celery
1 carrot (optional)
1 clove of garlic
3 bay leaves
Salt

For the sauce

3–4 tablespoons olive oil
Chilli powder to taste (optional)

Soak the chickpeas in water for a few hours or overnight. Put the chicken wings in a large saucepan of cold water and bring to the boil. Skim the surface, add the vegetables, garlic, bay leaves and drained chickpeas.

Simmer gently, covered, for at least an hour. When the chickpeas are tender, take out the chicken and bay leaves and season with salt. There should be plenty of liquid. Add the pasta and cook for 12 minutes, stirring occasionally. Take the meat off the wings and return to the stock.

To three or four tablespoons of the hot stock add the same amount of olive oil and some red chilli powder. Mix and pour it over the pasta.

LINGUINE CON LE NOCI

Linguine with walnuts

Serves 4

400g (14oz) linguine or spaghetti
Salt
2 cloves garlic, crushed
250g (½lb) walnuts, finely chopped
Good bunch of parsley, finely chopped
Good pinch of chilli pepper (optional)
175ml (6fl oz) olive oil

Boil the linguine or spaghetti in salted water until *al dente*. Beat the rest of the ingredients into the olive oil then mix well with the drained pasta.

AGNELLO AL FORNO

Roast lamb with mint

This lamb dish is from La Cucina dei Grandi Cuochi di Villa Santa Maria by Antonio di Lello and Antonio Stanziani. I met Signor Stanziani, who teaches at the Istituto Professionale of cooking, in the village square where older men sit and talk of their days cooking in the far corners of the world.

Serves 8

2kg (4¼lb) leg of lamb, boned
Salt and pepper
3–4 cloves garlic, crushed
1 large bunch mint, chopped
3 tablespoons olive oil
Juice of 1 lemon
1 stick of celery, finely chopped
1 carrot, finely chopped
1 onion, finely chopped

Open out the leg of lamb, season and cover with the garlic and half the mint. Roll it up and tie with string. Season outside and place the joint in a roasting tin, fat side up. Pour over oil and lemon juice. Surround with the vegetables and place in a pre-heated oven, 230°C (450°F, gas mark 8).

Turn the heat down at once to 220°C (425°F, gas mark 7). Roast for 30 minutes. Turn the heat down to 180°C (350°F, gas mark 4), add 300ml (½ pint) water and roast for a little over an hour. The meat should be crisp and brown, but very tender, pink, and juicy inside.

Strain the cooking juices. Skim off as much fat as you can. Mix in the rest of the mint and pour a little over each serving.

NOTE The vegetables, reduced to a purée to which you could add a glass of white wine to counteract the fat, make a good sauce in which to gently reheat any left-over lamb.

AGNELLO BRODETTATO

Lamb with egg and lemon sauce

An Easter dish, with echoes from Greece.

Serves 6

1 onion finely sliced
4 tablespoons sunflower oil
1kg (2lb) shoulder or leg of lamb, trimmed
of fat and cut into 2½cm (1in) cubes
½ bottle dry white wine
Salt and plenty of pepper
Good pinch of nutmeg
3 egg yolks
Juice of ½–1 lemon
Small bunch of parsley, finely chopped

Fry the onion in oil till soft. Add the meat and turn to brown the pieces all over. Then add the wine, salt, pepper and nutmeg and simmer gently, covered, for up to 2 hours until the meat is extremely tender, adding water to keep it moist. There should be a good amount of sauce.

When you are ready to serve, beat the egg yolks with the lemon juice and parsley in a little bowl and stir this into the stew. Leave very briefly on the heat, stirring constantly until the sauce thickens, but do not let it boil or the eggs will curdle.

COSTOLETTE DI AGNELLO ALLA BRACE

Grilled lamb chops

Grilling over embers is a popular way of cooking all over Italy, but it is more common in the south where they are masters of the art.

Serves 4

---

4 lamb chops
3 tablespoons olive oil
Juice of ½ a lemon or more
2 cloves of garlic, crushed
Sprig of rosemary
Pepper
Salt
1 lemon quartered
4 tomatoes

Marinate the chops in a mixture of olive oil, lemon juice, garlic, rosemary and pepper for about an hour. Then sprinkle with salt and cook for 10–15 minutes on a hot grill, turning over once until well browned but still pink and juicy inside. While the chops are cooking, heat the tomatoes on the grill until they soften and the peel can be pulled off easily.

Serve with lemon quarters and tomatoes crushed on the plate with a fork.

CONIGLIO IN TEGAME

Rabbit with wine and herbs

Serves 4

---

1 young, tender rabbit cut into pieces
2 tablespoons sunflower oil
Salt and pepper
Sprig of rosemary
Few sage leaves
150ml (¼ pint) dry white wine

Brown the rabbit pieces lightly all over in the oil in a large frying pan. Add salt and pepper, rosemary and sage and pour in the wine. Then simmer gently, turning the pieces over occasionally, for 15–25 minutes until very tender.

FAGIANO IN CASSERUOLA

Pheasant casserole

This, like the roast lamb recipe, is inspired by di Lello and Stanziani's collection of dishes.

Serves 4

140g (5oz) streaky bacon
2 young hen pheasants
2–3 tablespoons olive oil
1 small onion, chopped
1 clove garlic, chopped
Few leaves of sage
300g (11oz) black olives
Wine glass of red wine
Small glass of brandy
Salt and pepper
2–3 tablespoons chopped parsley

Fry the bacon in a casserole, remove it and turn the pheasants slowly in the fat, adding olive oil if necessary, until golden. Add onion and garlic and cook for a few minutes. Mix these with the pheasant livers, sage, half the olives and the chopped bacon and fill the cavity of each pheasant. Pour the wine over, season and cook in the tightly-lidded casserole in an oven preheated to 170°C (325°F, gas mark 3) for 1 hour. To serve cut the birds in half.

Strain off the casserole juices, add the brandy and the rest of the olives and heat through. Serve the meat with the stuffing, sprinkled with parsley, with the sauce poured over.

POLLO ALLA CACCIATORA

Chicken hunter style

Serves 4

1 chicken
4 slices of pancetta or unsmoked bacon,
chopped
3 tablespoons olive oil
2 cloves garlic, chopped
500g (1lb) tomatoes, peeled and chopped
150ml (¼ pint) dry white wine
Salt and pepper
Sprig of sage
Sprig of rosemary
2 bay leaves
250g (½lb) mushrooms, sliced

In a large pot or casserole, fry the pancetta in oil for a minute or so, then add the chicken and brown it all over. Add the garlic, and when the aroma rises add the tomatoes and the rest of the ingredients and simmer for 50–60 minutes or until it is tender, turning over once.

PALOMBA IN TEGAME

Casserole of wood pigeon

Serves 4

4 wood pigeons
3 tablespoons olive oil
¾ bottle red or dry white wine
½ litre (1 pint) chicken stock
4 tablespoons white wine vinegar
Grated rind of a lemon
2 sprigs of sage
2 sprigs of rosemary
2 bay leaves
2 cloves of garlic, crushed
5 cloves
1 tablespoon juniper berries, crushed
salt and pepper

In a casserole brown the wood pigeons all over in oil. Add the rest of the ingredients and simmer breast down with the lid on for 15–20 minutes or until done, turning them over once. Take the wood pigeons out, reduce the sauce by half and return the birds to heat through before serving with the strained sauce.

BROCCOLI AL LIMONE

Broccoli with butter and lemon

1kg (2lb) broccoli
Salt and pepper
2 tablespoons butter
Juice of 1 lemon

Rinse the broccoli, trim the stalks and divide into florets. Boil in salted water until the stalks are barely tender and drain. Put the broccoli back into the pan with the butter and lemon, heat through, and stir to coat. Sprinkle with pepper and serve hot.

Campania

Below Rome and the 'poverty line', where Italy becomes dry and almost entirely mountainous, is southern Italy which Italians call *il Mezzogiorno*. Once backward and primitive, it is still a different world from the north: warm, passionate, generous, steeped in religion and superstition, centred on the family and tradition. They say that history conspired with geography to make it poor.

Because it was unified under the same rulers – colonized by the ancient Greeks, then part of the Roman and Byzantine Empires and subsequently dominated by the Normans, Angevins and Aragonese – the regions of the south are fairly homogeneous compared with the rest of Italy, and belong more to the Mediterranean. The Greeks planted olive trees, vines and durum wheat; raisins and pine nuts, honey and almonds, orange blossom essence and the manner of stuffing vegetables came from the Arabs who ruled Sicily, and from Byzantium; and there is a very strong influence from France and Spain.

The south was a separate kingdom for much of its past: there was the Norman Kingdom of the two Sicilies, an Angevin monarchy, and the Spanish Kingdom of Naples. The land was owned by the king, the church and a few baronial families while the peasantry were disenfranchised serfs, the poorest in Europe, tied to the soil, living in abject poverty and oppression in caves and hovels. If you wonder about their legendary joy of living you are told that it was their way of living for the moment and of making the best of what they had. Making the best of the *piccole cose* (little things) they had is the basis of southern cooking.

At the end of the nineteenth century when their only hope was to emigrate, the peasants left by the million for America and Argentina and for countries around the Mediterranean such as Tunisia and Egypt. Of the five million Italians who went to America between 1880 and 1920, four million came from the south. No ethnic community has had as powerful an influence on American food as they have. Many went into the food business, bringing to it elements of their own home cooking. A new style, a blend from the different regions adapted to the tastes of the new world, and bearing little resemblance to the native tradition was born. And from there the pizzas and pastas and ice-creams of southern Italy went on to conquer the world.

Southern Italian food was considered poor and unhealthy (social workers were sent to encourage Italo-Americans to change their eating habits) until American dieticians discovered the merits of a healthy, low-cholesterol 'Mediterranean Diet'. Now it is one of the most fashionable cuisines: rich in grain, vegetables and pulses with plenty of fish, little meat and with oil as the cooking medium, it is full of flavours and aromas and what Italians call *fantasia*.

The cooking of Naples, the centre of power in the south since the fourteenth century, is the dominant influence and many dishes are common to all the regions of the south. But there is also great diversity in the form of local variations. It is a characteristic of the south that people did not spread out in the countryside but huddled together in towns and villages on hilltops to protect themselves from bandits, the traditional scourge of the area. The distances and lack of transport meant that, with little contact, everyone continued to cook in their own special ways.

The people of the coast adore fish and buy it fresh when the boats come in. Fishermen still go out to sea in their little boats at night and come back in the morning, but there is not much variety left in this part of the Mediterranean, so few can afford all the types of fish which restaurants offer. However there is plenty of blue fish – especially anchovies and sardines.

Although the south has the longest coastline in Italy, inland they hardly cook fish. In the past people feared the sea and were suspicious of its products. They lived high up on mountains, far away from the coast, next to castles and monasteries, as a protection against piracy and invasion. For peasants the sea did not exist.

The cooking of the hills and mountains, is based on dry hard-wheat, eggless pasta – spaghetti, macaroni, vermicelli (there are dozens more commercial types) – and the pasta they still make by hand by squashing tiny lumps of flour-and-water dough into little ears, hats, shells, snails and butterflies, or by rolling the dough round wires or knitting needles. They cook it until it is less than tender and add a little of the cooking water or a drop of oil (never butter) to keep it moist and slithering. They eat pasta twice a day but it is always different.

Doughy foods like pizza and focaccia are another staple of southern cooking. *Sfogliata rustica* and *pizza rustica* are big puff and shortcrusty pies, calzoni are half-moon shaped pasties. Panzerotti are like fried ravioli. *Torte* are made with a sweet shortcrust pastry and filled with pasta.

Vegetables are the triumph and glory of southern cooking. Campania's highly fertile black volcanic soil, which yields four crops a year in the plain above Naples, provides an unbelievably rich harvest, as does the Apulian plain. Vegetables – the familiar ones of the Mediterranean – are planted between olive and fruit trees which also serve as a trellis for vines which climb over them. They are eaten as a first or a main course. Preserved in oil – *sott'olio* – and pickled in vinegar – *sott' aceto* – they are real delicacies which make ready antipasti.

Fritto misto is an assortment of different vegetables all egg-and-breadcrumbed or dipped in batter and deep-fried. There may be courgette flowers, courgette slices and artichoke hearts, aubergines and potato croquettes. There may be, too, rice balls and cubes of cheese. It is an irresistible dish which is done for special occasions, because it is not easy as you must fry as you eat – *friggendo mangiando*.

Little meat is eaten in the south. In the past, most people ate it only once a year – at carnival time. It is mainly lamb (the mountains are full of shepherds and their flocks) and pork in the hilltop villages. But it is good meat, full of flavour because flocks and herds (there are some cattle too) graze on pastures rich in aromatic herbs and berries, and the small black pigs feed on acorns in the forests. Much of the cooking of meat is done directly over the fire with only herbs and a little olive oil. The lesser cuts are cooked long and slowly in stews. They are made into *polpette* (meat balls), or *involtini* (meat rolls). Every winter at pigsticking time, in the hills and mountains, pigs are turned into strongly flavoured cured and smoked hams, and all kinds of salamis. The fat is melted down and kept for cooking.

The classic fresh cheeses of the south, made with sheep's, goat's, cow's or buffalo's milk, are some of the best Italy has to offer. They are eaten as first or second courses and make wonderful melting cheeses for cooking. The most famous, *mozzarella di bufala*, is a speciality of Naples where they raise great herds of buffalo: they say these originated in India but they have been in the once marshy areas of Campania since Roman times. Mild, porcelain-white stringy mozzarella is pulled and made into small balls and plaits. Eaten fresh on the day it is made it is something really fabulous – nothing like the vacuum-packed exported variety. Made with cow's milk it is called *fior di latte*.

Mozzarella is eaten as it is, sometimes with a dribble of olive oil and a sprinkling of salt and pepper or as an hors d'oeuvre with tomatoes and basil. It is *impanata* when egg-and-breadcrumbed and deep-fried and *in carrozza* when fried between pieces of bread (the bread is sometimes dipped in milk). *Crostini* are slices of bread with mozzarella, chopped anchovy and tomatoes with a sprinkling of oregano put under the grill.

Caciocavallo, pear-shaped with a small ball at the top, is so called because the cheeses are tied up and hung in pairs astride a pole (*a cavallo*). It is semi-hard and strong-flavoured and can be eaten fresh, ripened or smoked. It can also be grilled or fried and used for cooking. Ricotta is eaten fresh and creamy or fermented and strong. Cacioricotta, hard salted ricotta, is used for grating. Goat's cheeses – caprini – are flavoured with herbs. Pecorini made from sheep's milk are mild or piquant and they are sometimes preserved in oil or left to dry and used for grating. Smoked provola and provolone, also belong to the south. Other specialities are tuma and butirro which has butter trapped in the middle.

Everyone in Campania seems to be crowded into Naples while the land around is empty, abandoned by everyone except the old for northern Italy, Germany and Switzerland. Exuberant, chaotic, desperately lively Naples of the Camorra (the local Mafia) and the decaying slums, was once the splendid, gay and powerful capital of the great kingdom of the south. The Spanish kings especially had a love of splendour and good living. From the time Alfonso, King of Aragon and Sicily, became king of Naples in 1442 and his court attracted scholars and artists, Naples remained a centre of good food. Although *spagnolismo* (Spanish high living) was restricted to those near the court, the nobility owned vast areas of land and ruled as despotic lords from their country retreats. Their dishes became the carnival and festive foods of the south.

The cooking of Naples took its present shape in the eighteenth century when the crops brought back from the Americas by the Spaniards became widespread. Peppers and tomatoes especially had a dramatic effect in the kitchen – from green to yellow, everything became red (today tomatoes are all-important – an ever-present ingredient, almost a religion). Tomatoes were married with pasta which had come as early as the thirteenth century from Sicily where the Arabs had introduced it. Soon the *mangiafoglie* (leaf eaters) became *mangiamaccheroni* (pasta eaters) and Naples became the queen of *maccheroni* (the general term for long pasta).

The glittering capital of the south was a magnet for the thousands who poured in from the countryside looking for work with the nobility. A tradition of street food sprang up to cater for these *disgraziati lazzaroni* (wretched good-for-nothings), as they were called, who lived on the street, waiting for work. Raw shellfish, snails bubbling in tomato sauce, tripe, entrails of every kind, pizza, fruit and pasta were sold from colourful stalls. *Maccheroni* were first seen here by visitors from abroad, many of whom wrote of their amazement at finding Neapolitans eating the long strips with their hands.

Even today people can remember *maccheroni* hanging on washing lines across the streets to dry. Sea towns had the ideal weather of alternating hot and cold air to dry pasta in the quickest possible time so that it could keep, and they became the centre of a thriving cottage industry. In 1840 the first large industrial pasta-making plant opened in Naples at Torre Annunziata. Hundreds more followed and exported their produce all over the world.

Pizza was also born in Naples when tomatoes were teamed with bread. It is the ideal fast food for a city where everyone is always out in the street. Neapolitans still make the best – very thin, crisp and brown outside and soft inside, with a light topping.

It is not all poor food in Naples. Something remains of the old Spanish Bourbon court cuisine. At the end of the eighteenth century King Ferdinand's queen Maria Carolina, dazzled by her sister Marie Antoinette's court of Versailles, asked her sister to send her the best cooks of France. So started an era of French influence with the Naples aristocracy. Those were the days when Sir William Hamilton was British ambassador and his wife Emma, the mistress of Nelson, was the bosom friend of Maria Carolina.

According to legend the king was a populist and insisted that *maccheroni* be served every day at the palace. His wife complained that palace etiquette did not permit eating with the hands so the palace cook devised dishes which could be easily eaten with a fork and did not need to be sucked in while the sauce splattered. These and some of the Naples sweets like *babà* and *sfogliatelle* (puff pastries filled with ricotta and candied fruit which are eaten hot), *pastiera*, the Easter cake which is now found all over Italy all the year round, *rococò*, orange-flavoured almond rings made at Christmas time, and *zeppole di San Giuseppe* (fritters stuffed with a pastry cream), *croccante* made with hard caramel and chopped nuts sculpted into extraordinary shapes, and the famous *zuppa inglese* with rum-soaked madeira cake and chocolate cream, came out of the old court kitchens.

Now everyone prefers the simpler foods but they all still make *ragù*, the prince of Neapolitan foods, which takes all day. Rolls of meat are stuffed with parsley, garlic, cheese, raisins and pine nuts and simmered slowly in wine with bacon and tomatoes. They call it *ragù del guardiaporta* (of the doorman) because it needs someone like a doorman to watch over it lovingly and to keep adding water while it simmers away. The sauce alone is served with pasta as a first course and then the meat rolls are served as the second.

Sweets play an important role on religious festive days. Many were once the speciality of convents. Most are made with almonds or ricotta, and there are walnuts, wine must, honey, orange blossom essence and dried and crystallized fruit. But the usual way to end a meal is with fresh fruit – there are citrus fruits, figs, apricots and peaches, cherries, grapes, melons, apples and pears – and ice-creams and sorbets of course, which are magnificent.

LE PIZZE ALLA NAPOLETANA

Classic Neapolitan pizzas

While more than half the regions of Italy now have their own special pizza, and an infinity of modern versions, many of them inspired by America, can be found throughout the country, old Neapolitan classics remain the favourites. A home-made pizza (basically a flat round of bread with a topping) cannot compete with one made in a wood-fired baker's oven but it can be very good providing your oven gets really hot enough.

Basic dough for 4 pizzas

500g (1lb) sifted plain flour, plus extra for flouring
¼ teaspoon salt
25g (1oz) fresh yeast or 15g (½oz) dried yeast
Pinch of sugar if necessary
About 250ml (8fl oz) warm water
About 3 tablespoons olive oil for the bowl and the baking trays

Put the flour in a large bowl with the salt. Crush and dissolve the fresh yeast in about half a glass of the measured water with a pinch of sugar to activate the yeast (or follow the manufacturer's instructions for dried yeast). When it begins to froth pour the yeast mixture into the flour, then pour in the rest of the warm water gradually, mixing first with a wooden spoon then working the flour into the liquid with your hands, add only just enough water so that the dough holds together in a ball. It is difficult to be too precise with quantities because flour varies from one country to another in its capacity to absorb water, and even flour made from wheat from the same field varies from year to year. Knead for 10–15 minutes until the dough is smooth and elastic, adding a little more flour if it is too sticky. Pour a tablespoon of oil in the bowl and turn the ball of dough in it to cover it well

with oil so that a dry crust does not form when it rises. Cover the bowl with a damp cloth and leave to rise in a warm place for 1–2 hours until doubled in size.

Punch the dough down and work it a little with your hands then divide into 4 balls to make 4 individual pizzas. Roll each ball of dough out on a lightly floured surface with a lightly floured rolling pin to a thickness of about ½cm (¼in), into a round about 23cm (9in) in diameter. Pinch the edges if you like to make a slight rim and place on well-oiled baking sheets or in round pie dishes.

Cover with one of the following toppings, the quantities are for one individual pizza, and bake in the hottest part of the oven at the hottest possible setting for about 20–25 minutes until the crust is crisp and coloured.

For *pizza aglio, olio e origano* (with garlic, oil and oregano) brush with 3 tablespoons of olive oil and sprinkle with 3 finely chopped cloves of garlic, 1 tablespoon finely chopped oregano (you can use the dried kind), salt and pepper.

For *pizza aglio, olio e pomodoro* (garlic, oil and tomato) do the same as above but add 150g (5oz) tinned peeled tomatoes, chopped and well drained of their juice.

For *pizza Margherita* spread with 2 chopped and well-drained tinned peeled tomatoes and sprinkle with half of a very good quality mozzarella, diced, 1 tablespoon grated pecorino or parmesan, a few torn basil leaves, salt and pepper and 3 tablespoons olive oil.

For *pizza Margherita bianca* use the same ingredients as above but without the tomatoes and with a whole mozzarella.

For *pizza alla marinara* spread with 2 chopped and well drained tinned tomatoes and sprinkle with ½ a tablespoon of capers, 1 tablespoon good-tasting pitted black olives, 4 chopped anchovies, salt and pepper.

PIZZA RUSTICA

Cheese and salami pie

This pizza is an unusual combination of sweet pastry and savoury filling.

Serves 8

For the pastry

100g (4oz) butter
50g (2oz) sugar – Italians use double
1 large egg
225g (8oz) flour

For the filling

6 eggs
450g (1lb) ricotta
50–100g (2–4oz) salami, cut very thick
50g (2oz) ham, cut thick
100g (4oz) mozzarella
100g (4oz) smoked mozzarella or other smoked cheese
2 tablespoons parmesan cheese
Salt and pepper

Cream the butter and sugar and beat in the egg, then add the flour gradually, mixing well, until you have a soft dough. Cover with cling-film and leave in a cold place for an hour.

For the filling, separate the eggs and beat one yolk at a time carefully into the ricotta. Chop the salami, ham, mozzarella and smoked cheese into small cubes and add them. Then add the parmesan and seasoning and gently fold in the stiffly beaten egg whites.

Butter and flour a 23cm (9in) tart pan. Divide the pastry into two pieces of one-third and two-thirds. Roll out the larger piece and line the mould. Add the filling. Cover with the rest of the rolled out pastry and seal the edges. Prick the surface all over with a fork.

Cook in a pre-heated oven, 190°C (375°F, gas mark 5), for about 50 minutes.

NOTE The top may be brushed with beaten yolk or milk to brown nicely.

TORTA RUSTICA CON SPINACI

Spinach and ham pie

Serves 6

For the pastry

300g (11oz) flour
50g (2oz) sugar
Pinch of salt
Zest of lemon
100g (4oz) unsalted butter
3 egg yolks
Beaten egg, to glaze

For the filling

500g (1lb 1oz) spinach
Salt and pepper
250g (9oz) tomatoes, peeled and sliced
175g (6oz) boiled ham, diced
400g (2 × 7oz balls) mozzarella, sliced

Mix the flour, sugar, salt and lemon zest. Rub in the butter, then add the egg yolks and mix briefly until the pastry holds together in a soft ball, adding a little water if necessary. Cover with clingfilm and leave in a cool place.

Cook the spinach, covered, until it crumples. Add salt and pepper.

Divide the dough into two with one part slightly larger. Roll out and line a 23cm (9in) greased and floured tart pan with it. Drain the spinach, squeeze dry and spread over the pastry shell. Lay the tomato slices on top. Sprinkle with ham and salt and pepper and cover with mozzarella.

Make a lid with the rest of the rolled out pastry and tuck it into the sides. Prick with a fork, brush with beaten egg and bake at 230°C (450°F, gas mark 8) for 10 minutes, then lower to 150°C (300°F, gas mark 2) and bake a further 30 minutes or until golden.

VARIATION Substitute for the spinach six frozen or tinned artichoke hearts, well drained and sliced.

INSALATA DI POMODORI E MOZZARELLA

Tomato and mozzarella salad

Serves 4

500g (1lb) ripe tomatoes, sliced
2 mozzarella cheeses, sliced
Salt and pepper
5–6 tablespoons olive oil
Bunch of basil, coarsely chopped

Arrange the tomatoes and mozzarella on a flat serving dish. Dress with salt, pepper and olive oil and sprinkle with basil.

ZUCCHINE SCAPECE

Fried courgette salad

Serves 4

500g (1lb) courgettes
Salt
Oil for frying
2 cloves garlic, cut in slices
1–2 tablespoons wine vinegar
Small bunch of fresh mint, chopped

Slice the courgettes, not too thinly. Salt them and leave them to lose their water for an hour, then rinse and dry them.

Fry quickly, a few at a time, in hot shallow oil, turning them over once, until lightly browned. Add the garlic towards the end.

Drain on kitchen paper then turn into a bowl, with mint, garlic and vinegar sprinkled between layers. Leave to marinate for a few hours before serving cold.

VARIATIONS For a peppery version, add half a small chilli pepper, finely chopped, to the frying oil.

A modern version is to marinate thinly sliced or chopped raw courgettes for a day in a mixture of oil, vinegar, salt, pepper, garlic and mint.

FAVE STUFFATE AL CACIO

Broad beans with fresh sheep's or goat's cheese

When broad beans have just come into season and they are very young and tender, they are eaten raw with their pods and skins removed. At the Ristorante Cappuccini Convento they served them cooked, and with goat's cheese. The restaurant is an old convent carved out high on the cliff top overlooking the Amalfi road. They like to cook vegetable dishes from the old convents of the region.

For centuries monasteries and convents had vast holdings and produced fruit and vegetables for the market. In the 18th century it was said that 'half the soil of Naples was held by the church'. With a population of fewer than 5 million the kingdom supported 21 archbishops, 165 bishops and abbots, 50,000 priests and as many monks and nuns.

Serves 4

1kg (2lb) fresh broad beans
1 large onion, chopped
4 tablespoons olive oil
Salt and pepper
250g (½lb) soft, barely salted sheep's or goat's cheese (caprini), cut into thick slices

Shell the broad beans. Fry the onion in the oil till golden. Add the beans, stir for a minute or two, then cover with water, season with salt and pepper, and simmer till they are very tender and the liquid absorbed.

Serve hot with the goat's cheese, warmed under the grill, on the same serving dish.

SARDINE ALLA SCAPECE

Sardines in spicy sauce

Alfonso, who has a little restaurant in a fishing cove at Praiano, gave this recipe.

Serves 8

1.35kg (3lb) fresh sardines
Juice of 1 lemon
Salt
Flour
Olive oil
900g (2lb) onions
150–200ml (6–8fl oz) vinegar
1 generous bunch mint, finely chopped
1 whole bulb garlic
2 hot chilli peppers (fresh ones are best)

You can simply gut and clean the sardines or remove the heads and backbones. Then soak them in water, lemon juice and one teaspoon salt for about 30 minutes to remove the strong flavour. Drain and pat dry. Dip them in flour, fry in olive oil, drain on kitchen paper, and sprinkle with salt.

Cut the onions into biggish rings and fry in two tablespoons fresh oil. When half-cooked, pour in the vinegar and cook until it has nearly evaporated. Chop the mint, garlic and peppers. Add to the onion and cook a little longer.

Place the sardines in a serving dish and cover with the sauce. Leave for several hours to marinate. Before serving, add a little more olive oil and some mint.

INSALATA DI FRUTTI DI MARE

Seafood salad

You can make a salad with only one or two of the following kinds of seafood, dressed with oil and lemon.

Serves 12 or more

2kg (4lb) mussels
1 small octopus weighing about 500g (1lb)
or baby ones (if you are lucky)
Salt
500g (1lb) small or medium squid
500g (1lb) uncooked prawns
6 large scallops
175ml (6fl oz) olive oil
Juice of 2–3 lemons
Pepper
Very large bunch of parsley, finely chopped

Clean the mussels, steam them open (see page 206) and remove them from their shells. Clean the octopus (see page 207) and simmer in the strained liquor of the mussels and clams with added water for 30 minutes or until tender. Clean the squid (see page 207), cut the body into rings and throw them in with the octopus. Then, 5 minutes later, add the prawns and scallops and cook moments only until the prawns turn red and the squid and scallops become opaque. Drain quickly.

Cut the octopus into small pieces and shell the prawns. Cut the scallops in half. Arrange on a serving dish with the squid, mussels and clams. Dress with a mixture of olive oil and lemon juice, salt and pepper. Leave to marinate in a cool place for at least an hour before serving. Sprinkle with chopped parsley.

POLPO AFFOGATO

Boiled octopus

This way of boiling octopus whole (*affogato* means drowned) is very popular all around the coast in the south. It is simple and attractive, especially when the double-tentacled *verace* are used. The tentacles curl up like the petals of a curious pink and white flower. It is usually served as an appetizer.

Serves 8

1kg (2lb) octopus (2 small ones or 1 large)
Salt
4 tablespoons or more olive oil
Juice of 1 lemon or more
2 cloves garlic, crushed
Pepper
Bunch of parsley, finely chopped

Clean the octopus (see page 207).

Blanch for a minute in boiling water to remove the scum which forms, then throw away the water and boil in fresh salted water until tender. Small ones weighing less than 500g (1lb) take between 25 to 45 minutes, large ones – they go up to 3kg (6lb) – can take up to 2 hours.

Drain and dress with olive oil and lemon juice, salt and pepper and a sprinkling of garlic and parsley. The octopus is served hot or warm – cut into slices – but it is also very good cold.

MINESTRA DI ZUCCHINE

Courgette soup

This easy soup is light, fresh and aromatic.

Serves 6

5 courgettes weighing about 375g (13oz),
finely chopped
1–2 tablespoons olive oil
1 litre (1¾ pints) light chicken stock
Salt and pepper
2 eggs
Small bunch of parsley, finely chopped
Small bunch of basil, finely chopped
Grated pecorino romano or parmesan

Fry the courgettes quickly in oil till lightly coloured. Add the stock, salt and pepper and simmer 15–20 minutes till tender.

Beat the eggs with the herbs and 3–4 tablespoons of grated cheese and pour into the soup, beating well, just before serving. Do not let it boil.

POMODORI GRATINATI

Neapolitan baked tomatoes

This Neapolitan way of cooking tomatoes has been adopted all over Italy.

Serves 4

4 large tomatoes, ripe but firm
4 tablespoons chopped parsley
1 clove garlic, crushed
4 tablespoons fresh breadcrumbs
4 tablespoons olive oil
Salt
A few sprigs of marjoram, chopped
1 tablespoon capers (optional)

Cut the tomatoes in half. Mix the parsley and garlic with the breadcrumbs, the oil, salt, marjoram and capers.

Place the tomatoes cut side up in a greased oven dish, cover them with the parsley and breadcrumb mixture and place in a pre-heated oven at 180°C (350°F, gas mark 4) for about half an hour. Turn up the oven to 190°C (375°F, gas mark 5) to crisp them. Do not let them get too soft.

Eat hot or warm.

PASTA AGLIO E OLIO

Pasta with garlic and oil

The poorest pasta dish of the south is one of the most popular.

Serves 4

400g (14oz) spaghetti or bucatini
Salt
4 cloves garlic, crushed
½ a small red chilli pepper, finely chopped or pounded (optional)
Large bunch of parsley, finely chopped
125ml (4fl oz) or more olive oil

Put the pasta in plenty of salted boiling water and start the sauce. Beat the garlic and, if you like, the chilli pepper (if this is used the dish is called *aglio, olio e peperoncino*) and salt into the olive oil, and when the pasta is cooked *al dente*, drain quickly and dress with the oil mixture and a generous sprinkling of parsley. Do not add grated cheese.

You may fry the garlic till slightly coloured in a little of the oil if you do not like it raw.

VARIATION Other herbs like basil and mint are sometimes added with the parsley. A restaurant in Trapani uses 13 including marjoram, oregano, thyme, sage and rosemary and calls it *spaghetti alle erbe*. Do try this.

SPAGHETTI CON POMIDORINI

Spaghetti with tomatoes

Spaghetti dressed with fried onion or garlic and tomato pulp cooked down to a smooth sauce has travelled around the world, but this way, with barely cooked cherry tomatoes served on top of the pasta, is more popular in Naples and the Italian south today.

Serves 4–6

450g (1lb) spaghetti or other pasta
Salt
3–4 cloves of garlic, chopped
3 tablespoons or more olive oil
1kg (2lb) small or cherry tomatoes, halved
1 teaspoon sugar
1 small hot chilli pepper, seeded and chopped (optional)
Good bunch of basil or parsley, coarsely chopped
Grated pecorino or parmesan

Cook the pasta in rapidly boiling salted water, stirring occasionally so that it does not stick, until only just tender. Drain.

Fry the garlic in the oil until golden. Add the tomatoes, sugar (our tomatoes need it), chilli and herbs, and cook until soft.

Serve the tomatoes on top of the pasta, moistening with a little cooking water or oil if liked. The last to be served are supposed to be luckiest because they get the best of the sauce.

VARIATION For another more usual tomato sauce: fry 1 chopped onion or 2 chopped cloves of garlic in 2 tablespoons oil till golden and add 1–1½kg (2–3lb) peeled and chopped tomatoes. Stir in 3 tablespoons of tomato paste if you like, season with salt, pepper and 1 teaspoon of sugar, and simmer till quite thick, then add a few sprigs of parsley and basil, finely chopped.

For *maccheroni al pomodoro al forno* (baked macaroni with tomato sauce) mix 500g (1lb) short pasta with a hole, such as bucatini, penne or rigatoni, cooked a little less than *al dente*, with the above tomato sauce and 150g (¼lb) grated parmesan in a baking dish. Stir in 300g (8oz) diced mozzarella and, if you like, also 350g (12oz) ricotta. Cover the dish with a sprinkling of breadcrumbs and a few shavings of butter and bake at 180°C (359°F, gas mark 4) for half-an-hour till golden.

SPAGHETTI ALLA 'PUTTANESCA'

Spaghetti with olives, capers and anchovies

No one knows the origin of this name which appeared forty years ago. Before that it was simply called *alla marinara*. The sauce is very popular all over Italy and is also served with vermicelli or linguine. Gaeta olives are used.

Serves 4

3 cloves garlic, chopped
4–5 tablespoons olive oil
500g (1lb) tomatoes, peeled and chopped
50g (2oz) capers, squeezed
100g (4oz) fleshy, tasty black olives, pitted
100g (4oz) anchovy fillets, finely chopped
1 small hot chilli pepper, chopped
Few sprigs of oregano
Good bunch of parsley, finely chopped
500g (1lb) spaghetti, vermicelli or linguine
Salt

Prepare the sauce: fry the garlic in 2 tablespoons olive oil till golden. Add the tomatoes, capers, olives, a little pepper and oregano and simmer for about 10 minutes, then add the rest of the oil. A minute before serving, add the anchovies and parsley, and salt if necessary (you may not need it).

Cook the pasta in boiling salted water until *al dente*, drain quickly and serve dressed with the sauce.

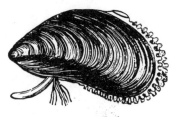

SPAGHETTI ALLE COZZE 'IN BIANCO'

Spaghetti with mussels

Spaghetti with shellfish (it is usually clams – *vongole*) is the most popular dish on the southern coast. Other pasta like *linguine* and *vermicelli* and other shells, like sea dates – *datteri* – are also used, and the sauce is made with or without tomatoes. There are those who like to remove the shellfish from their shells and those who prefer to leave them in.

Serves 4

1kg (2lb) mussels
400g (14oz) spaghetti
Salt
4 tablespoons olive oil
2 cloves garlic, chopped
Pepper
Bunch of parsley, finely chopped

Clean and open the mussels in a large pan (see page 206). Remove them from their shells or leave them in, as you wish. Strain the juices from the pan.

Cook the spaghetti in plenty of vigorously boiling salted water for 12–15 minutes.

In the meantime, fry the garlic in oil and add the strained mussel juice. Boil vigorously to reduce the liquor, then add the mussels, sprinkle with salt and pepper and cook for a minute longer – the mussels only need to be heated through.

Drain the spaghetti quickly when it is *al dente*, cover with the mussels and sprinkle with the parsley. Do not serve grated cheese.

VARIATION For a sauce with tomatoes – *spaghetti alle cozze coi pomodori* – add 350g (12oz) very ripe peeled and chopped tomatoes with the strained mussel juice to the garlic when it begins to colour. Simmer until reduced to a thick sauce, then continue as above.

CANNELLONI AI FUNGHI

Cannelloni with mushrooms

Cannelloni were born in Amalfi which was once a great naval power and important centre of trade with the East. The town made itself a free republic in 839, and boasts a style of cooking of its own.

Serves 6

For the pasta

Fresh egg pasta recipe page 84, using 200g (7oz) flour, a pinch of salt and 2 eggs or bought fresh or dry lasagne rectangles

For the filling

400g (14oz) mushrooms
1 clove garlic, crushed
3 tablespoons olive oil
400g (14oz) ricotta
2 tablespoons grated parmesan
Salt and pepper
Good pinch of nutmeg
50g (2oz) prosciutto crudo (raw ham) cut into squares
125g (4oz) Emmenthal cut in thin slices

For the béchamel sauce

600ml (1 pint) hot milk
3 tablespoons butter
3 tablespoons flour
Salt
Good pinch of nutmeg

To boil the pasta

Salt
1 tablespoon of oil

To garnish

2 tablespoons grated parmesan
25g (1oz) butter

Make the dough as described on page 84, roll it out thinly (not quite as thinly as for *taglia-telle*). Cut into 14 rectangles 15 × 10cm (4 × 6in). Or use bought lasagne rectangles.

Make the filling: chop the mushrooms coarsely and cook with the garlic in the oil for about 10 minutes, adding salt and pepper. Mash the ricotta and mix in 2 tablespoons parmesan, salt, pepper, nutmeg and mushrooms.

Make the béchamel sauce: melt the butter, add the flour and stir well with a wooden spoon to blend them. Then gradually add the milk and keep stirring until the sauce thickens. Add salt, pepper and nutmeg.

Now cook the pasta rectangles, a few at a time, in plenty of salted boiling water with a little oil to stop them sticking. While still a little firm, lift out with a slotted spoon, drain and lay them out on a slightly damp cloth.

Assemble the cannelloni: place a small slice of prosciutto (raw ham) in the centre of each pasta rectangle, cover with a slice of Emmenthal and top with a heaped tablespoon of filling, in a thin line. Then roll up the pasta.

Now spread 3 tablespoons of bechamel on the bottom of a baking dish and arrange the rolled cannelloni in a single layer over it. Cover with the rest of the sauce, sprinkle with grated parmesan and melted butter, and bake at 200°C (400°F, gas mark 6) for 30 minutes.

CANNELLONI ALLA SORRENTINA

Cannelloni stuffed with cheese in tomato sauce

Serves 6

fresh egg pasta recipe page 84, using 200g (7oz) flour, a pinch of salt and 2 eggs. Or use 14 bought fresh or dry lasagne rectangles

For the sauce

2 cloves garlic, finely chopped
2 tablespoons olive oil
1kg (2lb) ripe tomatoes, chopped
1 teaspoon sugar
Salt
Pepper or a good pinch of chilli pepper
Bunch of basil or parsley, or a mixture

For the filling

300g (10oz) ricotta
2 eggs
50g (2oz) grated parmesan or pecorino
Salt and pepper
Large bunch of parsley, finely chopped
250g (8oz) mozzarella, diced
75g (3oz) ham, finely chopped

Salt for boiling the pasta
1 tablespoon of oil for boiling the pasta
50g (2oz) grated parmesan or pecorino

Make the dough as described on page 84 and roll out thinly (but not quite as thinly as for tagliatelle) and cut into 14 rectangles 15 × 10cm (4 × 6in). Or use bought lasagne.

Make the sauce: fry the garlic in the oil till golden, add the tomatoes, sugar, salt and pepper or chilli pepper and simmer gently for about 10 minutes until reduced to a thick consistency. Then add basil and parsley.

Make the filling: mash the ricotta with the eggs. Add parmesan, salt, pepper, parsley, *mozzarella* and the ham, and mix well.

Boil the pasta rectangles, a few at a time. Drain while still a little firm and lay on a damp cloth. Place 2 tablespoons of filling in a line in the centre of each and roll up. Spread a few tablespoons of sauce at the bottom of a baking dish and arrange the rolled cannelloni in a layer on top. Sprinkle with parmesan or pecorino and cover with the rest of the sauce. Bake at 200°C (400°F, gas mark 6) for 30 minutes until browned and serve very hot.

VARIATION use a béchamel sauce (page 148).

TIMBALLO ALLE MELANZANE

Baked macaroni with aubergines in a mould

When Naples was ruled by a Spanish branch of the French Bourbons, the French cooks who came with them, called *monsù* by the Neapolitans, put pasta dishes into moulds for a more elegant presentation.

Serves 6–8

3 aubergines weighing about 750g (1½lb)
Salt
Olive oil for frying
2 cloves garlic, crushed
600g (1¼lb) tomatoes, peeled and chopped
Pepper
1 teaspoon sugar
Large bunch of basil, chopped
400g (14oz) short macaroni
450g (1lb) mozzarella, diced
6 tablespoons grated parmesan
300g (10oz) ricotta

Slice the aubergines lengthwise, salt and leave for an hour, rinse and dry. Fry in hot oil, turning over once until browned.

Make a sauce: fry the garlic in 2 tablespoons of oil, add the tomatoes, salt, pepper and sugar and simmer 15 minutes. Then add the basil.

Boil the macaroni in salted water till half cooked and drain. Line an ovenproof bowl about 15cm (6in) deep by 22cm (9in) diameter with overlapping aubergine slices. Fill with alternate layers of pasta, tomato sauce, and the three cheeses.

Cover with foil, gently press down and bake at 200°C (400°F, gas mark 6) for 45 minutes. Turn out.

SARTÙ DI RISO

Neapolitan rice cake with a meatball filling

Neapolitan cooking is a cooking of extremes – from extreme simplicity to grandiose baroque. When we made this dish I thought it was too much trouble and that I would not include it, but then it fed so many people and it was so appreciated that it stayed in. Other versions of *sartù* do not have the filling showing at the top as it is here, but have it in layers in the middle.

This used to be a festive dish but now you will find it in almost every self-service restaurant.

Serves 16

For the meatballs

250g (½lb) minced lamb, beef or pork
2 slices of bread soaked in milk and squeezed dry
4–5 tablespoons grated parmesan
2 eggs
2 cloves garlic, crushed
Salt and pepper
Bunch of parsley, finely chopped
Oil for frying

For the rest of the filling

1 onion, chopped
1 clove garlic, finely chopped
3 tablespoons olive oil
150g (5oz) mushrooms, cut into small pieces
2 small spicy sausages, skinned and cut into small pieces
125g (4oz) boiled small fresh peas or frozen petits pois
50g (2oz) prosciutto
6 tomatoes, peeled and chopped
Salt and pepper
125g (4oz) chicken livers, cut into small pieces
1 mozzarella cheese, cut into small pieces
2 hard-boiled eggs, cut into small pieces

For the tomato sauce

2 cloves garlic, finely chopped
2 tablespoons olive oil
1kg (2lb) tomatoes, peeled and chopped
1 teaspoon sugar
Salt and pepper
Large bunch of basil

For the rice

700g (1½lb) risotto rice
Salt
100g (3½oz) butter, cut into pieces
2 eggs plus 1 yolk, lightly beaten
75g (3oz) grated parmesan
Butter to grease the mould
Breadcrumbs to dust the mould

Prepare the filling first: put the meatball ingredients through the blender and shape the paste into little balls the size of large olives. Fry in hot oil, shaking the pan to brown them all over, then drain on kitchen paper.

For the rest of the filling, fry the onion in oil till soft, add the garlic and mushrooms and fry for about 5 minutes. Then add the sausage, drained peas, *prosciutto* and tomatoes, season with salt and pepper and simmer gently until the liquid is reduced. Then add the chicken livers and cook for a minute or two. Stir in the meat balls, the mozzarella and hard-boiled eggs and set aside.

Make the sauce: fry the garlic in oil till golden, add the tomatoes, sugar, salt and pepper and simmer till it thickens. Add the basil.

Now boil the rice in plenty of salted water for about 10 minutes until it is almost *al dente*, drain, turn into a bowl, and stir in the butter, eggs, yolk and parmesan. Grease a 31 × 8cm (12 × 3in) mould (I use one non-stick cake tin) with butter and sprinkle generously with breadcrumbs. Let the rice mixture cool and make a ring with three-quarters of it, packing it around the sides of the mould, leaving a hollow in the middle. Pour the filling into the hollow and cover with a layer of the remaining rice. Sprinkle lightly with breadcrumbs and bake at 200°C (400°F, gas mark 6) for about 25 minutes or until the top is lightly coloured. Turn out and serve with the tomato sauce.

CRESPELLE RIPIENE

Stuffed pancakes

French cooks introduced crêpes to the Naples court. They are still very popular on the Amalfi and Campania coast.

Serves 6–8

For the pancakes

150g (5oz) flour
375ml (13fl oz) milk
3 eggs
1 teaspoon salt

For a cheese filling

500g (1lb) ricotta
175g (6oz) mozzarella, diced
3 tablespoons parmesan
Salt and pepper
½ teaspoon nutmeg
Large bunch of parsley, chopped

For the sauce

750g (1½lb) tomatoes, peeled and chopped
2 tablespoons of oil
Salt and pepper
1–2 teaspoons sugar
Few sprigs of parsley, chopped

Oil to grease the frying pan and baking dish

To make the batter, gradually add the milk to the flour beating vigorously, then add the eggs, salt and 4 tablespoons of water (more if the batter seems too thick) and beat until smooth. Leave to rest for half an hour.

Into a greased heavy-bottomed or non-stick frying pan on medium heat pour half a ladleful of batter and move the pan so that the batter runs all over the bottom. As soon as the pancake sets and is easily detached, turn it over and do the other side. Repeat, stacking the pancakes in a pile.

For the filling, mash the ricotta, add mozzarella, parmesan, salt, pepper, nutmeg and parsley and mix well. It should be strongly seasoned as the pancake wrapping is bland.

Put a generous line of filling on each pancake then roll up and arrange side by side in an oiled oven dish.

For the sauce, simmer the tomatoes in oil until soft, seasoning with salt, pepper and sugar. Crush them with a fork and let the sauce reduce and thicken a little, then add parsley and pour over the *crespelle*. Bake at 220°C (425°F, gas mark 7) to heat through.

VARIATIONS

For a spinach and cheese filling: fry 1 large chopped onion in 2 tablespoons of oil till soft, mix with 550g (1lb 2oz) spinach or 275g (9oz) frozen whole-leaf spinach, boiled, squeezed dry and finely chopped, and 175g (6oz) ricotta and season strongly with salt, pepper, nutmeg and 2–3 tablespoons of grated parmesan.

For a mushroom filling: Lightly cook 500g (1lb) mushrooms – cut into pieces if they are too big (the fleshy shiitake and oyster mushrooms are particularly good for this) – in 4 tablespoons of oil. Add salt and pepper and 120ml (4fl oz) dry white wine and cook for about 15 minutes, raising the heat towards the end to evaporate the wine. Drain the mushrooms and finely chop in a food processor. Add 3 tablespoons of double cream and a large bunch of finely chopped parsley.

PARMIGIANA DI MELANZANE

Aubergines baked with tomatoes and cheese

You find versions of this dish all over Italy, usually with several layers of aubergines, but I particularly like this one.

Serves 4

---

2 large aubergines, sliced
Salt
1 clove garlic, crushed
Olive oil
500g (1lb) ripe tomatoes, peeled and chopped
1 teaspoon sugar
Pepper
Bunch of basil or mint leaves, chopped
1–2 mozzarella cheeses, diced
4 tablespoons grated parmesan cheese

Salt the aubergine slices and leave for half an hour to let the juices run out.

Make a tomato sauce. Fry the garlic in two tablespoons olive oil till the aroma rises. Add the tomatoes, sugar, a little salt and pepper and the herbs, and cook vigorously to reduce.

Now rinse and drain the aubergine slices. Dry them and deep-fry in hot oil, turning over once, and drain on absorbent paper.

Arrange the slices in an oven-proof dish or baking tray, cover with the tomato sauce, sprinkle with the cheeses and bake at 180°C (350°F, gas mark 4) for about 30 minutes.

GATTÒ DI PATATE

Potato cake

This delicious combination of creamy mashed potatoes baked with different cheeses and salamis is a good thing to make for a large number of people.

Serves 10 or more

1½kg (3lb) floury potatoes
Salt
125g (4oz) mozzarella, cut into small pieces
100g (3½oz) provolone, preferably a sharp one, cut into small pieces
65g (2½oz) mortadella, chopped
65g (2½oz) salami, preferably Neapolitan, chopped
100g (3½oz) grated parmesan
65g (2½oz) butter
4 egg yolks
Pepper
Good pinch of nutmeg
Breadcrumbs

Peel the potatoes, cut them in large pieces and boil them in salted water till soft. Drain and mash them to a purée. Mix well with the cheeses and salamis, the butter (leaving aside 1½ tablespoons) cut into bits, and the egg yolks and season with salt, pepper and nutmeg.

Butter a deep oven-proof dish or cake tin and dust with breadcrumbs. Pour in the mixture, sprinkle the top with butter shavings and breadcrumbs and bake at 180°C (350°F, gas mark 4) for about 30 minutes until golden.

Turn out and serve hot.

PASTIERA NAPOLETANA

Neapolitan Easter pie

This Neapolitan Easter dish is now sold in pastry shops all over Italy throughout the year. There are many versions. This one is a little unusual and comes from the ristorante Cappuccini Convento.

Serves 10

For the pastry

100g (4oz) unsalted butter
100g (4oz) granulated sugar
1 whole egg (large) or 2 yolks
225g (8oz) white flour

For the filling

450g (1lb) very fresh ricotta cheese
100g (4oz) granulated sugar
Ground cinnamon
1 lemon
4 tablespoons of orange flower water
100g (4oz) candied orange or mixed peel
6 eggs, separated
550ml (nearly 1 pint) milk
100g (4oz) vermicelli
Salt
Butter (for greasing dish)
1 egg yolk (optional)
Icing sugar for decoration

To make the pastry, cream the butter and sugar, add the egg or yolks and then the flour, gradually, mixing well to a soft dough.

For the filling, add to the ricotta all but two tablespoons of the sugar, plus a good sprinkling of cinnamon, the grated peel of half the lemon and its juice, the orange flower water and the chopped, candied peel. Add the egg yolks one at a time, beating them in carefully. (Save about half a yolk, if you like, or use another yolk later, to brush the top of the pie.)

Now boil the milk in a small pan and throw in the vermicelli. Gently simmer it in the milk with the remaining two tablespoons of sugar, a pinch of salt, a pinch of cinnamon and the grated peel of the other lemon half, until the vermicelli has absorbed all the milk. A teaspoon of oil in the liquid will prevent the pasta from sticking. While it is still warm, blend the pasta carefully into the ricotta mixture. Gently fold in the beaten egg whites.

Roll out two-thirds of the pastry and lay it in a 23 or 25cm (9 or 10in) springform mould or cake tin. Press the pastry into the base of the mould and round the sides. Pour in the filling.

Roll out the remaining pastry (you may have to add more flour to make a stiffer dough). Cut into long strips. Arrange these in a lattice on top of the filling. Brush the top with egg yolk (optional). Bake at 190°C (375°F, gas mark 5) for about 50 minutes, checking near the end of the time. Dust with icing sugar. Serve slightly warm, or cold.

GRANITA ALL'ARANCIA

Orange granita

1 litre (1¾ pints) freshly squeezed orange juice (you may use the bottled kind)
Juice of 1 lemon or 2 tablespoons orange blossom water
4–6 tablespoons sugar

Beat all the ingredients together. Taste for sweetness. Pour into ice-cube trays and freeze, covered with clingfilm.

Take the frozen orange cubes out when you are ready to serve and blend in the food processor to a fine, smooth, soft texture. The *granita* can go back into the freezer and be eaten later.

VARIATIONS You can do the same with mandarin and other fruit juices.

Apulia

Apulian food touches the heart, partly because Apulians are so incredibly warm and hospitable. Throughout Italy food is never just a matter of sustenance, it is part of the art of living, and there is always a sense of joy when you sit down to eat. In the 'heel' of the country, where emotions are heightened, the pleasures of the table are heightened too.

It may have something to do with the enchantment that this beautiful and ancient land produces with its endless coastline, its giant, contorted olive trees and white houses clinging together in clusters; with the mysterious beehive-shaped *trulli* – dwellings with conical roofs, and the magnificent Foresta Umbra in the mountainous promontory of the Gargano mountain.

The cooking evokes an ancient past and distant lands. My first experience of Apulian food was *'n capriata di fave*, mashed broad beans dressed with olive oil, which is exactly like a dish we made in Egypt. The second was *triya con i ceci* – pasta and chickpeas which is an Arab dish (*triya* is an old Arab word for pasta).

The coastal cities, because of their position in the middle of the Mediterranean, prospered through trade with the Near East and North Africa. Bari feels like a Levantine merchant city. The Arabs had a foothold in Apulia for a long time. Some came as traders, some as mercenaries, called in by warring cities and governing families, some had their pirates' nests there. When Sicilian Moslems failed to expand into the mainland, they raided constantly. That is why there are fortified towers around the coast and why many dishes echo those of Arab lands.

The earliest, most powerful and long-lasting influence in the area was Greek (the Greeks had colonies all along the coast), and it was renewed under the rule of Byzantium, which was the major force in the south until the tenth century. The fish soups found in every sea town are Greek, as are many words in the fishermen's jargon.

The golden age of a place usually leaves its mark on the kitchen, and for this part of Italy it was during the reign of Frederick II of Hohenstaufen in the thirteenth century. The splendours of his court and his banquets are constantly evoked in gastronomic conventions. It was a time when Apulia was rich and powerful: Frederick was King of Sicily, Holy Roman Emperor and King of Jerusalem (he led a Crusade). His throne and capital were in Palermo but he loved Apulia and had a palace in Foggia and a hunting lodge in Andria. Frederick brought a cosmopolitan feel to the kitchen. He liked to surround himself with philosophers, scientists and poets, who were mostly French, German, Arab and Jewish scholars. His cook Bernardo, who was famous for his *scapece* (preserved fish), prepared many foreign, especially Arab, foods. Although Apulia fell into decline when Naples became the centre of power in the south in the fourteenth century, the cooking of Frederick's glittering period remained. Apulia was also ruled by Normans, the Angevins and the Spaniards but they had little impact in the kitchen.

Until recently Apulian cooking was not considered worthy of interest because it was poor. In Milan a certain Peppino Strippoli had a successful chain of seventeen Apulian restaurants, but they offered modest fare. Today Apulian cooking is celebrated as the best example of what America calls the healthy 'Mediterranean Diet' and attracts chefs from abroad on gastronomic pilgrimages. It is humble food still, based on bread and pasta and things that grow wild in the fields. There is offal and horse meat and not very long ago donkey meat was used for sausages. *Maccheroni con il pesce 'fsciuto'* (dialect for *scappato*) means 'macaroni with the fish which escaped'. It is pasta with a sauce made from tomatoes, onions and stones from the bottom of the sea encrusted with microscopic molluscs and algae, which give the sauce a taste of seafood. But the cooking has great qualities. Its beauty lies in its sheer simplicity.

Apulia is rich now – it is the richest part of the south. The past twenty years have seen a profound economic and social transformation. Industries have mushroomed. There is pasta manufacturing, olive oil refining, canning, wine making, industrial cheese making, prosperous tobacco and clothing industries as well as steel and petroleum processing plants. Thousands have left the land, traditional farming has declined and modern agriculture with new technology has intensified. Young people have gone to the north of Italy where they settle, and to Germany and Switzerland as guest-workers. Towns have grown. Food habits have changed with the way of life. Young women go out to work and are no longer able or willing to spend hours making pasta by hand or watching the *ragù* as it simmers *da sole a sole*, from dawn to dusk.

But tradition *has* been kept up in the villages in the interior. The old carry on killing the pig and making sausages, drying tomato paste in the sun, preserving vegetables in oil and in vinegar, cherries in alcohol, figs in honey, olives in brine, fish in salt or vinegar. And the new middle class and the rich of Lecce, Taranto and Bari, which is the new industrial and commercial capital of the south, take pride in keeping up the traditional foods.

Apulia's advantage over its poverty-stricken neighbours is that the region is nearly all plain and highly fertile while they are entirely mountainous. The climate is hot and dry, but durum hard wheat, olives and vines, typical of the Mediterranean and needing little moisture, grow profusely. The long roots of the vines and olives seeking out water deep into the soil help them resist the attacks of Mediterranean winds. Apulia is the greatest olive-oil and wine-producing region of Italy. The giant olive trees yield excellent oil with a strong flavour and perfume, much of which goes to make up the blends of Tuscany.

Almond trees, for which Apulia is also famous, and fruit trees are squeezed in among the olives, and vegetables grow among the vines. There are few rivers, and water comes from an aquaduct fed by the river Sele in Campania – enough to produce splendid tomatoes, artichokes, fennel, cauliflower, broad beans, asparagus, radicchio and much more. The brilliant sun brings a great intensity of flavour and fragrance to the fruit – there are plums, peaches, cherries, figs, apricots, citrus fruit and melons – and to the vegetables.

Tomatoes especially are exquisite. People buy them in huge quantities from the growers and preserve them to last the winter. They boil them and turn them into pulp (*pomodori in bottiglia*) or put whole raw pieces, as they are, in jars which they sterilize (*pomodori a pezzi*) and use them to make sauces for pasta. *Conserva* is a salted concentrated paste which is left out on large terracotta plates to evaporate in the sun. Rows of plates are spread out on balconies and terraces. The paste becomes so strong that you only need a teaspoonful in a stew. For *pomodori sott'olio*, firm ripe tomatoes are halved, salted and left on boards to dry in the sun, cut side up. Then they are washed with vinegar and preserved in olive oil, sometimes with a chilli, garlic or capers and herbs. A variation is to put the halved tomatoes together with a little grated pecorino between them. *Pomodori a penduli* or *al filo* are tiny tomatoes, with hard but very edible skins, which are hung up in huge bunches with thread. They last the winter without spoiling and remain sweet and full of juice. Many vegetables, such as aubergines, mushrooms and artichokes, are preserved in oil.

A meal in Apulia usually starts with these preserves and an assortment of cured meats and salami. Capocollo is raw ham salted and covered in black pepper, smoked on oakwood, seasoned for six or seven months then washed in vinegar and wine, covered in red pepper and stuffed in a sausage skin for further seasoning. At Martina Franca, in the heel of Italy, hams are immersed in *vino cotto* (boiled down wine), covered in peppercorns, put into sausage casings then smoked and seasoned. The cervellata of Martina Franca is a mixed veal-and-pork sausage flavoured with fennel seeds.

Soppressata is a pork salami with lemon zest, cinnamon and cloves.

Cheese is eaten as an antipasto or as a meal. Apulia is a great cheese-making region with small artisan-type establishments and large industrial ones. They are spread out throughout the area but Gioia del Colle, Andria, Alberobello, Acquaviva delle Fonti and Foggia are important centres. They all make mozzarella as *bocconcini* (little balls) and *trecce* (plaits). Mozzarella is popular with the producers because it does not need ageing and does not trap capital investment. But, unless it is vacuum packed, it must be delivered immediately and eaten fresh on the day it is made. Caciocavallo and provolone are seasoned for at least 180 days. Pecorino has a delicious peppery flavour where the lentisk tree grows in the pastures.

Everything is eaten with bread which, with oil and wine, is a staple of the Apulian diet. Enormous amounts are consumed. One of the traditional breads is a giant, strong-tasting loaf which lasts several days and improves with time. Ciambella is a ring with a small hole. They cut it open, dry it out in the oven and it becomes the kind of dry food that shepherds and peasants take to the fields. They dip it in water and sprinkle on olive oil, salt and pepper and sometimes also chopped tomatoes and onion to make *bruschetta* or *frisedda*.

Peasants also make a cold soup, *cialledda*, in the fields by putting water, salt and olive oil in a bowl, cutting up tomatoes, onions, and cucumber, and breaking in the bread. Taralli are plain bread rings which are first boiled then baked. They are quite hard and meant to be dunked in wine.

People in Apulia still like to make pasta at home, with flour and water, and sometimes with flour and eggs. Their most famous pasta is their beloved orecchiette (little ears) which they eat every day. In dialect they are *recchie* or *recchietelle*. Every village has its special way of making them. They start by rolling the dough into a thin sausage and cutting it into little discs with a knife. Some indent them by pressing with their thumb, some squash them with the round end of a knife, some turn them inside out. Tiny ones are called chianchiarelle, larger ones pociacche. Pestazzule are little discs like orecchiette but not as deep. Cavatelli are like closed orecchiette. They also make turcinelli (little spirals), stacchiotte (like seashells) and fusilli (with a hole in the centre). Mignucchie are shaped like little gnocchi. Fenescecchie are macaroni rolled round a stocking iron. Strascenate (stagghiotti in Brindisi) are largish rectangles squashed on a piece of ridged wood. Troccoli are typical of Foggia. Women like to make all these sitting at a table in the street, when friends are around.

Pasta takes a long time to make but sauces are simple – barely cooked tomatoes, creamy, strong, fermented ricotta, toasted breadcrumbs and garlic, the liquor of a fish stew. The favourite is *cime di rape* – turnip tops with chopped anchovies. Others are made with broccoli and cauliflower, beans and chickpeas, fennel and rocket. The grand festive sauce for special occasions is *ragù* – meat stew with veal or horsemeat rolls.

Wild things, picked in the fields or found between the vines, have an important place in everyday cooking. *Lampasciuni* are curious tubers like hyacinth bulbs that grow underground like truffles. They have an unusual bitter flavour and are generally boiled and served with oil and vinegar as an hors d'oeuvre, roasted on the fire, cooked in *vino cotto* or put in an omelette or a stew. Wild chicory and fennel, rocket, cardoons, thin wild asparagus and an incredible variety of wild leaves and plants lend their strong, often bitter flavour to enhance some of the blander, plainer foods. Vegetables are eaten as a first or second course. Always simply cooked, they are little triumphs of gastronomy. There are herbs (no spices) and occasional embellishments like olives, anchovies, almonds, toasted breadcrumbs, egg and cheese.

With such a coastline and the sea always in the background, the importance of fish can be no surprise. One of the best appetizers of Apulia is raw seafood. It is a great thrill to buy it from the stands, *bancarelle di frutti di mare*, on the sea-front around Bari and Taranto where the enormous variety of shellfish includes oysters, scallops, mussels, clams, sea urchins, sea dates and razor shells. Vendors open them for you to eat raw, with only the perfume of the sea, or at most, a squeeze of lemon. Much of the seafood preparation, like everywhere in Italy, is as simple as possible to preserve the natural flavours.

Lamb and mutton, pork and game are eaten, but not in large quantities. Every year in the winter shepherds from the high plateaux of the Gargano and the Abruzzi and Molise bring down thousands of sheep to graze. They exchange cheese and lamb for olive oil, wine and vegetables. In many villages the butcher roasts the meat in his stone oven and sells it to his customers already cooked.

There is a great deal of diversity in the cooking of Apulia where peasants lived far away from their fields, huddled together in towns which remained isolated and separate (once upon a time they had fought incessantly). But the principal differences are between the coast, plain and mountains. At Monte Sant' Angelo, on the Gargano mountain in the spur of the Italian boot, people remember the time, before roads and television transformed their closed world, when you could tell who was a peasant, a shepherd and an artisan by the way they dressed and spoke and ate. Peasants and shepherds did not know how to cook fish. A few artisan families would wait for the mules laden with fish to arrive in the *piazza* after several hours' trek up from the sea, then make fish soup and sell it.

Many of the sweets can be found in all the southern regions. And the ubiquitous *zuppa inglese* is made here with sponge soaked with Alchermes and rum, covered with custard and cherries in syrup.

BRUSCHETTA AL POMODORO

Toast with tomatoes

This traditional shepherds' and peasants' lunch has become a fashionable appetiser.

Serves 4

8 small, thick slices of rough country bread
1 clove garlic, cut in half
Salt and pepper
Olive oil
2 large, very ripe tomatoes, roughly cut
1 small sweet onion, chopped (optional)
4 anchovy fillets (optional)

Toast the bread on both sides. Rub one with garlic, sprinkle with salt and pepper and olive oil. Cover with tomatoes and, if you like, a sprinkling of onion or a fillet of anchovy.

INVOLTINI DI MELANZANE ALLA MOZZARELLA

Aubergine slices stuffed with mozzarella

Serves 4–6

1 very large aubergine (400–500g, 14–18oz)
Salt
Oil for frying
250g (8oz) mozzarella
8 basil leaves
Freshly ground pepper

Slice the aubergine thinly, salt and leave to drain for an hour. Rinse and dry. Fry quickly in hot oil until tender and slightly browned. Drain on kitchen paper.

Cut the mozzarella into slices, place a basil leaf on each slice, sprinkle with pepper. Roll each aubergine slice around a piece of cheese and the basil and place in an oven dish. Grill until the cheese softens. Serve at once.

MELANZANE ALLA CAMPAGNOLA

Aubergines country style

The merit of this Apulian way of preparing aubergines is that the aubergines are not fried but grilled and marinated in olive oil. I first tasted them at the Vecchia Bari restaurant in Bari where Don Pepino and Anna de Grasta neither salt them nor brush them with oil before grilling. Other people extract the juices first by salting the aubergines. What matters is that they are cooked and marinated long enough – for up to 7 or 8 hours – before serving.

6 medium aubergines, peeled and cut into thin slices
Salt
150ml (¼ pint) olive oil
Pepper
6–8 cloves garlic, chopped
Few sprigs of fresh oregano, chopped
Small bunch of fresh mint, chopped
Few drops of wine vinegar (optional)

Sprinkle the aubergines with salt and let it draw out the juices for an hour; then rinse them and let them dry.

Lightly brush with oil and grill the aubergines over embers, on a lightly oiled grid or under the grill, until they are lightly browned, turning them over once.

Place them on a serving plate and sprinkle with pepper, garlic, herbs and if you like, with a few drops of vinegar. Finish with a generous dribble of olive oil and let them absorb the dressing for 4–5 hours before serving.

VARIATION A Sicilian version is sprinkled with a sweet and sour sauce made by boiling 2 tablespoons of sugar in 4 tablespoons of wine vinegar and then adding the raw olive oil. The Sicilians also like to fry their garlic and to add a pinch of hot chilli pepper.

INVOLTINI DI PEPERONI ALLA BARESE

Stuffed pepper rolls

Serves 12 or more

6 large green, red or yellow peppers
4 heaped tablespoons breadcrumbs
4–5 anchovy fillets (washed if preserved in
salt), finely chopped
1 tablespoon capers, chopped
2 tablespoons sultanas, chopped
2 tablespoons pine nuts, roasted
Small bunch parsley, chopped
Salt and pepper
3 tablespoons or more olive oil
4 tablespoons of juice (see recipe)

Wash and dry the peppers and put them whole, with their stems, on a tray in the oven set at the hottest possible setting for about 25 minutes till they are soft and the skin is slightly brown and blistered, turning them once to brown them evenly. Put them in a polythene bag, close it and leave them for 10 minutes. Peel them while still hot. Cut them in half lengthwise and remove the stems and seeds but try to keep some of their juice.

Mix the breadcrumbs with the rest of the ingredients, adding just enough oil and some of the juice to bind them into a paste. Put a tablespoon of filling on each half pepper and roll up. Arrange the rolls side by side on a serving dish and serve cold.

Or, to serve hot, put them in a lightly oiled ovenproof dish and bake at 190°C (375°F, gas mark 5) for 15–20 minutes.

VARIATION 120ml (4fl oz) olive oil, 6–8 tablespoons fresh toasted breadcrumbs, 2 tablespoons toasted pine nuts, 2 tablespoons sultanas, 24 pitted black olives, 2 anchovy fillets, chopped, 2 tablespoons capers, chopped, 2 tablespoons chopped parsley, salt and pepper. You might like this one best.

IL CRUDO

Raw fish

Absolutely fresh fish – particularly anchovies and sardines, but also other kinds such as red mullet, hake, smelts, picarel, bogue, goby – are eaten raw with a dressing of oil and lemon. Another way is to marinate them first in lemon juice which 'cooks' them in a way, and then to dress them.

Serves 4

500g (1lb) anchovies or sardines or other
very fresh fish
Juice of 2 lemons
1 clove garlic, crushed
4 tablespoons olive oil
½ mild onion, finely chopped
Salt
Black pepper or chilli pepper
Few sprigs parsley, finely chopped

Scale and gut the fish, remove heads, fins and tails and pull off the backbones. Wash and dry the fillets and marinate in the juice of 1½ lemons mixed with 1 crushed clove of garlic for a day, covered, in the refrigerator.

Drain and dress with a mixture of oil, the remaining lemon juice, the chopped onion, salt and pepper or chilli pepper. Serve sprinkled with parsley.

COZZE ARRAGANATE

Grilled mussels

Serves 6–8

2kg (4lb) large mussels
6 tablespoons of breadcrumbs
8 tablespoons olive oil
6 tablespoons parsley, chopped
Pepper
2 cloves garlic, crushed

Clean the mussels and steam them open (see page 206). Strain the liquid and reserve. Take off half of each shell and leave the mussels on the remaining halves.

Mix the breadcrumbs, 4 tablespoons of oil, parsley, pepper and garlic together, and moisten with a little mussel water.

Sprinkle each mussel with a little of the breadcrumb mixture and arrange in one or more roasting pans. Pour the rest of the oil over them and put them in a very hot oven 220°C (425°F, gas mark 7–8) for about 10 minutes until the breadcrumbs are golden, or put them under a grill for moments only.

VARIATION Dry white wine or tomato juice may be sprinkled on to the mussels.

PANZEROTTI

Little fried cheese pasties

Makes about 60

For the dough

450g (1lb) plain white flour
4 eggs
4 tablespoons oil
Salt

For the filling

225g (8oz) ricotta cheese
2 large eggs
100g (4oz) smoked provola or other strong cheese
Good quantity of parsley, chopped
225g (8oz) mozzarella cheese
225g (8oz) salami or ham
100g (4oz) parmesan cheese
Salt and pepper
Oil for frying

Make the dough (it is like pasta dough). Put the flour in a bowl; make a well in the centre and break in the eggs. Add the oil and the salt. Mix it all with a fork at first and then with the fingers. Knead well to form a smooth, elastic dough, dusting it with flour if it gets sticky. It should be smooth and silky. Wrap the dough in clingfilm and leave it to rest for at least half an hour in the refrigerator.

Meanwhile, make the filling. Put the ricotta into the bowl and break the eggs over the cheese. Then mix in all the other ingredients cubed or finely chopped. Season with salt and pepper.

Now roll out the pasta as thinly as you can, then cut into rectangles about 30 × 10cm (12 × 4in). Place little spoonfuls of the filling along one side about 1cm (½in) from the edge. Wet the edge slightly and fold the other edge over, making sure the edges stick together. Using a glass or round pastry-cutter, cut along the folded seam to make half-moon shapes. Decorate the cut edges.

Leave the pasties to rest for half an hour. Then lower them into very hot, deep oil and turn down the heat slightly so that they do not burn. Cook for a very short time: they will quickly turn brown and crisp. Turn them once. Remove and drain.

VARIATION Use pizza dough (see page 141). An alternative filling is mozzarella and chopped tomato with salt and pepper, or a mixture of ricotta cheese, cooked spinach and mozzarella.

ZUPPA DI PESCE

Fish soup

All kinds of fish and seafood are used, and every town and hamlet has its favourites. The Adriatic and Ionian seas yield a varied list. Any of these may be included: sole, flounder, turbot or brill, red mullet, bass, bream, monkfish, John Dory, hake, sardines, anchovy, eel, cuttlefish, squid, baby octopus, mussels, clams, prawns and mantis shrimp or lobster. *Scorfano* – a rockfish not available here – is often, but not always, included to give flavour to the liquor and then removed. You can substitute cod and any firm white fish that you like and make the soup as cheap and as easy as you like. The secret is to give each fish the right amount of cooking it needs and no more.

Serves 10

---

*2kg (4lb) assorted fish, cleaned and scaled,
left whole or cut up into steaks or fillets
750g (1½lb) squid or cuttlefish
500g (1lb) mussels or clams
250g (½lb) unpeeled prawns
2 onions, finely chopped
2–3 cloves garlic, finely chopped (optional)
5–6 tablespoons olive oil
2 small chillies, seeded and finely chopped
(optional)
750g (1½lb) tomatoes, peeled and chopped
Salt and pepper
250ml (8fl oz) or more dry white wine
2 tablespoons wine vinegar (optional)
1 teaspoon or more sugar (optional)
Bunch of parsley, finely chopped
10 slices of bread, toasted*

Clean and scale the fish or cut it into pieces. Clean the squid or cuttlefish (see page 207), and cut the bodies into rings (you can leave tiny ones whole) and divide the tentacles into small clusters. Clean and open the mussels and clams in a large saucepan (see page 206) and strain their liquor. Leave some in their shells – it looks good – and remove the rest.

In a very large casserole or a clay dish which goes on top of the fire, fry the onions and garlic in oil till golden. Add the chillies and then the tomatoes and cook gently for 10 minutes; then add the wine, the mussel water, salt, pepper and vinegar and cook 15 minutes more. Add sugar if the tomatoes are not sweet enough.

Now start putting in the fish and seafood, each according to the length of cooking time it requires – first the squid (tiny ones which take hardly any time should go in last) and the firmer-fleshed monkfish, then the delicate-fleshed fish such as the mullets and John Dory and the prawns, which need only minutes. The cooked mussels and clams go in at the end.

Sprinkle with the parsley and serve in bowls accompanied by toasted bread or *bruschetta* (page 131).

'NCAPRIATA

Bean purée

Dried broad bean purée was always poor food – the kind peasants took to the fields. Even in Roman times it was given to slaves and gladiators. Now it is very popular again and chic in Apulia, Sicily and Calabria.

In Calabria, where it is called *macco di fave*, and in Sicily, where it is *maccu*, the bean purée is combined with cooked pasta such as tagliolini or paternostri or with rice, while in Sardinia it is combined with tomatoes and cardoons and called *favata*. N'capriata partners the bland taste of the beans with bitter wild chicory or with spring onions and peppers. Although it is quite thick, it is served as a *minestra* or soup.

Serves 4

*300g (11oz) dried broad beans (buy them
already skinned)*
*2 sticks of celery, strings removed and
chopped*
1 large potato, chopped
2 medium onions, chopped
Salt
120ml (4fl oz) or more olive oil

Soak the beans in water overnight. Drain and
rinse and put them in a saucepan with the
celery, potatoes and onions. Cover with water
and cook on a low heat for about two hours.
During the last stages of cooking add salt and
a little oil, mixing well. Put the mixture
through a liquidizer, then beat in more olive
oil.

NOTE This purée is usually served with boiled
wild chicory – you may use curly endive,
dressed in oil. Or serve with fried peppers,
onions and tomatoes.

CALZONE PUGLIESE

Pizza pies

Calzone means 'pants'.

For 6 *calzoni*

Basic dough for 4 pizzas (page 141)
6 tablespoons olive oil
1 large onion, chopped
500g (1lb) tomatoes, peeled and chopped
50g (2oz) pitted black olives
1–2 tablespoons capers
8 anchovy fillets, finely chopped
Salt and pepper
Bunch of parsley, finely chopped

Prepare the dough as in the recipe on page
141, adding 4 tablespoons of olive oil and
working it in with the warm water.

For the filling, fry the onion in 2 tablespoons olive oil till soft, then add the tomatoes, olives, capers and anchovies. Season
with salt and pepper and cook for 10 minutes.
Then add the parsley.

Divide the risen dough into 6 balls. Roll
them out as thinly as you can, on a lightly
floured board with a lightly floured rolling
pin, into rounds about 23cm (9in) in diameter. Place them on well-oiled baking sheets
and spread the filling on half of each round,
leaving a 2cm (¾in) margin on the edge.
Moisten this margin with water and fold the
other half of the dough over the filling so that
the edges meet, making a half moon. Press
the edges firmly together and pinch and twist
them to seal the pies.

Bake in the hottest part of your oven for
about 25 minutes or until crisp and brown.
Serve immediately, hot and fresh.

VARIATIONS For *calzone con prosciutto* (with
ham), fill with layers of sliced ripe tomatoes,
mozzarella cut into slices, cooked ham cut
into strips, sprinkling each layer with salt and
pepper, grated pecorino or parmesan.

A *calzone di magro* – with onions only – is
made on the first day of Lent. The onions are
half-cooked in oil, then simmered in milk.
Sometimes, pitted olives and slices of fresh
cheese are added.

163

ORECCHIETTE E CIME DI RAPE

Pasta with turnip tops

This is the most typical of Apulian country dishes. Many who emigrate have bags of orecchiette sent to them regularly. Apulians grow turnips for the leaves. I have heard that some vegetable markets here sell turnip tops.

Serves 4

700g (1½lb) turnip tops
Salt
350g (12oz) orecchiette
3 tablespoons olive oil
1 clove garlic, crushed
2 anchovy fillets, chopped

Wash the turnip tops and remove any hard stems. Boil in salted water. After about 10 minutes add pasta and cook until *al dente*.

Put the oil and garlic in a pan and brown, add anchovies and break them up. Strain the pasta and toss it with the garlic and anchovy sauce. Stir and serve.

FRITTO MISTO DI MARE

Mixed fried fish and seafood

One of the most delicious ways of cooking fish and seafood in Italy is deep-fried with a light coating of flour in very hot olive oil. Every region and every sea town has its own particular assortment of mixed fry. In Naples and on the Campanian coast it is red mullet, baby cuttlefish, prawns and nothing else. In Liguria it can include sardines, anchovies, little soles, young hake, tiny octopus and squid. But the differences are blurred now because seaside restaurants put whatever they think is expected by tourists into their *fritto misto mare*.

Serves 4

1kg (2lb) fish and seafood chosen from these: red mullet, sardines, anchovies, sprats, whitebait, smelts, fillet of sole, baby hake, baby squid, large uncooked prawns
Salt
Flour
Olive oil for frying
2 lemons cut in wedges
Few sprigs of parsley

Scale, clean and gut small fish but leave the heads on. Wash, drain and dry on kitchen paper. Large fish can be filleted or cut into steaks. Leave baby cuttlefish whole (they do not need cleaning); clean squid and larger cuttlefish (see page 207) and cut the bodies into rings. Take the heads off prawns but do not remove the shells. Season with salt and roll everything except prawns in flour. (You can also peel the prawns and dip them in flour, then in beaten egg, so as to give them a thick protective crust.)

Use a large, high-sided pan so that the fish are not crowded and the oil does not boil over. Do medium-sized fish and steaks or fillets first – quickly, a few at a time, and of roughly the same size. Plunge in very hot oil (olive oil can reach higher temperatures than other oils without deteriorating and gives the very best results), then lower the heat to allow them to cook through without getting burnt. The temperature depends on their size. Lift out with a slotted spoon when cooked and crisp and golden. Drain on kitchen paper and keep hot in the oven while you fry tiny fish, prawns, squid and cuttlefish, all of which need moments only.

Serve very hot garnished with parsley, accompanied by lemon wedges.

GRIGLIATA DI MARE

Grilled fish and seafood

Cooking *ai ferri* or *in gratella* – on an oiled grill over the embers of a wood fire or, more commonly, *sulla piastra* – on a hot griddle, are popular ways of cooking fish and seafood all over Italy. Both methods are referred to as *grigliate*.

Although every kind of fish and seafood can be done in this way, each type needs a particular treatment. Some fish are grilled whole, large firm ones are cut into steaks. Unless they are very oily, like sardines and eels, they need marinating (preferably for half an hour) and brushing frequently with olive oil, melted butter or a marinade to prevent them from drying out. The fish is sometimes rolled in flour (in Sicily they use breadcrumbs) and then smeared with oil or melted butter or the marinade, which forms a crust that keeps the flesh moist. It is cooked, turning over once, over gentle heat, until the flesh turns opaque and just begins to flake.

To prepare fish for cooking whole, clean, scale and rinse but do not take off the head. For large and medium fish, make a few incisions diagonally with the point of a knife so that it cooks evenly and the skin does not burst. If the fish is very large (more than 1½kg (3½lb)) place it 15 to 20cm (6 to 8in) from the fire. If it is of medium size, place it 13cm (5in) away. Splitting the fish in half through the back cuts the cooking time and gives the smoky taste to a larger surface. The cooking time varies, depending on the size and type of fish, from about 15 minutes for a 1kg (2lb) lean fish to 45 minutes for a 5kg (10lb) oily one, and also according to the fire. Give the first side longer than the second and turn over more than once if the fish is large and firm enough. Place small fish 10cm (4in) from the fire and turn over once. (A hinged, double grill makes this easier.) They take from 5 to 12 minutes. Skewer eels rolled up in a coil.

Large fish with a firm flesh such as tuna, swordfish, monkfish and turbot are cut into steaks and grilled 8–10 minutes. They are also sometimes cut into 4cm (1½in) cubes which are threaded on skewers with a bay leaf between each piece.

Lobster is cut in half and grilled, shell side down for 10–20 minutes until almost done (the flesh brushed with olive oil or a marinade) then it is turned and the flesh side is given 1 or 2 minutes longer. Claws are left a few minutes more on the fire.

Prawns are grilled in their shells, with only their heads removed. King-sized *scampi* or *gamberoni* are cut open from the underside and flattened out so that they open out like a butterfly. They are marinated and grilled for only 4–5 minutes (mostly shell-side down).

Shellfish such as oysters, scallops, mussels and clams are also put on the fire for about 5 minutes until they open.

Small squid and cuttlefish are good on the griddle (cleaning instructions on page 207). They are dipped in olive oil and cooked for 5–10 minutes.

With a good selection of fish and seafood you can make a splendid *grigliata mista* (mixed grill). Serve sizzling hot with a sauce (it can also be the marinade), sprinkled with plenty of chopped parsley, accompanied by lemon wedges.

MARINADES AND SAUCES The usual marinade and sauce, which is poured over at the end or served in a bowl, is a mixture of olive oil, lemon juice, salt and pepper. It is the simplest and, to most tastes, the best.

In the north they often use melted butter instead of oil or a mixture of the two.

To the above mixtures add a little crushed garlic and chopped herbs such as marjoram, oregano, fennel, basil, rosemary, sage or bay leaf or add fresh tomato pulp; a little cayenne or chilli pepper; 2–3 finely chopped anchovies, or vinegar or white wine instead of lemon.

PESCE ALLA MARINARA

Fish in tomato sauce

Serves 4

2 cloves garlic, chopped
4 tablespoons olive oil
4 medium tomatoes, peeled, seeded and
chopped
Salt and pepper
1kg (2lb) fish (use small sea bass or other
white fish such as monkfish, hake, halibut,
skate and cod, whole or cut into steaks)
Bunch of parsley, finely chopped

Heat the garlic in the oil in a large pan. Add the tomatoes, salt and pepper and cook 10 minutes until the sauce is reduced. Add 300ml (½ pint) of water and cook 5 minutes longer.

Put the fish in and simmer gently with a lid on until it is done – from 4 minutes for fish steak to about 15 minutes for monkfish tails. The flesh should just begin to flake from the bone. Add parsley and serve.

POLPI IN UMIDO

Stewed octopus

In Puglia they mostly use baby octopus – *polipetti* – for this dish. I have not yet found them here but you can use the larger ones which are always about.

Serves 4

500g (1lb) octopus
2 tablespoons olive oil
2 cloves garlic, chopped
3 tomatoes, peeled and chopped
300ml (½ pint) dry white or red wine
Salt and pepper
2 teaspoons sugar
Bunch of parsley

To clean the octopus, see page 207.

Blanch for a minute in boiling water and throw out the water (this is to get rid of the scum that forms). The octopus firms and curls up. Cut into pieces and fry lightly in olive oil, turning them over once. Add garlic and, as it begins to colour, add the tomatoes, wine, salt and pepper and a little sugar. Cover with water and simmer until tender – it takes 20 minutes for baby octopus and up to 50 minutes for a medium one. Sprinkle with parsley.

VARIATION For *polpi arrabbiati* add 2 chopped anchovies, 2 small chilli peppers and 2 tablespoons of capers at the start.

TIELLA ALLA BARESE

Baked rice and mussels

Serves 6

2 medium onions, peeled and sliced
500g (1lb) tomatoes, sliced
500g (1lb) potatoes, peeled and sliced
300g (11oz) courgettes, sliced
4 tablespoons finely chopped parsley
2 cloves garlic, skinned and crushed
300g (11oz) arborio (risotto) rice
3–4 tablespoons olive oil
750ml (8fl oz) stock or water
Salt
500g (1lb) mussels

In a clay pot put alternating layers of onion, tomatoes, potatoes and courgettes, sprinkling parsley mixed with garlic in between each. Cover with rice. Pour in the oil and enough stock or salted water to just cover the rice.

Scrub and wash the mussels thoroughly and removed the beards. Open them by steaming them in 1.5cm (½in) water in a covered pan. Strain the liquor and pour it on to the rice.

Bake, with a lid on, in the oven at 180°C (350°F, gas mark 4) for about 40 minutes or until the rice is tender, adding water if necessary. Discard any mussels that haven't opened, take the rest out of their shells and put them back in half a shell each. Lay them on top of the rice and put the pot back in the oven for a few more minutes.

SPIGOLA AL FORNO

Baked sea bass

Sea bass is the grandest and most favourite fish – so appreciated in Apulia that only the minimum treatment is tolerated.

Serves 6

Sea bass weighing 1½–2kg (3–4lb)
Salt
Olive oil

Scale, wash and gut the fish but leave the liver and any roe. Sprinkle lightly with salt inside and out and rub with olive oil. Wrap loosely in a large sheet of silver foil, twisting the foil edges together so as to have a tightly closed but baggy parcel.

Bake at 220°C (425°F, gas mark 7) for 30–45 minutes. Eat it as it is, in its juices, with nothing to distract from the delicate flavour.

NOTE If you must, serve it with a sauce of olive oil beaten with lemon juice and a little salt.

BRACIOLE AL RAGÙ

Stew with stuffed meat rolls

This meat stew is a Sunday special in all the south. The sauce is served first with fusilli or other pasta, and then the meat rolls are served as the second course.

Serves 6

1.25kg (2½lb) beef topside, cut into thin slices (lamb, pork or veal can also be used)
Salt and pepper
100g (4oz) pecorino or provolone cheese
4 cloves garlic, crushed
Large bunch chopped parsley, or a few basil leaves
Olive oil
100g (4oz) streaky bacon (optional)
1 bunch spring onions or 1 onion, chopped
1kg (2lb 4oz) peeled and chopped tomatoes
2 tablespoons tomato concentrate
Glass or more of red or dry white wine

Flatten the beef slices and season.

Mix together the grated pecorino or thinly sliced provolone, 3 crushed garlic cloves, parsley or basil. Spread the mixture on the beef slices and, folding in the sides, roll each up into a small parcel and tie with thread.

Fry the rolls in two to three tablespoons of oil, turning them until they are nicely brown all over, then remove them. In the same oil, fry the bacon, onion and remaining garlic. Add the tomatoes, crush them, then add the tomato concentrate and the wine.

Put in the rolls and simmer, covered, on a very low heat for two hours, watching to make sure they do not burn and adding more wine or water to keep the meat covered. Or put in a low oven, 170°C (325°F, gas mark 3), tightly covered, for two hours.

Before serving, remove the thread.

VARIATION In Naples they put raisins and pine nuts in the meat rolls for their ragù.

Basilicata

Basilicata has much in common with her neighbours, especially Apulia. But she is the poor relative, being almost entirely mountainous, beset by floods and landslides, and having only a short coastline where the mountains rise abruptly from the sea. Basilicata has always been far from the centre of power.

Here, too, pasta made at home is the queen of the table. The difference is that here the sauces are very hot with chilli pepper. The cooks in Basilicata put _peperoncino_ (red pepper) into everything. There are many varieties which range from very hot to mild and sweet. They are used fresh, chopped up or whole, or dried (they can be seen hanging everywhere), or in powder form and in oil – this gives the oil a very powerful kick. In the days when there was malaria in this area, _peperoncino_ was thought to cure it.

The main characteristic of the cooking of Basilicata is the preponderance of pork. There is sheep, goat and game but every family has at least one pig. There is an old saying in dialect: '_Cu' si marita sta contentu 'nu jornu, cu' ammazza 'u porcu sta contentu n'annu_', which means, 'Who gets married is happy for one day, who kills a pig is happy for a year'. Pigs are reared for sausages, cured ham and salami. The people say they want something to give their children when they visit and something for them to take away. (Most of the children leave.)

The famous lucaneca (luganega in the north) which can be fresh, smoked or dry and is said to have been made since Roman times, derives its name from Lucania, the other name for Basilicata. Soppressata, a large flattened, oval sausage, with ginger and plenty of black and red pepper is preserved in oil. Sausages _sott'olio_ – preserved in oil, are typical of Basilicata where it is often too hot and sometimes not high and windy enough to age them.

Basilicatans make the usual cheeses of the south but they have a penchant for strong, sharp flavours and those that are meant to be aged are aged for even longer. Creamy fermented ricotta is so strong, it overpowers you when you open the jar.

INSALATA DI PEPERONI ARROSTITI

Roast pepper salad

I have eaten pepper salad all over Italy, sometimes dressed with oil and vinegar and with trimmings such as capers, chopped anchovies and garlic. But this simple way, with nothing to distract from their special flavour and texture, makes an ideal antipasto and a good accompaniment to all kinds of cold meats.

Serves 6

6 large fleshy peppers (preferably red and yellow)
Salt and pepper
4–5 tablespoons olive oil

It is easier to roast peppers in the oven than to grill them and they are just as good. Put them in a tray on the top shelf of a very hot oven, 240°C (475°F, gas mark 9) and bake for 20–30 minutes, turning them once on their side, until they are soft and the skin is blistered and browned in parts. Put them straight into a polythene bag, close tightly and leave for at least 10–15 minutes (this loosens the skins further and makes peeling easier).

When they are cool enough to handle, peel off the skin. Cut them in half, remove stems and seeds then cut the soft flesh into strips lengthwise (these can be wide or thin). Pour some of the juice that has collected in the paper bag over them and serve cold, dressed with olive oil, salt and pepper.

CIAUDEDDA

Broad bean stew

Serves 4

1 large onion, sliced
3 tablespoons olive oil
100g (4oz) pancetta (unsmoked bacon), chopped
1kg (2lb) broad beans, weighed before podding
4–8 artichoke hearts, quartered (tinned or frozen can be substituted)
500g (1lb) potatoes, sliced
Salt and pepper

Fry the onion in oil, with the bacon, until golden. Add the broad beans, artichoke hearts and potatoes, season with salt and pepper, barely cover with water and cook, stirring often, and moistening with a little water until the vegetables are done.

PATATE CON DIAVOLICCHIO

Potatoes with hot pepper

Serves 4

2 large potatoes
Salt
2 cloves garlic, crushed
1 small hot chilli pepper, finely chopped or ¼ teaspoon chilli powder
4 tablespoons olive oil
Few sprigs of parsley, finely chopped

Boil the potatoes in their skins in salted water. Peel, cut into slices. In 1½ tablespoons olive oil fry the garlic and chilli until the garlic colours. Take off the heat, stir in the rest of the oil and dress the potatoes. Sprinkle with salt and parsley and serve cold.

UOVA AL PIATTO CON MOZZARELLA

Fried eggs with mozzarella

Serves 2

1 clove garlic, chopped
2 tablespoons olive oil
1 mozzarella, cut into slices
2 eggs
Salt and pepper
Few basil leaves, chopped

Fry the garlic in oil in a frying pan till it begins to colour. Put in the mozzarella, break the eggs on top, season with salt and pepper and sprinkle with basil. Gently fry until the mozzarella bubbles and the eggs are cooked.

CUTTURIDDI

Lamb stew

Serves 4

1kg (2lb) lamb, leg, shoulder or fillet
2 tablespoons olive oil
4 little onions
2 cloves garlic, sliced
4 tomatoes, peeled
1 sprig rosemary
2 bay leaves
Salt
Good pinch of chilli pepper
300ml (½ pint) dry white wine

Cut the meat into pieces and remove as much fat as you can. Brown the pieces all over in hot oil in a large pan. Then put in the rest of the ingredients. Cover with water and cook, covered, for 1½ hours or longer, until the meat is very tender, adding water if necessary.

POLPETTINE FRITTE

Fried meat cutlets

These cutlets, which came to Basilicata from Sicily, make very good finger food for a party.

Serves 4

500g (1lb) pork, minced
4 tablespoons breadcrumbs
1 tomato, peeled and chopped
4 tablespoons grated parmesan
½ mild onion, grated
Salt and pepper
2 tablespoons raisins, coarsely chopped
2 tablespoons pine nuts, toasted
Oil for frying

Work all the ingredients together in a bowl: the meat could be blended first in a food processor with the breadcrumbs, tomatoes, cheese, onion and seasoning. Take lumps the size of a large egg, shape into little cakes and fry in hot oil until done, turning over once to brown them all over. Drain on absorbent paper before serving. You can dip the cakes in more breadcrumbs before frying.

CIPOLLE AL FORNO

Baked onions

Serves 6

3 large onions
3 tablespoons olive oil
1 tablespoon vinegar (optional)
Salt and pepper

Bake the onions (Spanish ones will do very well), whole and in their skins, at 200°C (400°F, gas mark 6) for 50–60 minutes or until they feel very soft. Peel them when they are cool enough to handle and cut into thick slices.

Dress with a mixture of oil and vinegar, salt and pepper, and serve warm or cold.

ERBE ALLA LUCANA

Mixed vegetables of the region

This is made in quantities to last over a few days and it is served hot or cold with bread or toast. Lucania is the old name for Basilicata.

---

2 aubergines, cubed
Salt
3 medium onions, sliced into rounds
2 large yellow peppers, seeded and cut into ribbons
Olive oil
2–3 cloves garlic, chopped
625g (1¼lb) tomatoes, peeled and chopped
1 teaspoon sugar
1 teaspoon powdered ginger
Good pinch of chilli pepper
Large bunch of basil, chopped
Large bunch of parsley, chopped

Salt the aubergines and leave them for an hour to degorge their juices. Then wash and dry them.

Fry the onions, peppers and aubergines separately in hot but not deep oil, turning them over once, till tender and browned a little (the onions and peppers should be crisp). Then drain on absorbent paper and sprinkle with a little salt.

Prepare a tomato sauce in a large pan: fry the garlic in 2 tablespoons of oil till the aroma rises, then add the tomatoes, salt, sugar, ginger (Basilicata is the only region of Italy which uses it) and chilli pepper, and simmer for 15 minutes or until the sauce thickens.

Now stir in the fried vegetables and the herbs and simmer gently for about 5 minutes.

LATTE DI MANDORLE

Almond milk

100g (4oz) blanched almonds
750ml (1¼ pints) water
3 tablespoons sugar or to taste

Chop or grind the almonds as finely as you can in the food processor. Add the sugar and water (as much of it as the processor will hold) and blend for a good amount of time until the water turns milky white. Pour into a jug and keep in the refrigerator, covered, for a few hours to infuse further. Strain through a fine strainer and serve very cold.

NOTE In Sardinia they add a tablespoon of orange blossom water.

CREMOLATA DI ALBICOCHE

Apricot ice

Serves 6

100g (3½oz) or more sugar
200 ml (7fl oz) water
Juice of 1 lemon
500g (1lb) very ripe apricots, pitted
1–2 tablespoons jasmine or orange blossom essence (optional)

Boil the sugar and water until the sugar melts (the amount depends on the sweetness of the fruit), add the lemon and let the syrup cool a little, then blend with the apricots to a cream. Pour into ice-cube freezer trays, cover with clingfilm and freeze for a few hours until hard. Just before serving put the frozen apricot cubes through the food processor, a few at a time, and blend to a very soft cream. You can put the ice-cream in a serving bowl and return to the freezer, covered with clingfilm, until a few minutes before you are ready to serve.

Calabria

Bordered by Campania and two seas, Calabria, the 'toe' of Italy, is largely mountainous – a quarter of it under forest, with great plateaux and plains and a few rivers; splendid in its great desolation; and stunningly beautiful, with mountains dropping into the sea, chestnut woods, lovely bays and medieval towns perched high above the water. Like the Sicilian coast, which is so near, the Tyrrhenian coast is lined with olive groves, citrus orchards and fig trees and tuna and swordfish are caught in large numbers. Tuna is preserved in oil and the roes are salted and pressed to make *bottarga*. On the Ionic coast the whitebait, which is caught in large quantities, is dried on wooden tables in the sun, dusted with hot, red pepper, then preserved in oil to make an explosive delicacy.

But Calabria is still a poor region from which emigration has always been heavy, with a cooking that is humble but full of rich, strong flavours. It is a land of home-made pasta. Aubergines and mushrooms are the most important vegetables – the tiniest village has its own way of making them – and swordfish is so common it is almost a symbol of the Calabrian coast. Cheeses are eaten for breakfast, lunch and supper. They have the mountain flavour of wild herbs heated in the sun and taste different in every village; shepherds still make their own.

There is lamb and the pig is celebrated. The little black, thin, hairy animals run free around the villages and are treated as though they were sacred. But in October their feasting ends and their owners' feasting begins and continues throughout the winter. The pig is a totem of the rural world in Italy and its killing is not a simple slaughter but a sacrifice involving the whole community. It is like a pagan, magic ritual.

Because the cooking is so primitive, echoes from distant lands take you by surprise. Pitta is a flat bread which must come from Greece; there is a dish called *patate alla tiana* which is like a Provençal *tian*; and the sweets are Arab even though they have names like *anime beate* (blessed spirits).

FUNGHI SOTT'OLIO

Mushrooms preserved in oil

This most popular Italian preserve makes a ready antipasto to serve with hams and salami. In Calabria it has a strong, peppery flavour.

Wash the mushrooms – porcini, shiitake or button mushrooms – well and simmer in a mixture of ⅔ water and ⅓ vinegar with salt to taste for 10–15 minutes, until tender. Drain well and let them dry on a cloth for an hour.

Pack into glass jars with a few garlic cloves, a tiny hot chilli pepper and herbs such as bay leaves, rosemary, thyme or oregano. Cover with olive oil.

The mushrooms should be ready to eat in a few days and will last for months.

CECI ALL'AGLIO

Chickpeas with garlic

This is a ritual Christmas dish which makes a good appetizer to serve with drinks. It is usually very garlicky and also peppery.

Serves 6

250g (½lb) chickpeas
Salt
4 or more cloves of garlic, chopped
100ml (3fl oz) or more olive oil
Black pepper or a touch of chilli powder

Soak the chickpeas in water for a few hours and drain. Then boil for at least an hour in water to cover until tender, adding salt when they begin to soften. Drain very well and return to the pan.

Fry the garlic in 2–3 tablespoons of oil until golden and mix into the chickpeas. Stir in the rest of the oil, sprinkle with salt and pepper, heat through and serve very hot.

This is also good cold.

INSALATA DI ARANCE

Orange salad

Serves 4

4 juicy oranges
Salt and pepper
4–5 tablespoons olive oil
4 spring onions or 1 sweet red onion, finely chopped

Peel the oranges and remove all the pith. Slice them thinly and lay the slices out on a serving plate. Remove the pips and sprinkle with salt and pepper, olive oil and spring onions.

FLAN DI ZUCCHINE

Courgette flan

This elegant version of a rustic dish is from Gaetano Alia of the Ristorante Alia at Castrovillari, Calabria.

Serves 6

6 medium courgettes, sliced
Salt
4 eggs, separated
170g (6oz) grated parmesan or pecorino
Pinch nutmeg
Oil to grease dish or ramekins

Blanch the courgettes in boiling salted water for no longer than 1½ minutes.

Mix the egg yolks with the cheese and nutmeg and stir the courgettes into the mixture.

Grease individual ramekins (or an ovenproof dish).

Beat the egg whites until stiff and fold into the mixture. Fill the dishes and bake for 25 minutes in a moderate oven, 180°C (350°F, gas mark 4), until puffed and golden on top. Serve hot.

POMODORI RIPIENI DI VERMICELLI

Tomatoes stuffed with vermicelli and herbs

The more usual fillings for stuffed tomatoes are based on rice or breadcrumbs. This 'poor man's' stuffing is quite delightful if you flavour it well.

Serves 4

4 large 'beef' tomatoes (each weighing about 300g (10oz))
100g (3½oz) vermicelli
Salt
3 tablespoons or more olive oil
Bunch of parsley, finely chopped
Bunch of mint, finely chopped
Bunch of basil, finely chopped
2 cloves garlic, crushed
Pepper

Cut a slice off the stem ends of the tomatoes and keep them to use as lids. Scoop out the inside with a spoon (this can be used for tomato sauce).

Crush the vermicelli into small pieces with your hands. (In Calabria they also use other pasta such as cannolicchi, rigatoncelli, ditalini rigati.) Cook in plenty of boiling salted water until it is not quite *al dente*, and drain quickly. Then dress quickly with a mixture of oil, herbs, garlic and plenty of salt and pepper. Mix well, and fill the tomatoes with this.

Place the stuffed tomatoes in an oiled baking dish and cover them with their tops. Bake at 160°C (325°F, gas mark 3) for about half an hour or until the tomatoes are soft – but not too soft or they will fall apart when you serve them.

VARIATION For a stronger tasting filling add 4 anchovies, 12 olives, a tablespoon of capers, all chopped, and a good pinch of chilli pepper to the cooked vermicelli.

CARCIOFI RIPIENI

Stuffed artichoke hearts

These days I would not make this dish myself with fresh artichokes. It takes too long to remove the leaves. I use the frozen hearts (they are much better than tinned ones) which I find in Middle Eastern shops.

Serves 4

8 frozen artichoke hearts
2 tablespoons oil (olive or sunflower)
250g (½lb) minced lamb, pork or veal
50g (2oz) grated pecorino or parmesan
Bunch of parsley, finely chopped
Salt and pepper
Juice of 1 lemon
1 tablespoon breadcrumbs
1 egg

Arrange the defrosted artichoke hearts in a lightly oiled baking dish.

Mix the minced meat, grated cheese, parsley, salt, pepper, lemon juice, breadcrumbs and egg very well and work into a paste. Fill each heart with a little mound of the mixture and brush the top with oil. Pour a little water in the dish to keep the artichoke hearts moist and bake at 180°C (350°F, gas mark 4) for 25 minutes until browned.

VARIATION Make a little tomato sauce (see page 150) and place the artichoke hearts in it in the baking tray.

PESCE SPADA O TONNO FRESCO ALLA MARINARA

Swordfish or tuna with tomatoes and olives

Tuna is brought in at several ports around the Calabrian coast and Bagnara specializes in swordfish. My own favourite is the swordfish. Luckily, it is now readily available here.

Serves 4

4 slices fresh swordfish or tuna, each weighing about 150g (5oz)
3 tablespoons olive oil
75g (3oz) black olives, pitted and chopped
1 tablespoon capers
400g (14oz) tomatoes, peeled and chopped
Bunch of basil, chopped
Salt and pepper or chilli pepper
2 tablespoons breadcrumbs

Brush an oven dish with oil and place the tuna slices in it. Cover with the olives and capers, the tomatoes and basil. Sprinkle with olive oil and breadcrumbs and bake in a 240°C (475°F, gas mark 9) oven for 20–30 minutes.

PESCE SPADA O TONNO AI FERRI

Grilled swordfish or tuna steaks

Serves 4

2 slices of swordfish cut into 4 pieces
2 tomatoes, peeled and seeded
4 tablespoons olive oil
Juice of ½ lemon
Few sprigs of marjoram, chopped
Salt and pepper or chilli pepper

Put the tomatoes, olive oil, lemon juice, marjoram, salt and pepper through the blender. Sprinkle the fish steaks with some of this sauce and cook over embers, under the grill or on a hot griddle for 6–10 minutes, until the flesh only just turns opaque (do not overcook), turning the fish over once and sprinkling with more sauce.

Serve at once with the remaining sauce.

COSCIOTTO DI AGNELLO ALLA BRACE

Boned leg of lamb on the grill

Serves 6

1 small leg of lamb
3 sprigs of rosemary or a bunch of mint
4 cloves garlic, cut into slivers
4 tablespoons olive oil
Juice of 1 lemon
Salt and pepper or chilli pepper

Have the butcher bone the leg of lamb or do it yourself. Remove the fat, open the leg out and flatten it. Pierce the meat with a sharp pointed knife in several places and push into each hole, and in a few places under the skin, a sliver of garlic and a few rosemary or mint leaves. Then marinate the meat for an hour in a mixture of olive oil, lemon juice, salt and pepper.

Place the lamb on an oiled grill over embers or under the grill in your oven, at least 7½cm (3in) away from the fire. After about 20 minutes turn the meat and cook another 15–20 minutes brushing occasionally with the marinade. It should be brown on the outside but still pink inside. Cut into the meat to see if it is done to your taste. If you want it well done, cook for another 15 minutes.

Alternatively, leave the fat on and cook the fat side first.

Sicily

In Palermo I remembered Egypt – the impromptu visits, the streams of relatives hugging and kissing and sitting in a circle, and piles of food. In the north they explained it as '*il culto della famiglia e del mangiare*' – the cult of family and food. Getting together is part of what the north envies as the southern 'joy of living'. Here, any event from a homecoming or birthday to saints' days and weddings is an occasion for a feast. The banqueting rooms in every tiny village are always packed. Feasting is also a matter of keeping up appearances, *la figura*, and extravagance (they call it *spagnolismo*, saying they learnt it from the Spaniards) can reach incredible heights.

The island is so poor that much of the male population has to leave in search of livelihood and yet not only is food important but the cooking is one of the most varied and exotic in Italy. The secret lies in the 2000 years of occupation. Being right in the middle of the Mediterranean, Sicily was always desirable when this sea was the centre of the world. She was colonized by Greeks and Romans, Arabs and Normans; governed from Spain, Austria and Constantinople, and occupied by the French, Germans and English (during the Napoleonic wars). She was not only conquered, but the seat of the conquering kings, which lends grandeur to anyone's cooking.

Sicilians do not break with the past. They can tell you that Greeks introduced honey and wine, olives and ricotta, *focaccia* (a kind of bread) and fish soup; that they cook *maccu*, a broad bean purée, as in Roman times; that the Byzantines brought sharp cheeses and spicy biscuits, the Normans salt cod and *involtini* (stuffed meat or fish rolls), the Spaniards tomato sauce and sweet and sour flavours, the English dessert wines and the Arabs much of what is theirs.

In 827 an army of Arabs – Berbers from North Africa and Spanish Moslems (Sicilians called them all Saracens) – landed on the island. They brought their laws and their language, their literature, arts and sciences and their religion; they irrigated the land and planted exotic fruits and vegetables around the cities. Used to nomadism, they encouraged sheep and goats. Stuffed vegetables, rice dishes, *cuscusu*, almond pastries, sorbets and even pasta are the relics of their civilization.

The fusion of cultures produced a rich and aromatic style of cooking where melted anchovies, garlic, hot red peppers, chocolate, wine (including sweet marsala), herbs (especially basil and mint), spices (including saffron), lemon and orange zest, olives and capers, almonds and pistachios, pine nuts and raisins, honey, orange blossom and jasmine all play their part.

Sicilian cooking is both very humble – there is a bread soup with only salt, garlic, a bay leaf and a sprinkling of olive oil – and sumptuous, an example of which is *cassata*, a cheese cake decorated with a fantasia of candied fruit and brightly painted marzipan. These extremes reflect the world of feudal landlords and serfs in which Sicily was locked until after the Second World War. Most of the land was owned by a powerful aristocracy which possessed feudal lordship over whole villages. They were absentee landlords who lived in town (Syracuse and Palermo were once among the largest and richest cities in the world), whose extravagant lifestyle and obsession with status are legendary. The *cucina nobile* (it is also referred to as 'baronial' and 'baroque') was based mainly on Arab and Spanish cooking and acquired a French touch in the eighteenth century when head cooks in noble households were French. *Galantines* of goose and pheasant pâtés appeared on tables; pastas were pressed into moulds and became *timbali*, or encased in puff pastry *in tortiera*; layers of rice were shaped into *gatto* and meat was cut into *médaillons*.

The mantle of noble cooking has been taken over today by a thriving catering trade with its never-ending round of parties and banquets for up to 400 people, many of which take place in the hired-out great old palaces of *Gattopardo* (*The Leopard*) fame. Some chefs are capable of extraordinarily elaborate centre-pieces, which would put Escoffier to shame. Mafia weddings, especially, can be mind-boggling affairs with meats and vegetables arranged in ornate, multi-coloured peacock shapes, and with monumental cakes.

In feudal days the great bulk of the population were shepherds, living in the mountains, many of them in huts with their animals, labourers and share croppers who surrendered more than half their produce in lieu of rent and still owed personal services to the master. It is their cooking (they call it *cucina povera*) or rather their festive dishes (for it was only on special occasions that they ate well), with a few borrowings from the aristocratic kitchen, that is the popular and fashionable food today. It is based on the produce of the land. Everything that grows in Sicily has a pure intense flavour because of the brilliant sun and the rich volcanic soil. Hard wheat which is easy to grow but difficult to mill is the main crop. Olive trees grow wild in the hills and there are so many huge orange and lemon orchards that their fragrance pervades the whole island. There are plenty of pistachio trees, hazelnuts, pine nuts and eighteen qualities of almonds. And large quantities of wine are produced.

Agriculture used to be backward and depressed because low investment monoculture of wheat, oranges and lemons suited the absentee landlords best, and because of the general anarchy of this arcane rural world, oppressed by vendettas and banditry. Harvests were often destroyed by drought and until recently, in modern Sicily, agriculture was subordinated to industry. But there is now a new dynamism and shift towards the intensive cultivation of vegetables.

There is sheep farming on the hills, a few cattle and some goats. Animals are left to wander everywhere, almost wild, to browse as they can. The frequent movement of the herds between coast and mountains to escape extremes of climate is bad for both their meat and milk, but the wild herbs they eat gives both a wonderful flavour, and the cows are of breeds which produce an enormous amount of milk. All the milk, including that of sheep and goats, is turned into cheese. They make caciocavallo, tuma and provola and the famous pecorino. Ricotta is made by boiling the whey left over from cheese-making – creamy granules float to the top and are skimmed off and put into plastic baskets to drain and become firm. Sicilians claim that only sheeps' milk ricotta has the perfect flavour and texture for making the sweets which are their forte. Hard pecorino and ricotta, dried in the sun, are used for grating.

A Sicilian way of making a meal of fresh pecorino or caciocavallo is to cut the cheese into slices, heat it very gently for a few minutes in a frying pan with a little garlic and a sprinkling of vinegar and oregano until it softens, and then dip bread into it. They also fry the cheese and break an egg on top.

Pigs feed on acorns and prickly pears which give them a special flavour. There is a tradition on the island of making sausages for cooking, rather than the more usual salami for eating raw, but in Nicosia they make a curious salami by mixing rabbit with pork.

Sicilians are famous for preserving fruit. Their crystallized fruit actually taste of the fruit. At Macchia di Giarre, at the foot of Mount Etna, they make marvellous cherries preserved in alcohol; at Caltagirone and Piazza Armerina they are known for their delicious perfumed quince paste.

The fishing industry is most important and ports specialize, Messina in swordfish, Trapani in tuna fishing. The *mattanza del tonno* is when the tuna is fished in great nets. About eighty men are employed for six months to do it. The method is supposed to give a better flavour. There is also a preserving industry: swordfish is dried, anchovies and sardines are preserved in salt, tuna in oil. Tuna roe is dried and pressed to make the highly prized delicacy *bottarga*. Fish is one of the glories of Sicilian cooking.

178

The cooking of Sicily is the most exuberant and colourful in Italy. On the whole you will find the same dishes all around the island but there are different versions in every town. The west coast is more oriental and exotic, with perfumes and spices, orange juice, sweet and sour flavours, and raisins and pine nuts everywhere. The region of Trapani, the one closest to Africa, specializes in *cuscusu*, a variant of the famous North African dish. A peppery fish couscous is the most famous one. On the east coast they are more restrained in their tastes and prefer to use only herbs.

Pasta came to Sicily with the Arabs (there is still a very thin type called by its old Arab name, *itriya*), acquired its best known shapes here and marched north, eventually taking the place of rice and polenta to become the national staple. Sicilian pasta is the dry kind made of the local hard wheat and water. *Pasta lunga* (spaghetti and macaroni) is preferred and little rings called anelletti. They make several kinds by hand including egg tagliatelle from the north.

There is a saying, '*cambia sempre come la salsa*' (changing always like the sauce), because the variety of sauces is so great. Most are incredibly simple examples of just how attractive *cucina povera* can be. Peasants fed themselves entirely on pasta so it had to be good, and they put in what they could. Typical sauces are made with almost every vegetable and with seafood – with black cuttlefish ink, with clams, mussels and prawns and with newly-born fish so small they look like a lump of jelly. These can be sardines, red mullet and other fish. Fishing them is forbidden most of the year (the fishermen use special nets) but they always seem to be about.

Although *antipasti* are not in the Sicilian tradition (Sicilians ignore them and can't wait for the pasta), restaurants serve a huge array, starting with simple things like very fresh ricotta, anchovies marinated in oil and lemon with garlic and hot red pepper, marinated caciocavallo or canestrato cheese, crushed green olives flavoured with mint, fennel and garlic, and *bottarga* cut into slices and eaten on bread with a squeeze of lemon.

There were rice fields in Trapani during Arab times, but they stopped cultivating the grain when the island became too dry (there were once several rivers running across it). There are still a few rice dishes. The most famous, orange-shaped, *arancini di riso* belong to the street, to the realm of the *friggitori* who fry all kinds of things; the beloved *panelle* like fat chips made with chickpea flour, *cazzilli*, potato croquettes, vegetable fritters, and aubergines cut into slices held together at one end called *quaglie* because they look like multiwinged quails.

Vegetables are more important here than anywhere else in Italy because for centuries they constituted the meal. Aubergines are special favourites. Introduced by the Arabs, they went out of favour when the Arabs left and were considered poisonous until the Renaissance when Carmelite monks, who had eaten them in their monasteries in the east, brought them back into favour. They say they have a hundred ways of doing them and as many for peppers.

Artichokes are very popular; an unusual variety with thorny leaves has a most delicious flavour. The most common way of dealing with vegetables such as aubergines, peppers, artichokes and pumpkin is to roast them over a charcoal fire and serve them with a sprinkling of olive oil, chopped garlic and parsley. Another is to cook them in a sweet and sour sauce, made with vinegar and sugar and a touch of mint, and to serve them cold.

Despite the changes since the boom years of the Sixties, despite the fascination after the war with grilled meat and salads and with frozen foods, and despite the attraction of fast foods for the young, traditional cooking has survived in the home. Food is tied to the rituals of life. Apart from Christmas, the New Year, Easter, the Day of the Dead and the Carnival, there is always a religious feast, a holy day, a saint's day and celebrations to commemorate a historical event, the arrival of the seasons and ancient superstitions and magic. And there is special food and always a pastry attached to each one of those days.

In the early Middle Ages cake-making was an accomplishment of nuns and they are still made by them today. Several monasteries all over Sicily and particularly in Palermo became famous for their sweetmeats.

Cloistered nuns are all old now and their eyes are not good enough for embroidery, which was another of their activities, but they can still make pastries and crystallized fruits and the marzipan sweets with extraordinary shapes and riotous colours. The almond paste differs according to the proportion of sugar and bitter almonds used and by the flavouring – lemon, cinnamon, orange or lemon zest and flower essence – and the sisters sometimes stuff it with 'secret recipe' jam. I was told that because nuns are not supposed to enjoy themselves too much some of their pastries have names like *brutti ma buoni* (ugly but good), *ossa di morti* (dead men's bones) and *sospiri* (sighs).

Sicily is famous for her *granite* and *sorbetti* (they are *sciarbat*, the Arab word for sorbets, in dialect). There is still talk of the way the Arabs fetched snow from Mount Etna to make them, and the habit of mixing sugar and jasmine essence in a glass full of snow goes back to those times. Sicilians became the great masters of the art of ice-cream making before anyone else in Europe and it was a Sicilian, Procopio Coltelli, who opened the Café Procope in Paris in 1686 which served ice-creams for the first time in France.

CARCIOFI ALLE MANDORLE

Artichoke hearts with almond sauce

I discovered several new artichoke dishes on my last Sicilian trip, including pasta with artichokes, and artichoke bottoms stuffed with sausage meat, raisins and pine nuts. Sicily has many different kinds of artichokes, including a mauve one with thorny leaves, and wild ones. In some varieties the leaves are so tender they can be eaten entirely.

Serves 6

6 artichokes
Salt
½ an onion, grated
1 clove garlic, crushed
3 anchovies, chopped
100g (3½oz) ground almonds
300ml (½ pint) light chicken stock
4 tablespoons olive oil
1 tablespoon vinegar
1 tablespoon sugar
Juice of 1 lemon
White pepper
2 tablespoons capers, chopped (optional)
2 small pickled gherkins, chopped
(optional)

With a sharp knife cut the artichokes across, about a finger above the base, then cut off the stems and trim the base. Throw away the top of the leaves. Boil the artichoke hearts and stems in salted water for about 30 minutes until the leaves pull off easily, then drain. Remove as many layers of what is left of the outer leaves as are not entirely edible and, with a pointed spoon, remove the choke from the middle. If the stems are really tender (they are often stringy and inedible), peel them and keep them for a soup or salad.

For the sauce, fry the onion till gold, then the garlic. Add the anchovies and let them melt, then add the almonds, pour in the stock, and simmer for about 15 minutes until thick and creamy. Beat in the oil, vinegar, sugar and lemon and a little salt and pepper, adjusting the quantities to taste.

Arrange the artichoke hearts on individual plates, pour the sauce over them and garnish with capers and pickled gherkins. Serve cold.

CAPONATA

Sweet and sour aubergine salad

This is made in large quantities by most families and kept in clay pots as a ready antipasto, or an accompaniment to cold meats and fish. Some people add a little bitter cocoa to the sauce.

Serves 4

4 medium aubergines, cut into cubes
Olive oil
1 onion, sliced
5 tomatoes, skinned and chopped
Salt and pepper
1 tablespoon capers
50g (2oz) green olives, pitted
3 celery sticks, cut into 3cm (½in) pieces
4 tablespoons wine vinegar
1 tablespoon sugar

Salt the aubergines and let the juices degorge for half an hour. Then rinse, dry and fry in hot olive oil until brown and tender. Drain on absorbent paper. Fry the onion in a little oil until golden, add tomatoes, salt and pepper and simmer for 15 minutes. Blanch the capers, olives and celery, drain, then add to the tomato sauce with the vinegar and sugar. Simmer for about 15 minutes until reduced a little, stirring occasionally, then mix with the cold aubergines. Leave to stand for at least 30 minutes.

NOTE Serve garnished, if you like, with chopped almonds and parsley.

PEPERONI RIPIENI DI RISO

Peppers stuffed with rice

Stuffed vegetables are almost a symbol of the Mediterranean, Arab in origin and infinitely varied. In Sicily they stuff aubergines, tomatoes and peppers and, though fillings vary, the base is usually breadcrumbs or rice.

Serves 4

6 small peppers (red, yellow or green)
1 onion, chopped
3 tablespoons olive oil
250g (½lb) Italian (risotto) rice
500g (1lb) tomatoes, peeled and chopped
Salt and pepper
1 teaspoon sugar
Good bunch of parsley, finely chopped
Bunch of mint, finely chopped

Cut a slice off the stem end of the peppers. Keep these 'lids' and remove the seeds.

For the filling fry the onion in 2 tablespoons of oil till golden, add the rice and stir until it becomes transparent. Add the tomatoes, season with salt, pepper and sugar, and cook, moistening with 4 or 5 tablespoons of water, for about 20 minutes until the rice is only slightly underdone. Stir in the herbs and fill the peppers with the rice mixture. Cover with their lids and pack into an oven dish.

Pour the rest of the oil and about a finger of water in the bottom of the dish, cover with foil and bake in a 200°C (400°F, gas mark 6) oven for 30 minutes or until they are tender. They are best served cold.

VARIATION You may like a stronger tasting filling with finely chopped olives (black or green), capers (with their vinegar squeezed out), a good pinch of hot chilli pepper and the juice of 1 lemon.

ARANCINI DI RISU E RICOTTA

Rice balls with cheese

You find these, the size of a small orange (*arancini* means little oranges) at the old-fashioned *friggitori* and at the *tavole calde* or modern fast food establishments. Tiny ones are prepared at home as party food to pass around. Some are mixed or stuffed with meat sauce and green peas, and sometimes the rice is cooked with saffron. This simple version with cheese (sometimes peas and ham go in) often features as part of a vegetable *fritto misto* throughout southern Italy.

Serves 6 as a starter

150g (5oz) Italian short-grain rice
Salt
100g (3½oz) ricotta, mashed
25g (1oz) grated pecorino or parmesan
3 eggs
Good bunch of parsley, finely chopped
Salt and pepper
Pinch of nutmeg
100g (3½oz) fresh tuma cheese or mozzarella, chopped
Flour
Fine breadcrumbs
Oil for frying

Boil the rice in ¾ litre (1¼ pints) of salted water for about 17 minutes until tender. Let it cool and dry out for a few minutes on a large plate. Then turn into a bowl and mix in the ricotta, grated pecorino or parmesan, 2 eggs and parsley, and season generously with salt, pepper and nutmeg. Work well until the mixture sticks together like a paste then work in the chopped tuma or mozzarella.

Wash your hands and wet them to shape the rice into small walnut-sized balls. Roll in flour, then in the remaining beaten egg and lastly in fine breadcrumbs. Deep-fry in medium hot oil till golden. The oil should not be too hot as the *arancini* must be in for 5

182

minutes to allow the cheese to melt and they could brown too quickly. Drain on absorbent paper. You can heat through in the oven when you are ready to serve.

VARIATIONS A little powdered saffron can go into the water where the rice is boiling. Chopped fresh mint gives the *arancini* a lovely fresh taste and gorgonzola (though not a southern cheese) makes a good alternative to tuma or mozzarella.

PANE CON LE OLIVE E CON LA SALSICCIA

Bread with olives and sausage

Large braided loaves covered with sesame seeds (the kind you find here in Greek shops) are typically Sicilian. In the small towns and villages, little bakeries bake bread which people make themselves, and there are some which contain bits of olives, cheese, salami, herbs and even vegetables which constitute a snack. This one is a speciality of Agrigento.

750g (1½lb) strong flour
1 rounded teaspoon salt
5 tablespoons olive oil
25g (1oz) fresh yeast or 1 sachet active (easy blend) dried yeast
Pinch of sugar (optional)
450ml (¾ pint) water
200g (7oz) black olives, stoned and chopped
200g (7oz) fresh soft salami, diced
Sprig of rosemary, chopped

Mix the flour, salt and 4 tablespoons of oil together in a bowl. If you are using fresh yeast, dissolve with the sugar in a little of the measured warmed water and leave to froth for about 15 minutes. Then mix into the flour mixture and add enough of the remaining water to make a stiff sticky dough. (If you are using dried yeast mix with the flour before adding water or follow the manufacturer's instructions.) Knead for about 10 minutes or until the dough is smooth and elastic, adding a little water or flour if necessary.

Put the remaining oil in a bowl, turn the dough in it to prevent a crust forming, and leave to rise in a warm place covered with a damp cloth, for 1–2 hours or until the dough doubles in bulk. Then punch it down and knead again, and divide it into four. Share the olive and salami and the rosemary between each and work them well into the dough. Make 4 balls, place them on an oiled baking tray and allow them to rise again to almost double their bulk. Bake in a preheated 200°C (400°F, gas mark 6) oven for about 45 minutes or until the loaves sound hollow when tapped.

INSALATA DI TONNO E PATATE

Tuna and potato salad

Serves 6

650g (1¼lb) potatoes, boiled, peeled and thickly sliced
250g (½lb) tinned tuna, broken into pieces
2 hard boiled eggs, quartered
1–2 tablespoon capers, chopped
50g (2oz) anchovy fillets, chopped
4 pickled gherkins, chopped
Handful of black olives, pitted and chopped
Juice of 1 lemon
Salt and pepper
4–5 tablespoons olive oil

Put all the ingredients in a serving bowl together and mix well.

VERMICELLI ALLA SIRACUSANA

Vermicelli with peppers, tomatoes and aubergines

Serves 4

1 largish aubergine, cubed
Salt
1–2 fleshy yellow peppers
3 tablespoons olive oil or more if needed
1 clove garlic
2 anchovies, finely chopped
4–5 tomatoes, peeled and chopped
Pepper
8 black olives, pitted and cut into pieces
1 tablespoon capers, their vinegar squeezed out and chopped
Small bunch of basil, chopped
400g (14oz) vermicelli
Grated caciocavallo or pecorino cheese (optional)

Sprinkle the aubergine cubes with salt, and let the juices run out for an hour, then rinse and dry them. Roast the pepper by turning it under the grill until the skin is brown and blistered. Put it in a polythene bag, close it, and after about 10 minutes peel it (putting it in the bag makes it easier). Remove the seeds and cut the pepper into ribbons.

In a large pan fry the aubergine cubes in oil turning to brown them all over. Add the garlic, and when the aroma rises, the anchovies, then the tomatoes. Season with salt and pepper and simmer about 15 minutes until the aubergines are tender. Then add the olives, capers, basil and the yellow pepper, and cook a minute longer.

Boil the vermicelli in plenty of salted boiling water till cooked *al dente*, drain and serve topped with the sauce and pass the grated cheese around.

PASTA A PICCHI PACCHI

Pasta with raw tomato sauce

I first had this splendid pasta – a relatively new one – at a restaurant called PG in Trapani where a whole football team ordered what sounded like *pik pak*. No one can explain where the name comes from and it is sometimes called *pasta al pesto* because some of the ingredients are pounded with a pestle and mortar.

All the sauce ingredients are raw. Everyone explains them differently: sometimes there is very little tomato; sometimes there are no almonds and sometimes they are toasted; various other herbs can join basil in the *pesto*, and opinions are divided as to whether you should add grated cheese.

Serves 4

1kg (2lb) tomatoes, peeled, chopped and well drained
4 tablespoons olive oil
50g (2oz) blanched almonds, very finely chopped or pounded (not ground almonds)
2–3 cloves of garlic, crushed
Good bunch of basil, chopped or pounded
Salt and pepper
1 teaspoon sugar (optional)
½ a small chilli, finely chopped, or a pinch of chilli powder (optional)
400g (14oz) spaghetti or bucatini
Grated pecorino or caciocavallo cheese (optional)

Prepare the sauce: put all the ingredients except the pasta and cheese in a bowl to macerate, covered, for an hour at least so that the flavours have time to infuse (pounding extracts more of the basil's fragrance).

Cook the pasta *al dente* in boiling salted water, drain quickly and dress with the raw sauce (which should be at room temperature). Many, as I do, prefer to eat this without cheese.

PASTA CON LE ZUCCHINE E LE MELANZANE

Pasta with tomato sauce served with courgettes and aubergines

There are many pasta dishes with aubergines and courgettes. In Palermo I was offered a plate with two small, whole deep-fried aubergines sitting on top. They were cut into slices, but not right through, so they remained attached at one end and opened out like fans (they call them 'quails' because they look like multi-winged birds). I also had spaghetti topped with courgettes cut into little sticks and fried. A famous speciality of Catania, *pasta alla Norma*, has aubergine cubes mixed into a tomato sauce. But the following way of serving both vegetables in an accompanying plate is the popular one of the moment.

Serves 4

*2 large aubergines, cut in half lengthways
and sliced thin (into half-moons)
6 courgettes, sliced thin lengthways
Salt
1 onion, chopped
Olive oil
750g (1½lb) tomatoes, peeled and chopped
2 cloves garlic, finely chopped
½ a small chilli pepper, finely chopped
(optional)
Pepper
½ teaspoon sugar
Good bunch of basil, chopped
400g (14oz) spaghetti*

Sprinkle the aubergines and courgettes with salt and leave them for an hour to drain.

Make a tomato sauce: fry the onion in 2 tablespoons of oil till soft, then add the tomatoes and garlic; season with salt, pepper and sugar, and cook for about 25 minutes until the sauce has reduced to a thick consistency, adding the basil towards the end.

Press the aubergines between two plates to squeeze out as much juice as possible. Rinse and dry the aubergines and courgettes. Then deep-fry quickly in hot oil till lightly browned and tender and drain on absorbent paper. Arrange on a flat heat-resistant dish and heat through in the oven before serving.

Boil the pasta in plenty of salted boiling water until *al dente*, then drain quickly and dress with the tomato sauce. Present the vegetable slices separately.

NOTE You can sprinkle the courgettes and aubergines with flour and shake them in a colander before frying.

DITALI COI BROCCOLI

Pasta with broccoli

Serves 4–6

*700g (1½lb) broccoli, or 1 large cauliflower
Salt
350g (12oz) ditali (short macaroni)
4 tablespoons olive oil
1 clove garlic, finely chopped
8–10 anchovy fillets, chopped
125g (4oz) green olives
1 red chilli pepper, finely chopped
(optional)
6 tablespoons freshly toasted breadcrumbs*

Trim and cut the broccoli or cauliflower into florets. Boil in plenty of salted water until tender and drain, reserving the cooking water. Use the water to cook the pasta in for 10–12 minutes.

Heat the oil with the garlic in a small pan until the aroma rises, then add the anchovies and mash them well. When the pasta is *al dente*, drain and mix quickly with the anchovy sauce, adding a little more olive oil if you like. Add the olives, pitted if you prefer, broccoli or cauliflower and chilli pepper and serve sprinkled with breadcrumbs.

PASTA CON LE SARDE

Pasta with sardines

This is the most typical of Sicilian pasta dishes. The wild fennel leaves, which lend a distinctive flavour, can be substituted here with cultivated fennel leaves.

Serves 6

12–14 fresh sardines
Salt
1 medium onion, chopped
Olive oil
Good bunch green fennel leaves, chopped
50g (2oz) pine nuts
25g (1oz) raisins, soaked in water
Flour
500g (1lb) spaghetti
6 tablespoons fine breadcrumbs, toasted

Scale, clean and bone the sardines and remove the heads. Open them out flat. Wash and salt them.

Fry the onion in two tablespoons of oil until golden, then add the fennel and cook gently. Add the drained raisins and pine nuts and cook through.

Flour the sardines lightly and deep-fry in oil. Boil the spaghetti until just tender (10–12 minutes) and drain quickly. Mix the spaghetti with the fennel mixture and add a spoonful or two of raw olive oil if you like and one or two of pasta water. Arrange the sardines on top.

Pass the breadcrumbs round for everyone to sprinkle some on. (Breadcrumbs were known as 'the poor man's parmesan' and were sprinkled over pasta by the poor, who could not afford the real thing.)

RISU E MILINCIANI 'A PALERMITANA

Aubergine and rice mould

Rice is not an everyday dish in Sicily as it is in the Veneto, Lombardy and Piedmont. Apart from the little *arancini*, it is a festive dish reserved for special occasions. It is often said that although the unification of Italy meant a conquering of the south by the north, in gastronomic matters the conquests went the other way – pasta and pizza went north but polenta and risottos were never adopted in the south. In the *Guida all'Italia Gastronomica*, Massimo Alberini and Giorgio Mistretta trace the southern aversion for rice to the First World War, when southern soldiers fighting in the trenches received disgusting rations of gluey rice and swore never to eat risotto.

But Sicily does have her own much-liked rice dishes. This one is a speciality of Palermo.

Serves 6 or more

2 large aubergines, sliced
Salt
Olive oil
2 medium onions, chopped
500g (1lb) tomatoes, peeled and chopped
Pepper
1 teaspoon sugar
Few sprigs of parsley, chopped
Small bunch of basil, chopped
250g (½lb) Italian short-grain risotto rice
About 1¾ litres (3 pints) light chicken stock
40g (1½oz) grated caciocavallo or salted dry ricotta

Sprinkle the aubergine slices with salt and leave for about an hour, then press between two plates to squeeze out as much of their juice as possible. Rinse and dry, then fry in hot olive oil, turning them over once, until tender and lightly browned. Lay them on a

33. Little tomatoes hanging up to dry remain juicy inside
34, 35. Maize is hung up to dry then it is ground into meal for polenta. Polenta, the poor food of the north, is now popular again there, and it is served in all the grand restaurants.

36 (overleaf). Boiled vegetables served with oil and lemon (p26), broad beans with goat's cheese (p143), the very popular rocket salad (p113), and focaccia (flat bread) with olives (p26)

37. Grape harvest in the Chianti hills
38. Relaxing after work in the vineyards
39. Friuli vineyards

40 (overleaf). A bowl of mixed berries, a fresh fruit tart with a delicately flavoured custard (p115), baked pears (p45), Florentine flat bread with grapes (p30)

41. Sicilian sweets: cassata Palermo style (p24), coffee granita with whipped cream (p24), and 'almond blossom' – an almond pastry (p190)

few sheets of absorbent paper with more paper on top and press gently to get rid of excess oil.

Make a tomato sauce: fry the onions in 2 tablespoons of oil till very soft and golden. Add the tomatoes, salt, pepper and sugar and simmer for 15 minutes till reduced, then take it off the heat and add the parsley and basil.

Now boil the rice in plenty of chicken stock for about 15 minutes, or until tender but still firm. Drain, throwing away the excess stock.

Line a round mould or heatproof bowl with the aubergine slices and fill with alternating layers of rice and tomato sauce with sprinklings of grated caciocavallo or salty ricotta. Bake covered with foil in a 200°C (400°F, gas mark 6) oven for about 25 minutes. Serve hot, turned out of the mould.

PESCE SPADA ALLA SICILIANA

Swordfish steaks in white wine with tomatoes

The Messinese are masters at cooking swordfish. This is one way they have of cooking the delicious firm-fleshed fish.

Serves 4

1 small onion, chopped
1 celery stalk, chopped
1 clove garlic, finely chopped
2 bay leaves
2 tablespoons olive oil
3 tomatoes, peeled and chopped
1 teaspoon sugar
About ½ pint or more dry white wine
Salt and pepper
2 slices of swordfish, skin removed

Fry the onion, celery and garlic and the bay leaf in 2 tablespoons olive oil till softened.

Add the tomatoes and a little sugar and cook, stirring, for 1 minute. Then pour in the wine, season with salt and pepper, simmer for 5 minutes and put in the swordfish. Poach for less than 10 minutes, until the flesh becomes opaque, turning the slices over once.

Serve hot or cold.

CALAMARI (O SEPPIE) IMBOTTITI

Stuffed squid or cuttlefish

Serves 4

8 medium or 16 tiny cuttlefish or squid
4 tablespoons olive oil
50g (2oz) fresh breadcrumbs
2 anchovies, finely chopped
Bunch of parsley, chopped
2 cloves garlic, crushed
Salt and pepper
5 tomatoes
200ml (7fl oz) dry white wine
1 teaspoon sugar (optional)

Clean the cuttlefish or squid (see page 207).

For the filling, mix the breadcrumbs with the chopped tentacles, anchovies, parsley and garlic, add salt and pepper and 2 tablespoons of oil, and moisten with a few drops of water to form a paste. Fill the cuttlefish or squid three-quarters full with this filling (they shrink and the filling expands when they are cooked so it will spill out if they are too full). One is usually advised to sew up the openings but I do not bother. Fry gently on all sides and remove. Make the sauce in the same pan – add the tomatoes and white wine, a little salt and sugar and cook 10 minutes. Then add the fish and simmer gently until tender, from 5 minutes if they are very small to 15–20 minutes if medium. Serve hot or cold, sprinkled with parsley.

SARDE A BECCAFICU

Stuffed sardines

Serves 6

900g (2lb) fresh sardines
1 medium onion, chopped
Olive oil
225g (8oz) fresh breadcrumbs
Good bunch of parsley
75–100g (3–4oz) pitted green olives,
chopped
50g (2oz) capers
Juice and zest of 1 orange and 1 lemon
Salt and pepper
12 bay leaves
1 lemon

Scale, gut and clean the sardines, split them open and remove the head and backbone. Fry the onion gently in three tablespoons of oil. When golden add breadcrumbs, parsley, olives and capers, moisten with orange and lemon juice, add the zest and season well. Place a spoonful on each sardine and roll up, starting from the neck.

Arrange in an oiled ovenproof dish, alternating each with a bay leaf. Sprinkle a little more oil and the juice of one lemon over the dish and bake, uncovered, at 180°C (350°F, gas mark 4) for 10–15 minutes. Serve hot or cold.

VARIATIONS from the Eastern part of Sicily: Omit the olives, capers and orange juice and add instead 2 tablespoons pine nuts, 2 tablespoons raisins and 6 finely chopped anchovies.

In Messina they use thin slices of swordfish instead of sardines and grill them.

COZZE AL LIMONE

Mussels with lemon

Serves 6

1kg (2lb) mussels
Juice of 1 lemon
100ml (4fl oz) or more olive oil
Salt and pepper
Bunch of parsley, finely chopped

Prepare the mussels as described on page 206. Remove the top part of the shell. Mix the rest of the ingredients. Pour a little into each half shell.

FRITTEDDA (O FRITELLA)

Braised vegetables

Serves 4

250g (9oz) spring onions, coarsely chopped
500g (18oz) fresh broad beans (before
podding)
500g (18oz) fresh peas (before podding)
4 artichoke hearts, quartered
Salt and pepper
About 4 tablespoons olive oil

Put all the vegetables in a pan with the oil and cook very gently for a few minutes. Season and add a ladleful of water and cook, stirring occasionally and adding a little more water now and then, for about 25 minutes or until vegetables are tender.

This is served alone as a first course or a side dish, as a soup with stock or as a sauce with pasta.

VARIATION This can be eaten cold, in which case a little lemon juice, sugar and a few leaves of mint are added during the cooking.

SCALOPPINI CU LA MARSALA

Veal escalopes with Marsala

Serves 4

---

4 × 175g (6oz) veal escalopes
Flour
50g (2oz) butter
1 tablespoon sunflower oil
1 glass dry Marsala
Salt and pepper

Coat the veal with flour and quickly fry in 25g (1oz) butter and the oil until brown. Add the Marsala, evaporate a little, then remove the meat from the pan, season and keep warm. Reduce the sauce, whisk in the remaining cold butter, cut into pieces, and pour over the veal.

You may omit the flour and use only oil without butter.

VARIATION Fillet of pork is cut into medallions and cooked in the same way.

FICATU ALL'AGRU E DUCI

Liver in sweet and sour sauce

This is from Paolo Cascino's book *Cucina di Sicilia*. He is considered the greatest cook in Sicily. Now he teaches at the hotel and catering school in Palermo, where students learn how to plan feasts of 30 and even 40 dishes.

Serves 4

700g (1½lb) calves' liver, thinly sliced
Sunflower oil
Salt and pepper
Breadcrumbs
3 cloves garlic, skinned and crushed
1 tablespoon sugar
3 tablespoons wine vinegar
1 teaspoon fresh mint, chopped

Season the liver and dip in breadcrumbs. Fry very quickly two to three minutes each side in oil, put on a plate and keep warm.

Fry the garlic and sugar in 2 tablespoons oil until golden, being careful they do not burn. When the sugar is caramelized, add the vinegar, let it evaporate and add the mint.

Pour over the liver and eat hot or cold.

CONIGLIO ALL'AGRODOLCE

Sweet and sour rabbit

Serves 4

---

1 onion, sliced
2–3 tablespoons olive or sunflower oil
1 young tender rabbit, cut into pieces
Flour
300ml (½ pint) red wine
1 bay leaf
Sprig of rosemary
1 tablespoon sugar
2 tablespoons white wine vinegar
2 tablespoons pine nuts, toasted
1 tablespoon raisins
2 tablespoons pitted and chopped green or black olives

Fry the onion in oil (I prefer using sunflower oil here) till soft and golden. Roll the rabbit pieces in flour and fry lightly, turning to brown them all over. Cover with red wine, add the bay leaf and rosemary, salt and pepper and simmer for 20 minutes. Add sugar and vinegar, the pine nuts, raisins and olives and raise the heat to evaporate the vinegar for a minute or two (its taste should not be too powerful).

FIOR DI MANDORLA

Almond blossom – a pastry

Most of the pastries in Sicily are Arab in origin and based on almonds. Angelo Lauria, pastry-maker of Licata near Agrigento, offers a huge and delicious range. These were my favourites.

Makes about 27

400g (14oz) ground almonds
200g (7oz) sugar
100g (3½oz) honey
1 teaspoon cinnamon
Zest of 1 lemon
2 egg whites
Icing sugar

Mix the ground almonds, sugar, honey, cinnamon and lemon zest and add only just enough egg white to make a soft firm paste (it is important not to add more than you need).

Start kneading the mixture when it is still dry, like damp sand, and the oil in the almond will help to hold it together.

Shape into little cakes about 5cm (2in) in diameter and place on greased foil on a baking tray. Bake in a pre-heated oven at 150°C (300°F, gas mark 2) for 20 minutes.

Let them cool, place on a serving plate and dust with icing sugar.

GRANITA AL MELONE

Melon granita

Sicily's ice-creams have conquered the world and they still have an enormous place in Sicilian life. They are made by pastry makers who also make confectionery, almond pastries and savoury pies. Curiously, many of these are of Swiss origin and they have added their own ways of making ice-cream with eggs and cream to the Sicilian classics like *cassata*

and granitas. There are always new flavours, new *bombe* and new styles – now ice-creams are stuffed into *brioches* for eating in the hand. But old favourites, like melon granita, remain, and people still make them at home.

Choose a sweet, perfumed and very ripe melon. This is the kind of sweet you should make to taste, adding the amount of sugar according to the sweetness of the melon.

2 ripe melons (preferably cantaloup) making
750ml (1¼ pints) pulp
65–75g (2½–3oz) sugar or more according
to taste
Juice of 1 lemon
1–3 teaspoons jasmine or orange-blossom
essence (optional)

Cut up the melon, peel it and remove the seeds. Blend the pulp to a liquid, adding sugar, lemon and flower essence if you like. Jasmine essence is hard to get (I have only found it in Sicily and Thailand) but orange-blossom water is available in oriental and Indian stores (you can use the larger quantity as it is sold here in diluted form).

Pour into an ice-cube tray, cover with cling-film and let it freeze hard. Just before serving turn the cubes to a light frothy ice-cream in a food processor or blend in advance and put the cream back in the freezer, covered, for serving later.

GRANITA AL CAFFE CON PANNA

Coffee granita

1 litre (1¾ pints) good strong black coffee
4 tablespoons sugar or to taste
300ml (½ pint) whipped cream (optional)

Dissolve the sugar in the coffee while it is still

hot (it is best made not too sweet). Let it cool then pour into ice cube trays. Cover with clingfilm and put in the freezer for several hours.

Just before serving take out the required amount of ice cubes and blend in a food processor to a soft or crunchy consistency. Serve in glasses, topped, if you like, with cream.

SEMIFREDDO ALLE MANDORLE O ALLE NOCCIOLE

Almond or hazelnut ice-cream

Antonio Tantillo, chef at the Charleston in Palermo, gave me this recipe.

Serves 6

100g (4oz) blanched almonds or hazelnuts
75g (3oz) granulated sugar
600ml (1 pint) double cream
2 eggs, separated
100g (3½oz) icing sugar
2 tablespoons maraschino

To make the praline: toast nuts lightly in a dry frying pan, shaking the pan. Add sugar and stir until melted and golden brown. Pour on to a lightly oiled tray and, when cool, break into pieces and blend for a few seconds to pulverize.

To make the ice-cream: beat the cream until thick. Beat the egg yolks with 25g (1oz) icing sugar until pale. Beat the whites until stiff, then add the rest of the icing sugar and beat until the mixture stands in stiff peaks. Fold the yolks into the cream, then fold in the meringue mixture and the praline and stir in the maraschino.

Line a mould with foil, spoon in the ice-cream, level and cover with foil. Freeze for 24 hours. Leave to stand for a few minutes before turning out.

CASSATA PALERMITANA

Cassata Palermo style

Confectioners cover this Sicilian classic with marzipan, fondant icing and baroque decorations. The icing given here is simpler.

300g (11oz) sponge cake, thinly sliced
3–4 tablespoons rum or Marsala (optional)
300g (11oz) ricotta
100g (4oz) caster sugar
Few drops vanilla essence
50g (2oz) candied fruit or pumpkin, chopped
50g (2oz) candied orange peel, chopped
50g (2oz) chopped or grated bitter chocolate
350g (12oz) icing sugar
Few drops pistachio green food colouring
200g (7oz) candied peel or glacé fruits

Line the sides and bottom of a 20cm (8in) mould with foil, then line with sponge cake, keeping some to cover the top. Sprinkle with half the rum or Marsala (if used).

Put the ricotta, caster sugar and vanilla through the blender. Stir in the pumpkin or candied fruit and the peel and chocolate. Spoon the mixture into the mould, cover with the remaining sponge slices and sprinkle with the rest of the alcohol. Cover with foil and press down well, then refrigerate a few hours.

Melt the icing sugar in a double saucepan with a drop or two of green colouring and a few tablespoons of water. Stir continuously with a wooden spoon and be careful it does not brown. Turn out the cassata and cover with the icing.

Decorate with mixed candied peel or glacé fruits and serve in very thin slices.

Sardinia

'It's a prehistoric dish,' explained the owner of a small restaurant at Cabras near Oristano, referring to a grey mullet preserved with a herb from the *laguna*. I had arrived through a landscape dotted with the remains of cone-shaped towers (the *nuraghi*) dating from 1200 BC and the menu in Sardinian, which sounds like Latin, reinforced the sensation of the remote past. But the development of luxury hotels, villas and yachting basins on the Sardinian coast has brought a mushrooming of restaurants which offer what they think tourists want. The first seafood restaurant opened in Cagliari twenty years ago; now there are two hundred there. They claim that the inspiration for the new cooking of the sea came from local fishermen.

Sardinians are people of the interior. They hate the sea and they don't like fish. Those who live on the coast are from outside or of mixed ethnic ancestry. Fishermen are Genoese, Neapolitan, Sicilian (they have taken over tuna fishing), Arab and Catalan (they still speak thirteenth-century Catalan). Their influence can be detected in the dishes and cooking terms: *burrida* and *ciuppin* are Genoese for fish stew, *scabeccio* is Spanish and a Neapolitan fish soup has a Spanish name, *cassola*, derived from the pot. The result is a very varied list of fish and seafood, simply cooked and delicious.

Sardinia had many foreign invaders and conquerors, starting with the Phoenicians, Carthaginians and Romans. They stayed on the coast while the Sardinians retreated into the interior, and they left few traces in the kitchen. *Fregula*, semolina granules made by moistening the grain and rolling it gently with the fingertips, which go into fish soups, are supposed to have been introduced by the Romans. The Byzantines introduced ways of making cheese. The Arabs brought rice, milk puddings and almond pastries. Spanish domination lasted four centuries and peopled Alghero with Catalans. Saffron, meat pies (*empanadas*), and the mixed meat stew *lepudrida* (in Spanish *olla podrida*) are part of the Hispanic heritage.

192

Italian civilization (and dishes) came for the first time since the Romans with the Pisans and Genoese in the eleventh century. The two struggled for control of the island until the arrival of the Spaniards in the fourteenth century. Cagliari became the centre of Pisan power in the south-west (where you can still hear medieval Tuscan) and Sassari became the bastion of Genoese influence in the north-west. Prominent Pisan and Genoese families married into the native aristocracy. The merchant classes flourished. Monks settled from Italy and developed agriculture.

In the eighteenth century Sardinia was acquired by the House of Savoy and the Duke of Savoy became the King of Sardinia. The bonds between Sardinia and Piedmont became close when the court of Savoy, driven from Turin by Napoleon, found refuge in Cagliari in 1799. They introduced stuffed pasta – their *agnolotti*, which were transformed into *culingiones* and *angiolottus*. The King of Sardinia, Vittorio Emanuele II, became the first king of Italy in 1861. But Sardinia remained isolated from the mainland and her regional cooking is the most distinctive in Italy. The true Sardinia, the mountains and the forests and the silent lonely life of the shepherd, has not changed much in spite of television and industrialization, road-building and marinas. Hidden in remote villages where life seems to have stopped a hundred years ago, people have clung to their old traditions, many of which are of extreme antiquity, and their cooking reflects their simple and archaic way of life.

There are shepherd villages and peasant villages but every family produces its own olive oil (trees grow wild) and wine (mostly sweet wine for festive occasions) and *acquavite*, and grows its own vegetables. The main industrial crop of the island is durum wheat, and there is fruit. The climate is very hot and dry and winds tear at the land which makes it difficult for cultivators. Every family kills a pig or two and makes cured ham and sausages. The Sardinian diet is based on meat (mainly lamb and pork) including game (wild boar, hare, partridge), cheese and bread. The flesh of the animals has a delicate flavour derived from the wild herbs and berries tangled in the scrub which covers the mountains. The most typical food is suckling pig (*porceddu*) roasted in the open until the crust is brown and crackling. Baby lamb or kid and wild boar are done in the same way. Salt is the only seasoning; the flavour comes from the burning wood (juniper, holm oak, myrtle and vine) and from the branch which serves as a spit, traditionally stuck upright into the ground. At the end, the roast may be wrapped in myrtle leaves and wild herbs so that their perfume permeates the meat. Another way, laying the meat over heated stones in a pit lined with myrtle, rosemary, thyme and other herbs, with a fire burning on top, is still used by hunters to cook wild boar to melting tenderness, and was originally how animal thieves and poachers hid their booty while it cooked.

Myrtle leaves are a favourite flavouring. According to legend the plant was brought by the Jews (who used it for ritual purposes) when they were deported to the island by the Roman emperor Tiberius. A delicacy is boiled chicken or birds left in a bag with the leaves for at least a day until the perfume is absorbed.

Cheese is still made by shepherds in their sheepfolds in the hills. They make dozens of different kinds. Soft and fresh, they are used for cooking – for making soups and in pies and savouries. Pecorino, a mature, hard cheese which can be used for grating, is one of Italy's most popular and is exported all over the world. Several types of ricotta include salted, fermented and baked ones. One of the best cheeses I have ever eaten is *casumarzu*, which means 'rotten cheese'.

The most typical Sardinian bread is the crisp paper-thin *pani carasau* made in large round sheets and called *carta di musica* by mainland Italians because of the noise it makes when you eat it. It keeps well and shepherds have always taken it with them when they spend months away from the village, wandering with their flocks from highland to lowland pasturage. (Now most are motorized and can go home for the night.) Brushed with oil, baked again and eaten hot, it becomes delicious *mazzamuru*. Softened in water, it is layered or rolled up like lasagne or cannelloni to make *pani fratau* with tomato or meat sauce filling and topped with grated cheese and a poached egg.

Every village has its own special breads (there are supposed to be 500 types) and its own biscuits and cakes. On festive occasions villagers work their breads into fine lacy, sculptured designs featuring leaves and flowers and little birds or animals. Some motifs have ancient religious and magical significance. In this religious and superstitious land, every saint's day, holy day and pagan event is a festive occasion and sweets are part of the celebrations.

Crowded in little towns and villages (it was once for protection from brigands), in clans of relatives (they all have the same names), with a powerful communal spirit, isolated from their neighbours with little contact and perpetually feuding, Sardinians have preserved their individual cultures (including banditry and vendetta), their local dialects and their dishes. That is why, although it is simple, the cooking is extraordinarily rich in regional specialities. 'If a village grows potatoes,' I was told, 'they have a hundred ways of preparing them. Sardinian food is poor food because many live at subsistence level. But can roast meat served with raw tender artichokes and fennel dipped in vinaigrette, stews with wine and herbs, pasta dough mixed with saffron, plates of wild mushrooms and asparagus be called poor food?

I don't know if it is because Sardinians are unbelievably generous and hospitable and their land so beautiful, or because their food evokes the simple life or the remote past, or because it is simply so good, but it provokes strong emotion of the kind you never forget.

CULINGIONES

Cheese ravioli

Natalina Laconi and her sister make these beautifully crafted little ravioli at their restaurant Su Meriagu at Quartu Sant Andrea, Cagliari, with a variety of different fillings (including mashed potatoes or spinach).

Serves 4

Fresh egg pasta, see page 84
600g (1lb 6oz) fresh pecorino or
well-drained mashed cottage cheese
2 eggs
Bunch of mint, finely chopped
Salt and pepper
Zest of half an orange (optional)
Grated nutmeg (optional)
½ packet saffron powder dissolved in a
drop of hot water (optional)
2 tablespoons or more melted butter
Grated pecorino

Mix the cheese, eggs, mint, salt and pepper, zest, nutmeg and saffron in a bowl. Roll out the dough to a thin sheet on a lightly floured surface. Cut into 6.5cm (2½in) rounds with a pastry cutter. Put a heaped teaspoonful of filling in the centre (a little to one side) of the rounds. Fold over to make a half-moon shape then pinch the edges together and twist to make a tight, festooned edge. Boil the ravioli in plenty of boiling salted water for five minutes and drain as soon as they are done. Coat with butter and serve with grated pecorino cheese, or with fresh tomato sauce and grated cheese (see page 150).

PASTA CON FRUTTI DI MARE

Seafood pasta

Serves 6

1kg (2lb) mussels or clams
4 scallops (optional)
250g (½lb) small squid or cuttlefish
250g (½lb) scampi or prawns
3 cloves garlic, finely chopped
3 tablespoons olive oil
1 hot red chilli, fresh or dried, finely
chopped or crumbled or a pinch of powder
(optional)
4 tomatoes, peeled and chopped (optional)
300ml (½ pint) dry white wine
Salt and pepper
Bunch of parsley, finely chopped
600g (1¼lb) spaghettini, tagliolini (thin
noodles) or tagliatelle

Clean the shellfish and steam them open (see page 206). When they are cool take them out of their shells and filter the remaining liquid in the pan (keep it for the sauce). Cut the scallops into 2–4 pieces. Clean the squid and cuttlefish (see page 207) and cut the bodies into rounds. Shell the prawns.

Fry the garlic in oil till it just begins to colour. Add chilli and tomatoes if you like, the liquid from the shells and the wine. Season with salt and pepper and simmer for 10 minutes to reduce a little. Then add the squid and prawns and cook a few minutes only until the prawns turn pink and the squid turns opaque. Add the mussels or clams and scallops and the parsley and heat through when the pasta is ready to serve.

Cook the pasta in plenty of boiling salted water until *al dente* and serve with the sauce.

VARIATION A pinch of saffron occasionally gets into the sauce.

In Venice at Cipriani's they make a shellfish sauce with champagne and add cream.

PASTA CON SUGO DI LEPRE

Pasta with hare stew

A similar sauce for pasta is made in several regions; in Sardinia hare is still plentiful.

Serves 4–6

50g (2oz) streaky bacon, rinded and chopped
4 tablespoons olive oil
1 small hare, cut into pieces
2 medium onions, peeled and sliced
2 cloves garlic, peeled and crushed
1–2 tablespoons flour
1 bottle of red wine
Salt and pepper
3 cloves
1 teaspoon cinnamon
Sprigs of rosemary or thyme
500g (1lb) spaghetti
Grated pecorino cheese

Fry the bacon in oil, add the pieces of hare and turn, to brown them all over. Remove from the pan and gently fry onion and garlic until soft. Stir in the flour and add the wine. Return the hare pieces, add salt and pepper, the cloves, cinnamon and rosemary or thyme and simmer for one hour, stirring occasionally. Finish the cooking on a high flame if necessary to reduce the sauce. Cook the spaghetti in plenty of salted boiling water until *al dente*, strain and dress with the hare stew and pecorino cheese.

NOTE The hare can also be lifted from the sauce, which is then served with the pasta as a first course, and the hare served separately.

GAMBERONI IN TEGAME

Fried king prawns

Serves 4

500g (1lb) giant uncooked prawns (frozen ones will do)
2 cloves garlic, crushed
½ small chilli pepper, chopped (optional)
4 tablespoons olive oil
Salt
Bunch of parsley, finely chopped
About 4 tablespoons acquavite or grappa

Wash the prawns and remove the heads and little legs. Fry them quickly with the garlic and chilli pepper in the oil for a few minutes until they turn pink. Sprinkle with salt and parsley. Just before serving, pour in the acquavite or grappa and set it alight.

AGNELLO CON OLIVE

Lamb with olives

Lamb with olives is a very Mediterranean combination. The wine, garlic and hot pepper give it a Sardinian touch.

Serves six

1.4kg (2½lb) lamb, leg or fillet, cut into 2.5cm (1in) cubes
4–5 tablespoons olive oil
2 medium onions
½–1 fresh red chilli (seeds removed), or a good pinch chilli powder
1 clove garlic, peeled and chopped
100ml (4fl oz) or more red or dry white wine
175–225g (6–8oz) richly flavoured black olives
Salt

Cook the lamb in a pan in two to three table-spoons of oil on a medium flame until brown. Remove from the pan. Chop the onions, chilli and garlic in a food processor to a very fine pulp and add it to the pan with a little more oil.

Cook, stirring, until golden brown, add the wine, stir and increase the flame to let it evaporate. Then reduce the flame to the lowest possible and add the olives and lamb.

Season, cover and cook, adding water or more wine if it becomes too dry. It needs about 40 to 60 minutes for the meat to be very tender and suffused with the sauce.

SEBADAS

Fried pastries with cheese and honey

This is the most popular sweet in Sardinia. The combination of pastry, hot melting cheese and honey is most appealing.

For the pastry

500g (1lb) strong flour
4 eggs
Pinch salt
50g (2oz) butter (softened)

For the filling

500g (1lb) mozzarella, cut into small cubes
500g (1lb) ricotta or cottage cheese
Grated rind of 2 large oranges

1 egg white or yolk (optional)
Vegetable oil for frying
225g (8oz) honey, to serve

Mix the flour with the eggs and salt and knead well before adding the butter a little at a time so that it is absorbed thoroughly. Knead well to a soft elastic dough, adding a little water if necessary: it should be firm but not sticky. Roll out the pastry thinly and cut out 10cm (4in) circles.

For the filling blend the cheeses and orange rind. Put two teaspoons in the centre of half the pastry rounds and put the remaining rounds on top as lids. Seal the edges well: it is much easier to do this if you moisten round the borders of the pastry bottoms with water or egg white or yolk, using your finger.

Fill a large pan with oil and deep-fry the pastries over a medium heat, two at a time, taking care they do not brown. They only take a few minutes. Serve immediately and pass round clear honey (warmed if you like) for everyone to help themselves. In Sardinia, they sometimes use melted bitter honey.

DOLCE DI RICOTTA

Ricotta pudding

This is a little different to the Roman cake made with ricotta.

Serves 6

100g (4oz) almonds, finely chopped
Two bitter almonds or a few drops of
almond essence
300g (11oz) fresh ricotta
300g (11oz) good scented honey
3 eggs
Butter to grease the dish
2 tablespoons breadcrumbs
Juice of 1 orange

Put the ricotta through the blender, then add the almonds, almond essence, 200g (7oz) of the honey and the eggs.

Grease a flan dish with butter and dust with breadcrumbs, then pour in the ricotta mix-ture. Bake at 200°C (400°F, gas mark 6) for about 45 minutes or until firm and the top is golden. Turn out. Beat the orange juice into the remaining honey and pour over.

Serve cold. It is even better the next day.

Planning a Meal

I have grouped the recipes by region, but you are meant to pick from all over when you plan a meal. To make it easier for you to choose, the dishes are listed here in sequence, but bear in mind that they are flexible. Many *antipasti* make a perfect second course or a side dish or they can be part of a buffet, and many dishes can be served on their own as a meal in itself.

A formal meal in Italy is a succession of courses, with no main course, starting with an hors d'oeuvre or appetiser (*antipasto*), followed by a first course (*primo*) of either pasta, risotto or soup, and a second course (*secondo*) of meat, poultry or fish, accompanied by one or two vegetable side dishes (*contorni*). Then there is salad (*insalata*), sometimes cheese, and the meal ends with fruit or dessert (*dolce*).

Antipasti used not to play an important part in Italian eating. Not long ago they would consist only of a few slices of cured meat or salami, and these are still the favourites. *Antipasti* are meant only to whet the appetite, so do not make too much. For most people in Italy the first course is the most important, and pasta is the favourite food. Although most favour the simplest treatment – olive oil and garlic with fresh raw tomato and basil or a dressing of butter melted with sage leaves, sprinkled with freshly grated black pepper and parmesan, the versatility of pasta is extraordinary. Risotti and other rice dishes, gnocchi and canederli (bread dumplings) are also versatile. Soups can be a meal in themselves or light and delicate.

With so much coast, Italy has a wide range of fish and seafood. Until recently fish was considered to be a Friday dish only, and not grand enough to serve to guests, but now it is one of the most popular foods.

Meat and poultry dishes are mostly grills, roasts and stews; there are lovely game dishes and offal is particularly good. Egg or vegetable dishes can also be served as a second course. Vegetable dishes are an important part of every meal so make good use of the repertoire. Salad can be green leaves or boiled vegetables dressed with olive oil and lemon juice. Then cheese may be served. The usual way to end a meal is with fruit. In Italy, desserts are rarely served at home, but if I did not offer a sweet, I believe my guests would feel cheated.

GLI ANTIPASTI E ALIMENTI VARI

Appetisers and Hors d'oeuvres

Bruschetta   131
Garlic toast

Bruschetta al pomodoro   159
Toast with tomatoes

Crostini di olive   113
Olive toast

Crostini di fegatini   99
Chicken livers on toast

Pâté di fegato   11
Liver pâté

Crostini di midollo   123
Bone marrow on toast

Antipasto di salumi   83
A plate of raw ham, cured meats and salami

Verdure in pinzimonio   99
Raw vegetables dipped in olive oil

Bagna cauda   11
Hot garlic and anchovy dip for vegetables

Panzanella   99
Tomato and bread salad

Insalata di arance   173
Orange salad

Funghi crudi   83
Raw mushroom salad

Funghi sott'olio   173
Mushrooms preserved in oil

Prosciutto con fichi o melone   83
Parma ham with figs or melon

Insalata di pomodori e mozzarella   143
Tomato and mozzarella

Asparagi con salsa zabaione   56
Asparagus with zabaglione sauce

Insalata di peperoni arrostiti   169
Roast pepper salad

Peperoni alla piemontese   12
Pepper salad with anchovies and tomatoes

Melanzane alla campagnola   159
Aubergines country style

Zucchine scapece   143
Fried courgette salad

Patate con diavolicchio   169
Potatoes with hot pepper

Fave stuffate al cacio   143
Broad beans with goat's cheese

Flan di zucchine   173
Courgette flan

Ceci all'aglio   173
Chickpeas with garlic and chilli

Cipolline in agrodolce   127
Sweet and sour onions

Carciofi alle mandorle   181
Artichokes with almond sauce

Peperonata alla veneta   56
Peppers Venetian style

Caponata   181
Sweet and sour aubergine salad

Frittata di patate romana   123
Potato cake

Insalata di cappone   37
Chicken salad

Insalata di carne cruda   15
Raw meat salad

Lingua in salsa rossa   16
Tongue with red sauce

RIPIENI
Stuffed vegetables

Involtini di melanzane alla mozzarella   159
Aubergine slices stuffed with mozzarella

Involtini di peperoni alla Barese   160
Stuffed pepper rolls

Peperoni ripieni di riso   182
Peppers stuffed with rice

Zucchine ripiene   123
Baked courgette boats

Pomodori ripieni alla cipolla   83
Tomatoes stuffed with onion and herbs

Pomodori ripieni di vermicelli   174
Tomatoes filled with vermicelli

Cipolle ripiene   13
Onions stuffed with meat

Cipolle ripiene di magro   13
Onions stuffed with pumpkin

Funghi ripieni   28
Stuffed mushrooms

Carciofi ripieni   174
Stuffed artichoke hearts

FRITTI
Fried Morsels

Fiori fritti   100
Courgette flowers fried in batter

Panzerotti   161
Little fried cheese turnovers

Arancini di risu e ricotta   182
Rice balls with cheese

Pollo fritto   105
Chicken pieces fried in batter

Polpette alla fiorentina   106
Meat or chicken cutlets

Crochette di pollo   107
Chicken croquettes

Il fritto misto Piemontese   14
Mixed fried delicacies

FORMAGGI E UOVA
Cheese and Eggs

Fonduta   12
Cheese fondue

Caciocavallo o scamorza alla brace   131
Grilled cheese

Uova al piatto con mozzarella   170
Fried eggs with mozzarella

Uova in camicia   12
Poached eggs with tomatoes and basil

Uova alla fiorentina   102
Eggs Florentine

Frittata   70
Omelette

ANTIPASTI DI MARE
Seafood Hors d'œuvres

Il crudo   160
Raw marinated fish

Cozze al limone   188
Mussels with oil and lemon

Cozze arraganate   160
Grilled mussels

Calamaretti e gamberoni fritti   56
Deep-fried squid and prawns

Calamari o seppie imbottiti   187
Stuffed squid or cuttlefish

Granseola alla veneziana   57
Crab in the shell with oil and lemon

Insalata di frutti di mare   144
Seafood salad

Insalata di tonno e patate   183
Tuna and potato salad

Polpo affogato   144
Boiled octopus

Sardine alla scapece   144
Sardines in spicy sauce

Pesce in saor   58
Baby soles in a sweet and sour sauce

PIZZE, FOCACCE E TORTE
Pizzas, Bread Pies

Focaccia   27
Flat bread

Focaccia con le olive   27
Flat bread with olives

Pane con le olive e la salsiccia   183
Bread with olives and sausage

Le pizze alla napoletana   141
5 Neapolitan pizzas

Calzone pugliese   163
Stuffed pizza pies

Pizza rustica   142
Cheese and salami pie

Torta rustica con spinaci   142
Spinach and ham pie

I PRIMI
First Courses

PASTE ASCIUTTE
Pasta Dishes

Spaghetti alla carbonara 124
Spaghetti with eggs and bacon

Salsa al gorgonzola 87
Gorgonzola sauce for pasta

Fettuccine con prosciutto di Parma e panna 88
Fettuccine with raw ham and cream

Ragù di carne alla bolognese 88
Bolognese meat sauce

Paparele e figadini 59
Tagliatelle with chicken livers

Pasta con sugo di lepre 196
Pasta with hare stew

Tortelli alle erbette 86
Ravioli stuffed with cheese and spinach beet

Schlutzkrapfen 49
Ravioli with spinach and ricotta

Culingiones 195
Cheese ravioli

Pansoti con salsa di noci 30
Triangular herb ravioli with walnut sauce

Salsa di noci 31
Walnut sauce

Tortelli di zucca 38
Pasta stuffed with pumpkin

Timballo alle melanzane 149
Pasta mould with aubergines

Cannelloni ai funghi 148
Cannelloni with mushrooms

Cannelloni alla sorrentina 148
Cannelloni stuffed with cheese and tomato sauce

Lasagne al forno 87
Baked lasagne with meat sauce

Mandilli di sea 30
Pasta squares with pesto

Crespelle ripiene 151
Stuffed pancakes with 3 fillings

GNOCCHI
Dumplings

Gnocchi di patate 72
Potato dumplings

Gnocchetti di zucca 72
Pumpkin dumplings

Gnocchetti di ricotta al gorgonzola 59
Gorgonzola cheese dumplings

Malfatti 39
Cheese and spinach dumplings

Gnocchi alla romana 126
Semolina gnocchi

Canederli ai funghi porcini 48
Bread dumplings with mushrooms

Canederli tirolesi 48
Tyrolean dumplings with *Speck*

RISOTTI

Risotto con gli asparagi 40
Risotto with asparagus

Risi e bisi 60
Rice with peas

Risotto con la zucca 39
Risotto with pumpkin

Risotto ai frutti di mare 60
Risotto with seafood

Risotto al Barolo 17
Risotto with red wine

Antico risotto sabaudo 17
Risotto with ham and cheese

Risotto alla milanese 40
Saffron risotto

Tiella alla barese 166
Baked rice and mussels

Risu e milianciani 'a palermitana 186
Rice mould with aubergines

Torta di riso e spinaci 31
Rice and spinach cake

Sartù di riso 150
Neapolitan rice cake with a meatball filling

POLENTE

Polenta 64
Maize flour porridge

Polenta e gorgonzola 41
Baked polenta with gorgonzola

I SECONDI
Second Courses

PESCI E CROSTACEI
Fish and Shellfish

Gamberoni in tegame   196
Fried king prawns

Seppioline nere   61
Cuttlefish in their ink

Polpi in umido   166
Stewed octopus

Sogliole alla fiorentina   102
Sole Florentine-style with spinach

Triglie alla ligure   32
Red mullet with olives

Spigola al forno   167
Baked sea bass

Pesce alla marinara   166
Fish in fresh tomato sauce

Pesce spada o tonno ai ferri   175
Grilled swordfish or tuna steaks

Pesce spada o tonno alla marinara   175
Swordfish or tuna with tomatoes and olives

Pesce spada alla siciliana   187
Swordfish steaks in white wine with tomatoes

Sarde a beccaficu   188
Stuffed sardine rolls

Baccalà alla vicentina   62
Creamed stockfish with olive oil and milk

Trota con salsa verde   114
Trout with green sauce

Trote alla panna acida   50
Trout with sour cream

Anguilla in tegame   73
Stewed eel with wine and vinegar

Anguilla in umido   88
Eels in tomato sauce

Fritto misto di mare   164
Mixed fried fish and seafood

Grigliata di mare   165
Grilled fish and seafood

Zuppa di pesce   162
Fish soup

Brodetto alla marchigiana   117
Fish soup of the Marches

Rane in guazzetto   43
Frogs cooked in wine

CARNE, POLLAME E SELVAGGINA
Meat, Chicken and Game

Grigliata mista di carne e selvaggina   103
Grilled meat and game

Scaloppini cu la Marsala   189
Veal escalopes with Marsala

Rostin negàa   41
Veal chops in wine

Lombata di vitello   89
Veal escalopes with ham and cheese

Saltimbocca alla romana   124
Veal cooked with ham and sage

Osso buco alla milanese   41
Braised shin of veal

Brasato al Barolo   20
Beef braised in Barolo wine

Braciole al ragù   167
Stuffed meat rolls with meat sauce

Il bollito misto   18
Mixed boiled meats

Bagnet verd   19
Green herb sauce

Mostarda d'uva   20
Fruit preserve in grape juice

Porchetta   104
Roast suckling pig

Arista alla fiorentina   104
Crown roast of pork

Maiale al latte   62
Pork cooked in milk

Costolette di agnello alla brace   134
Grilled lamb chops

Agnello al forno   133
Roast lamb with mint

Agnello arrosto   103
Roast leg of lamb

Cosciotto di agnello alla brace   175
Boned leg of lamb on the grill

Agnello brodettato 133
Lamb with egg and lemon sauce

Agnello con olive 196
Lamb with olives

Cutturiddi 170
Lamb stew with white wine

Polpettine fritte 170
Fried meat cutlets with raisins and pine nuts

Grigliata di cervo 50
Grilled venison

Salsa di cren 51
Horseradish sauce

Fegato alla veneziana 63
Liver Venetian style

Ficatu all'agru e duci 189
Liver in sweet and sour sauce

Rognoni trifolati 20
Sautéed kidneys

Animelle in agrodolce 42
Sweet and sour sweetbreads

Cervella al limone 127
Brains with butter and lemon

Trippa alla fiorentina 105
Tripe with tomatoes and parmesan

Coda alla vaccinara 125
Oxtail stew

Zampone con lenticchie 89
Stuffed pig's trotter with lentils

Salsiccia con lenticchie 114
Sausages with lentils

Pollo alla diavola 106
Grilled chicken

Pollastri pini e boni 63
Roast chicken stuffed with cheese and herbs

Cappone lesso 90
Boiled chicken

Salsa verde emiliana 90
Green sauce Emilian-style

Salsa rossa emiliana 90
Red sauce Emilian-style

Padellata di pollo e peperoni 125
Chicken with peppers

Pollo ai funghi 106
Chicken with mushrooms

Fegatini di pollo al Marsala 21
Chicken livers with Marsala

Tacchino di Natale 42
Christmas turkey

Faraona alle erbe al cartoccio 114
Roast guinea hen with herbs

Anatra di Palmina 21
Duck stewed in wine

Anatra all'aceto balsamico 42
Duck breasts with balsamic vinegar

Anatra arrosto 73
Roast duck

Oca con mele e castagne 64
Goose with apples and chestnuts

Piccione ripieno 118
Stuffed pigeon or poussin

Pollo alla cacciatora 135
Chicken hunter style

Palomba in tegame 135
Casserole of wood pigeon

Fagiano in salmi 22
Pheasant in red wine

Fagiano caldo in carpione 22
Soused pheasant

Fagiano in casseruola 134
Pheasant casserole

Quaglie su crostone di polenta 23
Quail on grilled polenta

Risotto con le quaglie 43
Risotto with quails

Coniglio in tegame 134
Rabbit with wine and herbs

Coniglio in casseruola nel peperone 107
Peppers stuffed with rabbit

Coniglio all'agrodolce 189
Sweet and sour rabbit

Lepre in salmi 23
Hare in wine sauce

I CONTORNI, INSALATE E VERDURE

Side Dishes, Salads and Vegetables

Insalata verde 108
Green salad

Insalata mista　128
Mixed salad

Radicchio con rucola　66
Radicchio and rocket salad

Fagiolini all'agro　107
Green beans with oil and lemon

Verdure assortite all'agro　113
Mixed vegetables with oil and lemon

Broccoli al limone　135
Broccoli with butter and lemon

Piselli al prosciutto　108
Peas with ham

Endivia belga lessa　128
Poached chicory

Pomodori gratinati　145
Neopolitan baked tomatoes

Finocchi gratinati　90
Baked fennel with cream and parmesan

Spinaci all'uvetta passolina e ai pinola　32
Spinach with raisins and pine nuts

Funghetti al vino　65
Mushrooms in white wine

Funghi trifolati　127
Mushrooms with garlic and parsley

Cipolle al forno　170
Baked onions

Patate al forno　108
Baked potatoes with rosemary and garlic

Gattò di patate　152
Potato cake

Fagioli all'uccelletto　108
Beans in tomato sauce

Ciaudedda　169
Broad bean stew

Fritedda O Fritella　188
Braised broad beans, peas and artichokes

Erbe alla lucana　171
Mixed vegetables of Basilcata

Parmigiana di melanzane　152
Aubergines baked with tomatoes and cheese

I DOLCI

Desserts

Frutti di bosco　118
Wild woodland fruit

Fragole al limone　128
Strawberries with lemon and sugar

Pesche al vino　44
Peaches in wine

Pesche ripiene　44
Stuffed peaches

Albicocche ripiene　44
Stuffed apricots

Pere al forno　45
Baked pears

Cotogne in composta　32
Quinces in syrup

Frittelle di mele　91
Apple fritters

Mascarpone　45
Rich cream cheese

Tiramisu　66
Cream cheese and rum pudding

Ricotta al caffè　115
Ricotta with coffee

Dolce di ricotta　197
Ricotta dessert with honey and orange juice

Budino di ricotta　128
Ricotta cake

Panna cotta　91
Cream custard

Tartarà dolce　24
Almond pudding

Bonèt　24
Rum and chocolate custard

Crostate di frutta　115
Fresh fruit tarts

Früchtepudding　51
Fruit pudding

Apfelnusstorte or torta di mele　51
Apple and nut cake

Pita di mele　74
Apple pie

Torta di riso　91
Rice cake

Basics

To clean and prepare live mussels

You can keep mussels (uncleaned) for a day in the refrigerator or longer in a bucket of cold salted water. Sandy ones will disgorge some of their sand in the water.

To clean mussels, scrub them, pull off their 'beards' (the stringy bits that hang out of the shell) with a knife, and wash in several changes of water. Test them to see if they are alive: discard any which are broken and those which are too heavy or too light or which do not close when they are tapped or dipped in cold water.

To steam them open, put the mussels in a saucepan with about 1½ fingers of water at the bottom – enough to produce steam. Put the lid on and bring to the boil. The shells will open in 1–5 minutes. Take off the heat and discard any which remain closed.

You can also open (and cook) mussels by putting them on a hot grill or griddle or in a hot oven for a minute or two.

Clams and other shells are prepared in the same way.

To clean and prepare squid

Pull the head away from the body pouch and discard the soft innards which come out with it. Cut out the eyes (being careful that the ink does not squirt out at you) and the small round cartilage at the base of the tentacles. Discard the insides of the pouch: the ink bag if any (carefully, without breaking), the icicle-shaped transparent cuttlebone and the soft gelatinous innards. You do not need to peel off the reddish membrane which covers the pouch nor cut off the fins from the body (though some people do for aesthetic reasons). Rinse very thoroughly in running water.

To clean and prepare octopus

Octopus is now almost always sold already cleaned and tenderised and all you need to do is cut out the eyes and gristle with the help of a sharp knife.

If it has not already been cleaned and tenderised, cut part way through the muscle which unites the tentacles to the inside of the head and discard all the contents of the head cavity – pull out the ink bag carefully without breaking, the hard oval 'beak' and the gelatinous innards. Cut out the eyes, then beat the tentacles with a mallet until they feel soft and have lost their spring. Remove any scales which may be left on the suckers. Wash thoroughly in cold running water.

Only a very large octopus needs to be skinned; otherwise the skin acquires a lovely pinkish colour when it is cooked.

To cook pasta *al dente*

The main thing about cooking pasta is not to overcook it. It must be *al dente* – firm to the bite, not soft and mushy. Southern Italians like it even a little hard and complain that northern Italians overcook theirs and turn it into *colla da manifesti* (poster glue).

For 4 people and 400g (14oz) of pasta, bring about 4 litres (7 pints) of water to the boil. Add salt, let it come to a rapid boil and put in the pasta all at once. Bend long hard pasta in the middle with a wooden spoon or by pressing it down, so that all the pasta is quickly under water and cooks evenly.

Stir and put the lid on so that the water comes more quickly back to the boil. Then take the lid off and cook at a lively boil. Stir the pasta to keep it from sticking together and very quickly start trying it for doneness. The cooking time depends on the type of pasta and varies from 2–3 minutes for fresh egg tagliatelle to about 10–12 minutes for spaghetti and macaroni. Drain quickly in a colander as soon as the pasta is tender enough to bite through – it is best drained slightly underdone as it continues to soften out of the boiling water. Southern Italians do not drain their pasta too well and leave a tablespoon or so of cooking water to keep it moist. Mix in the sauce and serve at once.

To make broth (*brodo*)

Broth in Italy is much less concentrated, lighter and more delicate in flavour than stock. It is made with meat – beef, veal and chicken are used – and with a few bones, but you may use a chicken carcass and less meat.

For 2 litres (3½ pints) of broth

750g (1½lb) beef or veal (use the cheapest cuts)
1 or more beef and some chicken bones
1 stick celery, cut into large pieces
1 carrot, cut into large pieces
1 onion, cut in half
1 tomato
Few parsley stalks
Salt

Put the meat and bones in 3 litres (6¼ pints) of cold water and bring to the boil. Remove the scum, then add the rest of the ingredients and simmer for 3 hours. Strain. If there is too much fat, use a ladle and kitchen paper to remove it from the surface, or cool in the refrigerator and remove the fat when it solidifies.

VARIATIONS You may add 2 bay leaves, and sprigs of thyme, sage and rosemary.

I have seen a cook add a glass of white wine and the result was good.

Ingredients

With few exceptions, all the ingredients you need for cooking Italian dishes are available here. But make sure that they are of the best quality and that they taste good. There are plenty of olives that taste bad, stale pine nuts and walnuts, too vinegary capers, slightly 'off' ricotta and mozzarella, and they will spoil your dish.

Bread

Bread is one area where mass production has brought uniformity where once there was diversity. Throughout Italy now you find soft, elongated rolls (*panini*), called *banane* because of their shape, to make into sandwiches, and little hard, crusty rolls, light and airy or half empty inside, whose name, according to their shape, is *michetta*, *rosetta*, *ciriola*, *parigina*, *fisarmonica*, *treccia* and *torcigliato*. These are the original breads of the north of Italy – of Lombardy, the Veneto and Piedmont. Because polenta once reigned there and took the place of bread, bread was a luxury food, small, elegant, and insubstantial. In the south, starting in Tuscany, the bread was large and the further south you went the larger it became. The rough country loaf called *pagnotta* is heavy and compact and made to last at least a week. This coarse solid bread was one of the most important ingredients in cooking. It was used as a bed for food, in salads, soups and stews, in dumplings, fillings, puddings and cakes. Bakers have now started to make it again, as they have many other popular regional breads which had disappeared, but it is never like the old home-made kind which had a strong taste and rich texture which is the bread needed for recipes like *bruschetta*, *panzanella* and *pappa al pomodoro*.

To name a few of the many regional breads still to be found, there is the ring-shaped *ciambella*, the Sardinian paper-thin *carta di musica*, Sicilian sesame bread, a rye bread of Alto Adige with cumin seeds, the famous twisted *manine* of Ferrara, the flat focaccias of Tuscany and Liguria, the thin unleavened *piadina* of Romagna baked on a grid, the Friulan *pan de frizze* with bits of bacon, the Tuscan *panini al rosmarino* with rosemary and raisins and the Apulian hard baked *frisedda*.

Ritual breads are still made for weddings, baptisms, Easter, the *Carnevale* and every type of feast and festival, while a whole new range of modern breads, such as those with walnuts, olives and onions, are offered in restaurants.

Pasta

Pasta is the most important food of Italy. There are hundreds of different types, shapes and sizes and at least 2,000 dialect names, from the fresh noodles such as tagliatelle, tagliolini, fettuccine and the wider pappardelle, stuffed pasta like ravioli, cappelletti, tortelloni and the large lasagne and cannelloni, all made with egg and soft wheat, to the dry hard-wheat pasta. In this category you find spaghetti, spaghettoni and spaghettini (depending on their diameter), vermicelli and all the versions of pasta with a hole: ziti, maccheroncelli, bucatini with tiny holes, penne which are short and smooth, rigatoni which are ridged, and a whole world of shells, ears, snails, hats, tubes, twists, corkscrews, quills, birds' tongues, little stars, ribbons, bow ties, butterflies, coins and wheels.

There is no unity of nomenclature. Every region uses its own names and industrial production has not always made it easier. The same industrial pasta is called cravattine, farfalle or gasse, trenette or linguine. Pasta illustrates more than anything the anarchic independent spirit of Italy which unification did not change. The importance of shapes and textures has to do with the amount of sauce they can collect and hold. Every region has its favourites. In the Veneto and Alto Adige they sometimes mix whole-wheat, rye or buckwheat flour with white flour. Many types are available in Britain now and it is worth experimenting and finding your own favourite combinations of pasta and sauce.

There are differences in quality in commercial pasta. For hard-wheat dry pasta, it is far better to get Italian brands, but they too vary in quality. The test is if they cook perfectly *al dente*.

Olive oil

It is always worth buying 'extra virgin' olive oil. The blander, cheaper kind of 'extra virgin' now available in our supermarkets is not much more expensive than that simply labelled 'olive oil' and is very good for cooking and deep-frying fish and vegetables. For salads, and when it is to be used raw, you should experiment and taste some of the very best quality 'extra virgin' oils which are sometimes so strong that you are only meant to use a little drop. Many Italians prefer to use a light vegetable or seed oil like sunflower oil for cooking meat and dishes where olive oil would overpower the delicate flavours. I do too. See also page 96.

Parmesan cheese

It is far better to buy a good piece and to grate it yourself than to buy it already grated.

See also page 77.

Tomatoes

Italians used tinned peeled tomatoes a great deal. My recipes call for fresh, ripe, peeled tomatoes because that is what I like to use. Although tomatoes here are never as good as those grown and ripened in Italy, we are much luckier now in the quality and taste of those we get, and a teaspoon of sugar improves their flavour. But good quality tinned tomatoes are far better than fresh tomatoes with a bad taste or with no taste at all. So in all the recipes which use fresh tomatoes for cooking, you can use tinned ones instead.

Stock cubes

In all the kitchens I visited I saw the cooks use stock cubes for dishes like soup and risotto, so there is no reason why you should not use them too, except when a specially good broth is required.

Pepper

Where I say 'pepper' in recipes it always means freshly ground black pepper. For hot red pepper you can use any of the little chilli peppers, fresh or dried. You will have to be careful with the amounts you use. You can use them whole and leave them in the ingredients while they are cooking for a short time only, if you do not want the dish to be too hot.

Herbs

Use fresh herbs if you possibly can – you can find them now all the year round. Parsley in Italy is the continental flat-leafed kind but you can use the ordinary one.

Anchovies

In Italy, the anchovies used in cooking for flavouring are those preserved in salt. They are whole and much larger than the fillets in oil available here, and they have a better flavour. The quantities I give in the recipes are for our fillets in oil which are sometimes a quarter of the size of the ones in Italy. If you have these, wash the salt off under running water, then scrape off some of the skin and lift the fillets from the bone with a pointed knife.

Prosciutto

When Italians say *prosciutto*, which means ham, they always mean *prosciutto crudo* – raw ham. They use the less prestigious parts of this, cut thickly, for cooking. It is much more expensive than *prosciutto cotto* – boiled or baked ham, but its distinctive flavour makes a difference to a dish.

Pancetta

Pancetta is unsmoked bacon cured in a way that makes it sweeter than bacon, but you can use unsmoked bacon instead.

Choosing the Wine

In Italy no meal is complete without wine. It is good to combine the food and wine of the same region, because they have been paired traditionally and some, like the Piedmontese, are natural partners. But just as I have encouraged you in this book to mix dishes from all over Italy in the eclectic way that Italians do now, there is no reason why you should not cross regional borders with wine. The important thing is to please your taste and to choose the right one for the food and the occasion. Until recently all the Italian wine available here was cheap, but there is now a choice of fine wines, and you can even find some of Italy's best in our wine shops and supermarkets.

Italy produces huge quantities of wine – more than any other country in the world, and 20% of the world output. There are seas of grapes everywhere and every region is wine country. But most of the wine is merely drinkable _vino di tavola_ to be consumed on the spot, or it is wine used for blending abroad or for distilling. Only a very small proportion (10–12%) represents quality wines which qualify for DOC (_denominazione di origine controllata_) status – Italy's _Appellation Contrôlée_, which governs geographic origin, grape variety, yields per acre, methods of vinification, alcoholic strength and ageing requirements.

This area of quality wines has seen extraordinary developments over the last decade or so. There has been a revolution – some call it a 'Renaissance'. Until the Sixties, when the profits of wine-making were shared equally between peasant farmers and landowners under the system of the _mezzadria_, there had been little incentive for either to produce good wines – and anyway the world only wanted cheap wines from Italy. But now quality wines are in demand and people are prepared to pay high prices for them; there are new men in the field, a new attitude and spirit in wine-making, and much excitement and activity.

Famous French grape varieties, such as Chardonnay, Sauvignon, Merlot, Cabernet and Pinot, have been introduced and French methods emulated; new techniques from California, where many wine-makers are of Neapolitan origin, have been adopted; wine industries have been transformed from rustic to high-tech, and producers have come up with stylish, new wines, particularly fresh, light, fragrant whites which they now produce in large quantities.

Traditionalists who have persisted with wines in the old heroic mould with local grapes have improved their wines to suit modern palates and, with better methods of planting and growing, a little blending, and more rigorous standards of perfection, have brought about unexpected refinements. Some have even revived abandoned traditions and re-introduced long-neglected grapes.

Wherever I went, in every part of Italy, even in the much maligned southern regions where the heat produces powerfully alcoholic wines, I found some very pleasant satisfying wines and, occasionally, also memorable ones. The leading regions which produce great wines are Piedmont and Tuscany, which are rivals for the best reds (Italy is traditionally red wine country), and Alto Adige and Friuli which are famous for fine whites. Italy's reputedly greatest wine is the long-ageing, strong, complex red Barolo of Piedmont. I will never forget the flavour and scent of one I drank in a village near Asti. Other great reds are the softer, more delicate Piedmontese Barbaresco and the famous and very attractive Chianti Classico from the top estates in the Chianti region of Tuscany. The white aperitif-style Pinot Grigio is a favourite in Alto Adige and the sweet white dessert Picolit is the most outstanding of the Friuli hills.

Other fine wines are Vino Nobile di Montepulciano of Abruzzi, Brunello di Montalcino of Tuscany, the sparkling white Albana di Romagna, Oltrepo Pavese of Lombardy, Amarone of Verona, Taurasi of Campania, the frothy sweet Asti Spumante of Piedmont, and Vernaccia di Oristano of Sardinia. The list is endless. There are more than four thousand different wines and several hundred of them are DOC (there are 219 DOC denominations, but some are umbrella denominations which cover several wines in a region). The unbelievable variety reflects differences in terrain, grape varieties and micro-climates and also local wine-making traditions and the independent, individualistic, sometimes anarchic, spirit of producers who want to follow their own way and forge their own style. It makes the world of Italian wines perplexing, many splendoured and extraordinarily fascinating.

Although only a fraction of this great variety of wines is available here, it is worth finding out about them. For this, read Burton Anderson's *Pocket Guide to Italian Wines* (Mitchell Beazley) and his *Vino, the Wine and Wine Makers of Italy* (Little, Brown); Victor Hazan's *Italian Wine* (Penguin); Bruno Roncarati's *Viva Vino* (Wine and Spirit Publications), and David Gleave's *The Wines of Italy* (Salamander).

Acknowledgements

My greatest debt is to Brenda Jones and Philip Clarke who sent me to Italy to write 'A Taste of Italy' for the *Sunday Times Magazine*. They made it possible for me to visit most cities in every region, to try every dish and discover the local produce and to meet hundreds of people connected with food. Without their support this book could never have been written. Brenda advised and encouraged me and I owe her more than I can ever repay her.

I owe a great deal to Massimo Alberini, the culinary historian and journalist, who made information available and introduced me to cooks and gastronomes all over Italy. I cannot thank him enough. He has just turned eighty and still rushes around the country attending and putting on events, choosing menus and encouraging cooks as Vice-President of the Accademia Italiana della Cucina. The Accademia was founded in 1953 by Orio Vergani, the sports writer who, while covering the Tour de France, realised how France was making the most of her regional cooking traditions while Italy was neglecting hers. The aim of the Academy is to save the culinary heritage and maintain the standard and authenticity of regional cooking.

Because I travelled alone, without plans and pre-arrangements, I depended greatly on the help of people I met for guidance. I cannot name all those whose food I ate, who gave me recipes and information, who let me see them at work and took me to see cheese and salami and pastry makers, who extended the hospitality of their homes and taught me about Italy, but I am grateful to them all, and something of what they told me is in this book. I cherish every contribution, and all the warmth which came with it.

I have very special thanks for the following who gave generously of their time and their knowledge and expertise: Gianna Modotti who teaches cooking in Udine; Renzia Sebelin who teaches in Treviso; Gianni Gosetti of Tolmezzo in Friuli; in the Veneto, Sergio Luciano Preo, Giuseppe Carlotto, Dino Boscarato, Francesco and Jenny Rizzo; Cipriani's Natale Rusconi; in Bolzano, Giorgio Grai; in Merano, Horst Auerbach; Piero Bolfo in Pavia; Fulvio de Santa at the restaurant Peck in Milan; Franco Colombani at the Albergo del Sole at Maleo; Antonio and Nadia Santini at Dal Pescatore in Runate near Mantua; Giorgio Gioco of the 12 Apostoli in Verona; Vito Quaranta and Attalo Paparello of Verona; Vittorio Bisso of Da 'O Vittorio in Recco, near Genoa; Giovanni Goria in Asti; Anna Maria Alvano; Signor Giardino of the Enomotel il Convento, and Danilo of La Crota in Rodi d'Alba; Pierro Bertinotti of Pinocchio in Borgomanero; Paola Buldini and Bruno Simoni in Bologna; Giorgio Fini and Giuseppe Giusti in Modena; Rino Azzali of Al Tartufo in Salsomaggiore; Giancarlo Ceci of the Ristorante Maria Luigia in Collecchio, Parma; Gianfranco Neri in Parma; Carla Schuani of Sandri in Perugia; Vittorio Battilocchi in Norcia; in Tuscany, Mariapaola Dettore, and Lorenza Stucchi de' Medici; Professor Corrado Barberis in Rome; Dottore Nello Oliviero in Naples; Dottore Aielli of the Ristorante Cappuccini Convento on the Amalfi coast; Nico Blasi in Martina Franca in Apulia; Franco Frassinato of Otranto; Paola Pettini who has a cookery school in Bari; Antonio Stanziani and the teachers at the Cookery Institute at Villa Santa Maria in the Abruzzi; Paolo Cascino in Palermo; Salvatore Schifano in Agrigento; Giuseppe Catalano of the Hotel Moderno in Erice; Fiorella Badalucco in Trapani; Maria Guccione in Isola Favignana near Trapani; the Mother Superior of the Monastero Santo Spirito in Agrigento; Franco Azzolini of the Palm Beach Hotel in Villa Grazia di Carini; Angelo Lauria of the Pasticceria Italia in Licata near Agrigento; the Canuscio family in Palermo and Corleone; Antonio Tantilo at the Charleston in Palermo; in Sardinia, Natalina Laconi of Su Meriagu Sant Andrea at Quartu S. Elena, Cagliari; Cesare Murgia of Sa Cardiga e Su Schironi at Maddalena, Cagliari; Giancarlo Deidda of the restaurant Dal Corsaro in Cagliari; Signora Sacchi of Monte Ortobene; Antonio Licheri of the Scuola Alberghiera near Nuoro.

I thank Nico Passante, of the Gritti Palace in Venice, for an invitation to a banquet with the regional chefs who demonstrate at the hotel's cookery school, and to Avvocato Giorgio Bernardini of Parma Alimentare for the splendid Renaissance banquet in Parma for the presentation of the Maria Luigia prize for journalism.

I am grateful to Dottore Francesco Varola Ancillotti who wrote from Rio de Janeiro and Rome correcting spelling and points of geography and history in my *Sunday Times* pieces and to Mr Gianfranco Spaggiari and Dottore Massimo d'Amico of the Italian Trade Centre in London for their advice. I have special thanks for Marion Maitliss, Jenny Cowgill and Alec Chanda – Alec particularly – who cooked and ate the dishes with me, and for Maxine Clarke who prepared the dishes for the photographs. I am grateful to my editor Hilary Laurie for her help and for seeing the book through at great speed and squeezing as much as she could in with gentleness and good humour, and I want to thank Kate Poole for a really lovely design.

I wish to acknowledge my debt to a wide collection of regional cookery books which I have used for reference, among them Jeanne Carola Francesconi's *La Cucina Napoletana* (Edizione del Delfino), the equally monumental *Le Ricette Regionali Italiane* (Casa Editrice Solares) by Anna Gossetti della Salda which has been my bible, and *Le Migliori Ricette della Scuola del Gritti* (Edizioni Acanthus) from which several of the chefs' recipes have come.

Publishers' acknowledgments

For the illustrations thanks are due to the following:

PLATE SECTIONS
Anthony Blake 2, 13; Cephas Picture Library 39; Serge Chirol 3, 8, 21; Fiorepress 34, 35; Robert Harding/John G. Ross 38; John Heseltine 4, 15; Marka 10, 26, 27, 29, 30, 31, 33; Grazia Neri 9, 16; Dave Paterson 14, 19; Rapho/De Seynes 5, /Pasquier 22, 25; Eckhard Supp. 20

TITLE PAGE
Mary Evans Picture Library

Picture research by Philippa Lewis

The publishers wish to thank Maxine Clarke and Helen Payne for their help with the food photography.

Index by Dorothy Groves

Index

214

216